D0742411

World Accumulation
1492–1789

World Accumulation 1492–1789

Andre Gunder Frank

Monthly Review Press
New York and London

Library of Congress Cataloging in Publication Data
Frank, Andre Gunder, 1929–
    World accumulation, 1492–1789.
    Bibliography: p. 273.
    Includes index.
    1. Economic history.   2. Capitalism—History.
I. Title.
HC51.F68   330.9   77–091746
ISBN 0–85345–442–6

Monthly Review Press
62 West 14th Street, New York, N.Y. 10011
47 Red Lion Street, London WC1R 4PF

Manufactured in the United States of America

10 9 8 7 6 5 4 3 2 1

To the memory of
my student, friend, and compañero in Chile

Dagoberto Perez Vargas and his comrades

who put these theoretical concerns behind them
to fight and die to end
accumulation through expropriation
and exploitation

The inquiry into this question would be an inquiry into what the economists call Previous, or Original Accumulation, but which ought to be called Original Expropriation.

— Karl Marx,
"Wages, Price and Profit" (1969:56)

Indeed, the booty brought back by Drake in the Golden Hind may fairly be considered the fountain and origin of British Foreign Investment. Elizabeth paid off out of the proceeds the whole of her foreign debt and invested a part of the balance (about £42,000) in the Levant Company; largely out of the profits of the Levant Company there was formed the East India Company, the profits of which during the seventeenth and eighteenth centuries were the main foundation of England's foreign connections; and so on. . . . this is quite sufficient to illustrate our argument . . . that the greater part of the fruits of the economic progress and capital accumulation of the Elizabethan and Jacobean age accrued to the profiteer rather than to the wage-earner. . . . . Never in the annals of the modern world has there existed so prolonged and so rich an opportunity for the businessman, the speculator and the profiteer. In these golden years modern capitalism was born. . . . Thus the rate at which the world's wealth has accumulated has been far more variable than habits of thrift have been. . . . It is characteristic of our historians that, for example, the Cambridge Modern History should make no mention of these economic factors as moulding the Elizabethan Age and making possible its greatness. . . . We were just in a financial position to afford Shakespeare at the moment when he presented himself! . . . It would be a fascinating task to re-write Economic History, in the light of these ideas.

— John Maynard Keynes,
A Treatise on Money (1930)

Contents

Preface

I think authors ought to look back and give us some record of how their works developed, not because their works are important (they may turn out to be unimportant) but because we need to know more of the process of history-writing. Historians today generally recognize, like social scientists, that their scholarship is an activity in which they are themselves participants. Writers of history are not just observers. They are themselves part of the act and need to observe themselves in action. Their view of what "really" happened is filtered first through the spotty and often hit-or-miss screens of available evidence, and second through the prisms of their own interest, selection, and interpretation of the evidence they see. The result can only be an imperfect approximation. Fortunately, no one has to regard it as the last word. Once an author looks back at what he thought he was trying to do, many perspectives emerge. Foremost is that of ignorance, at least in my case. A book that to its author is a mere antechamber to a whole unwritten library, bursting with problems awaiting exploration, may seem to his readers to have a solidity which shunts their research elsewhere. It is useless to assure them that the book is really full of holes.

—John King Fairbank,
Trade and Diplomacy on the China Coast (1969)

In this preface, I shall first try to look back and give some record of how this work developed, before saying something about what this book is about. In a way, I shall reminisce and dialogue in my own

11

way with this book on history, pursuing problems of today and not of yesterday.

In the preface to *Capitalism and Underdevelopment in Latin America*, dated nine years ago today (July 26, 1965) I wrote about:

> the need in the underdeveloped and socialist countries for the development of a theory and analysis adequate to encompass the structure and development of the capitalist system on an integrated world scale and to explain its contradictory development which generates at once economic development and underdevelopment on international, national, local and sectoral levels. (Frank 1967: xv)

That book itself, of course, did not intend or pretend to fill this need. It sought, as the same preface further states, only to provide the historical context—or perhaps to propose an approach which places Chile and Latin America in the historical context—in which contemporary "underdevelopment" should be studied and from which certain political conclusions could and should be drawn. This approach, which encompasses my own later writings along with thousands of others on Latin America, became associated with the "new dependency" school of theory and praxis that emerged in Latin America during the 1960s. These writings were, if I may quote this time from the preface of my second book, *Latin America: Underdevelopment or Revolution*, "the expression of the changing times and problems that gave them birth, filtered through the also-changing prism of the author's and others' conscientization and understanding . . . [in the] attempt, like millions of others, to assimilate the Latin American Revolution and the inspiration it finds in the Cuban Revolution" (Frank 1969: ix).

Beginning in 1967, simultaneously with, if not directly in response to, Che's call for "two, three, many Vietnams," and in collaboration with my friend, comrade, and colleague from India, Said A. Shah, I sought to apply or extend this "dependency" approach to the study of underdevelopment in Asia, the Middle East, and Africa, as well as Latin America. Since we ourselves did not know enough to write a book encompassing all these areas of the world (and their relations with the "metropolis"), we undertook to edit a reader or anthology assembling other people's writings on underdevelopment. Unlike other readers, this one did not intend to be representative of anything or anybody, but rather sought to use existing partial analyses to construct, as in a jigsaw puzzle, an emergent "dependence approach," or even "theory," distilled out of the bits and pieces of experience from each of these areas of the world, and from subcontinents within them, such as India. Volume I of this projected two-volume reader was to be historical and, based on the proposition that "theory is history," it tried to show the development of underdevelopment in each of these areas taken separately, in order to conclude that underdevelopment is the product of capitalism. Volume II was to be contemporary and, analyzing imperialism, class structure, politics, and ideology, it sought to conclude that the only way out of underdevelopment is through national liberation.*

In 1969, after some reformulations of "dependence" in Latin America published as *Lumpenbourgeoisie: Lumpendevelopment*, I undertook to write a theoretical introduction to the historical volume (I) of the underdevelopment reader, attempting to formulate the dependency thesis on a tricontinental scale. The fifty-page first draft, however, exceeded the bounds of an introduction, at least in length. Moreover, the second draft (expanded to one hundred pages in the process of grappling with certain theoretical problems) also began to exceed the scope of an introduction to the theory of dependence in that it sought to deal with the determination of the modes of production in the periphery by the exchange relations between the periphery and the metropolis. Several friends read and criticized this draft, and two critiques in particular determined the reformulations in the third draft. One was that of Giovanni Arrighi, who wrote (as he further developed in two articles [1970, 1972]) that I had inverted the direction of determination: as Mao observed in his essay, *On Contradiction*, from the same external heat applied to a stone, nothing emerges, while from an egg a chicken is born—thus the internal contradictions in a thing, and not its external environment, are determinant in its development. Similarly, Arrighi ar-

---

* Volume I was completed in 1969, but to this date it has not been published, since progressive (and therefore financially impoverished) publishers found the book, which consisted of eighty-eight selections, including many translations, on nearly 1,000 pages, too expensive to produce, while commercial and university publishers refused on the same grounds, but also had political objections against its publication. Volume II was never completed.

gued, it is the "internal mode of production" that determines the "external exchange relations," and not vice versa, as I had maintained for the underdeveloped areas (circulation determining production in the periphery of the capitalist system, as Ruy Mauro Marini would later formulate it in "dialectics of dependence" [1973]). The other most influential critique was that of Samir Amin, who wrote that in treating dependence separately in Asia, the Middle East, and Latin America (as was done in the anthology itself) I was not only looking at the rest of the world with Latin American eyes, but also neglecting the historical stages in the development of capitalism and the differences among dependent modes of production that were the result, for example, of Latin America's incorporation into the process of capital accumulation in the sixteenth century, and of part of Africa's incorporation in the twentieth century.

The third draft* completely abandoned the idea of an introduction, both in length and in scope. Instead it tried to contribute to "the development of a theory and analysis adequate to encompass the structure and development of the capitalist system on an integrated world scale," for which I had pleaded five years earlier. This draft was a short history of world capitalist development from the transition from feudalism to the early twentieth century and made the traditional distinctions, demanded by Amin, between mercantile, industrial capitalist, and imperialist stages. In it, I sought to analyze the transitions between these stages, while at the same time rising to the challenge of, if not accepting, the argument of Arrighi (and increasingly of other critics of "circulationism") by undertaking an analysis of the *mutual* (dialectical?) relations between the changing "external" (but with respect to the capitalist system still internal) relations of exchange and the transformations of the relations of production "internal" to each of the major regions of the world at each of the three historical stages of capitalist development on a world scale. Prompted in part by an assignment to contribute to the "comparative study of American societies," I devoted particular attention to the comparative analysis of the relations between differing exchange and productive relations in various parts of the

---

* One hundred fifty pages, presented to the Thirty-ninth International Congress of Americanists' meeting in Lima in August 1970 under the title "Toward a Theory of Capitalist Underdevelopment."

Americas during the mercantile period, with special attention to New England.

After the publication of Arghiri Emmanuel's *Unequal Exchange*, and the reading in draft form of Amin's *Accumulation on a World Scale*, I devoted renewed attention to problems of international exchange and their relations to the development of the internal market in the imperialist period. Moreover, stimulated by S. B. Saul's *Studies in British Overseas Trade 1870–1914* (1960) and Folke Hilgerdt's *Network of World Trade* (League of Nations, 1942), I inquired particularly into the importance of multilateral trade imbalances and the contribution of the underdeveloped countries' merchandise trade surpluses (but balance of payments deficits) in the process of world capital accumulation and international investment.* The confused and transitional nature of this draft, which reflects my struggle with the "internal production–external exchange" problem and straddles my earlier concern with regional "underdevelopment" and emergent concern with "accumulation" on a world scale, induced me to withhold it from publication (although the mimeographed version was cited as an "advance" by Ernest Mandel and Samir Amin, among others) pending the constantly felt need to revise it as soon as possible. After partial revision of the more *theoretical* sections of this 1970 manuscript, I have decided to exclude them from the present book and to publish them, together with some short historical sections, as a separate but complementary book under the title *Dependent Accumulation and Underdevelopment*.

At the same time, I exhumed my first book-length work on the problem, "*On Capitalist Underdevelopment*" (1975), which was even more primitive, since it had been written as early as 1963. The required revisions, however, would have amounted to a new book, and this new book had already been written in the 1970 draft, which itself was still in need of revision. Other matters and events (not least among them the 1970–1973 Popular Unity government in Chile, where I had been living since 1968), delayed the revision of the more *historical* material again and again—but permitted a further evolution of my concerns—until the third draft of the 1970 manuscript was again revised in 1973.

---

*This study, in subsequently revised form, is now separately entitled "Multilateral Merchandise Trade Imbalances and Uneven Economic Development."

In the resulting fourth draft (the present book), the historical account goes only as far as 1789 (1793 in India), but the historical treatment of the mercantilist period has been expanded and deepened from 20 to 250 manuscript pages in six chapters. The historical period now emphasizes (perhaps even overly so) the cyclical and crisis-ridden process of world capital accumulation, with special reference to the differing participation of various "underdeveloped" areas of the world at different times in this historical process. I intended to take this account up to the present, and indeed into the foreseeable future of another major and long crisis in capital accumulation. However, progress was slow and time became short, particularly for the Allende government in Chile. So I decided to stop at the Industrial Revolution, adding a theoretical account that goes beyond that time.

Thus I have to leave for the future both the later period and a treatment of the unequal structure and uneven process of capitalist development (and underdevelopment) from the Industrial Revolution to the present economic and political crisis of capitalism. At the same time, I shall be able to follow (and pass on) the good advice of John K. Fairbank, which I had not learned to follow when I was writing the first four drafts: "*Never* try to begin at the beginning. Historical research progresses backward, not forward. . . . The rule seems to be, if you want to study the mid-period . . . begin at the end of it and let the problems lead you back" (Fairbank 1969: ix). My concern (as the prefaces to earlier books testify) has always been with the present and future, the problems of which have led me back to their previous history. I now realize that in order to progress at all not only the concern for, but also the analysis and the writing of, history must progress backward, not forward, pursuing problems that are problems of today.

Since I was ignorant of Fairbank's rule, the present work is a historical account of the process of capital accumulation, centered in Western Europe but increasingly encompassing other parts of the globe, beginning around 1500 and ending in 1789. I was obliged by circumstance, however, to follow Fairbank's rule unwittingly and to back up momentarily to the twelfth, thirteenth, and fourteenth centuries. Part I thus examines the sectorally unequal and temporally uneven process that was already occurring at that time and takes the account up to the Glorious English Revolution of 1688–1689, which is taken as a political mark of transition to a new epoch. Chapter 1, "The Sixteenth-Century Expansion," relates the transition from feudalism in parts of Western Europe to both the simultaneous development of "second serfdom" in Eastern Europe and the incorporation of large parts of the New World into a single world process, including the expanded production of silver through the total transformation of the indigenous relations and modes of production of the New World. It is observed that, at the same time, trade relations were expanded with the Far East without as yet substantially affecting the Asiatic mode of production there. Chapter 1 concludes with an analysis of the consequences of this transformation and expansion for the process of so-called primitive accumulation of capital in Western Europe and other parts of the world. Chapter 2, "The Seventeenth-Century Depression," continues the analysis of accumulation by examining the long contraction and reorganization of economic activity and the accompanying political transformations that were reflected in the "decline" of the Mediterranean regions, the short-lived commercial ascendancy of Holland, and the development of manufacturing in England, as well as the more autonomous development of large parts of Asia, Africa, and Latin America.

Part II examines the political economy of rivalry and war, particularly between Britain and France, against the background of the major economic fluctuations or cycles until the Peace of Paris in 1763. Chapter 3 analyzes the Brazilian gold rush and its use by Britain through the latter's special relationship with Portugal, the eighteenth-century development of the sugar plantations in the Caribbean, and the associated slave trade and its repercussions in Africa. Chapter 4 reviews the transformation of productive, commercial, and social relations in India through the conquest of political power by Britain after the Battle of Plassey in 1757. The simultaneous and related depression elsewhere between 1762 and 1789 is interpreted in Chapter 5 as the immediate determinant or detonator of the American and French revolutions, as well as the immediate (if not the "final") cause of what has since come to be known as the Industrial Revolution. The historical account ends in Chapter 6 with a review and some attempt to account for the way in which the commercial revolution, including the triangular and slave trades

with the colonies and the commercial wars on their account, combined with the technological developments and transformations in
productive relations over the eighteenth century as a whole, to
culminate in a crisis for the process of capital accumulation, out of
which, beginning in the 1760s, developed the Industrial Revolution.

The more abstract analysis of two sets of theoretical problems
examined in earlier drafts of the present book have been placed in
Dependent Accumulation and Underdevelopment. One of these involves
the question of why different New World colonies took off in
different directions of development and underdevelopment as early
as in colonial times. By comparing the combinations of internal
productive relations and external exchange relations of the mining
economies of Mexico and Peru, the yeoman farming areas in the
Spanish possessions, the plantation systems in Brazil, the Caribbean, and the (later) U.S. South, and the special case of New
England, I argue that the combination of colonial productive and
exchange relations made for the beginnings of the development of
underdevelopment and that the absence of these colonial relations
through "benign neglect" was necessary but not sufficient to permit
the development experienced by New England, but not by other
yeoman societies. What further distinguished New England was its
particular "semi-peripheral" intermediate (Wallerstein's terms) or
"proto-subimperialist" insertion and participation in the process of
world capital accumulation, associated with its particular role in the
triangular trade, which permitted an important merchant capital
accumulation and its subsequent investment in industrialization in
the New England and Middle Atlantic colonies.

The other set of theoretical problems concerns the development of
the internal market, especially in its relation to the international
division of labor and the domestic relations of production. What
determines the development of the internal market, and why did it
develop at some times and places and not in others? What are the
relations between the production and export of raw materials and the
development of an internal market and domestic production of manufactures and capital goods? These questions are analyzed by (1)
critically examining some unsatisfactory classical, neoclassical, and
reformist international trade theses on comparative advantage free
trade, and the terms of trade; (2) discussing the extent and formation

of the internal market in terms of the "dualism" thesis, the staple theory, linkages, infant industry and import substitution policies, and technological gaps; and (3) examining the internal market in relation to sectoral divisions and class interests in the process of capitalist production and accumulation.

The aim throughout the present book has been to devote attention to different areas of the world and particular periods in the process roughly in proportion to the importance they had in and for the world process of capital accumulation. Thus, the Spanish American silver mining regions receive more attention in the sixteenth century and again at the end of the eighteenth century than they do in the intervening time, in which they played a minor role. Gold mining in Brazil and its importance for Portugal and Britain are examined for the half-century before 1760, in which they were particularly crucial. Discussion of the plantation economies of the Caribbean and the associated Atlantic slave trade is, however, largely confined to Chapter 3, even though they existed prior to their eighteenth-century culmination. Thus, particular parts of Asia and Africa are examined if and when they come to have a substantial function in, or assume a particular relevance for, the global process of accumulation. For this reason also, Japan, China, and Russia, which played virtually no role in this process before the late eighteenth century or later, are hardly discussed. Nonetheless, some areas are also neglected more than they deserve, in proportion to their role in the process. Russia, for example, which was marginalized for a long time, did eventually enter the process, but it is not examined here. Much of Eastern Europe receives scarce attention after the seventeenth century. The Turkish and Arab areas, after "involuting" in the seventeenth century, also drop out of the account, along with Germany, and France receives less analysis than it deserves. Certain periods, especially the seventeenth century and the period of crisis after 1762, as well as particular decades within these, receive preferential treatment, proportional to what I consider to be their importance. But other periods of crisis, in the sixteenth century and before, are barely examined. These holes in the account are due to the inadequacy of the literature available to me, or simply to my ignorance, and to my inability to pursue this work further after the coup in Chile in 1973.

Perhaps more important than the relative coverage, and most important from a historiographic or theoretical point of view, is the time, or timing, perspective used in this analysis: an attempt is made throughout to examine the whole of the accumulation process and world system at each significant point in time and to analyze how different events in various parts of the same world process and single world system influence or even determine each other at that point in time. Thus, for example, the discussion of the American Revolution in Chapter 5 notes how the Indian famine of 1770–1772, brought on by the rape of Bengal that the British had been carrying out since the Battle of Plassey in 1757, threatened the British East India Company with bankruptcy. The company's subsequent petition to parliament for aid, which—after Clive's replacement by Hastings in 1772—they received in the form of the Tea Act of 1773, in effect granting them monopoly privileges to dump tea on the American market, provoked the Americans to dump the same tea in Boston Harbor. This and the subsequent British reprisal for damages in the Intolerable and Quebec Acts of 1774 were instrumental in leading to the American Revolution of 1776. More fundamentally, the discussion of the period from 1763 to 1789 in the same chapter seeks to analyze how the events leading to the American and French revolutions were related to each other, to developments in the Iberian empires in the Americas and in the Caribbean plantation economies, and to events in India, which after the exclusion of the French "replaced" the accumulation from the then declining Caribbean sugar plantations; and how all of these processes were mutually related and partially determined through the crisis of accumulation in Europe, including the related agricultural enclosures and Industrial Revolution in Britain.

Throughout this book the attempt is made to examine successively simultaneous historical events and to analyze the processual or systemic connection between them in different parts of the world *at the same time*, that is, in the same decade or year, and particularly during the same period of crisis. Implicit, if not explicit, in this approach is the supposition of the existence of systemic connections in a single historical process by the sixteenth century, if not earlier. For example, the relation between the production of precious metals in the Americas and the oriental trade by way of the inflation in Europe and the decline of serfdom in its western regions, as well as the rise of the "second serfdom" in its eastern parts, is analyzed in

Chapter 1. This approach examines not so much the past as the historical process. The author considers this emphasis on the examination of different parts of the world at the same time to be the historiographically most significant approach to the writing and *understanding* of history, past, present, and future. This emphasis on the examination of production, distribution, political and military power, social institutions, culture, religion, ideology, etc., in their simultaneous mutual interconnections distinguishes this approach to history from others that examine a single place or problem at different times, and especially from those that go so far as to argue that:

> In this study, there is no such thing as a uniform temporal medium: for the *times* of the major Absolutisms . . . were, precisely, enormously diverse . . . no single temporality covers it. . . . [On the other hand] such fundamental phenomena as the primitive accumulation of capital . . . the advent of industrialization—all of which fall well within the formal compass of the "periods" treated here, as contemporaneous with various phases of Absolutism in Europe—are not discussed or explored. Their dates are the same: their times are separate. (Anderson 1974: 10)

Although the value of different approaches in the historical division of labor is obvious and I have only benefited from the others in the preparation of this study, such a rejection of the historical process as "chronological monism" in which "events or institutions appear to bathe in a more or less continuous and homogeneous temporality" must be rejected in turn. Anderson's apparent attempt to make historiographic virtue out of empirical necessity when he argues that the historical times of events are different though their dates may be the same must be received with the greatest of care—and alarm. For however useful it may be to relate the same thing through different times, the essential (because it is both the most necessary and the least accomplished) contribution of the historian to historical understanding is successively to relate different things and places at the same time in the historical process. The very *attempt* to examine and relate the simultaneity of different events in the whole historical process or in the transformation of the whole system—even if for want of empirical information or theoretical adequacy it may be full of holes in its factual coverage of space and time—is a significant step in the right direction (particularly at a time in which this generation must "rewrite history" to meet its need for historical perspective and understanding of the single historical process in the one world of today).

Beyond the omissions of fact, this book is really full of holes of a much greater theoretical importance. It is bursting with a whole unwritten library awaiting exploration, and with respect to which—at least in my case—the foremost perspective is ignorance. Therefore, at the last minute I have added a long theoretical conclusion and euphemistically called the holes of my ignorance questions that remain unresolved. Although they arise out of the examination of the process of capital accumulation in the text, often these questions, not to mention their answers, are perhaps conspicuous by the absence of their treatment in the text itself. These questions concern: (1) the transitions and relations between so-called primitive, primary, and capitalist accumulation; (2) the extension of capitalist accumulation of capital in view of its unequal structure of production, circulation, and resolution; (3) the uneven process of accumulation as manifested in its stages, cycles, and crises; and (4) the class struggle over accumulation through the state, war, and revolution as well as the relation between infrastructure and superstructure through ideology, culture, and scientific or technical progress. In posing such questions I am inviting the reader not only to draw on the perspectives from his or her own experience and concerns in reading this book, but also to read it from a vantage point of a theoretical perspective that the author in large part did not possess at the time of writing it. On the other hand, the theoretical conclusion serves, once again, to emphasize explicitly a political perspective that *did* guide the writer, and that I hope will guide the reader. This perspective is that of Marx's twelfth thesis on Feuerbach—the point is not simply to interpret the world, but to change it—and the relevance of this point to a sort of sociohistorical Heisenberg principle of indeterminacy: How does interpreting the world also change it? How does the study of history make it? More specifically—since a rendition of the past need not be historical, and history does not end with the past—how does, can, and should historical knowledge of the past intercede in the praxis of the present to affect the course of history in the future? These questions informed this inquiry into the history of capitalism; they occasion my audacity to present it, and even more so only half of it, in published form; they underly the writing of this preface and the conclusion; and it is the author's intent that these questions should be explicit in every reader's dialogue with this book, be it each in his or her own way . . .

Acknowledgments

My political, intellectual, and personal debts to many persons are reflected in the preface, text, conclusion, and bibliographical references. They are too numerous to acknowledge individually. Suffice it, therefore, to mention collectively the *compañeros* and *compañeras* in Latin America with whom I suffered and learned from dependence; the many critics there and elsewhere who, perhaps themselves driven on by circumstance oblige us all to move to overcome the limitations of our "dependence" perspective; my *compañeros* and *compañeras*, now almost all in exile, with whom I worked, thought, and fought at the Centro de Estudios Socio-Economicos (CESO) of the University of Chile before it was closed down by the military junta; and the students, colleagues and my family with whom in seminars and other sessions these ideas were presented, discussed, rejected, and revised, first in the Escuela de Economía in Santiago, then in the Lateinamerika-Institut at the University of Berlin, and now at the Max-Planck-Institut in Starnberg, Germany—in all of which places I have been under the political and intellectually critical scrutiny of my family. I am also most grateful to Margaret A. Fay at the Max-Planck-Institute, who not only vastly improved the English typescript of the six historical chapters by editing and retyping it, but who—far beyond the call of duty—helped me eliminate various errors and inconsistencies, and to Karen Judd at Monthly Review Press for additional editorial work. This work, as well as my own revision, was made financially possible through the support of the Max-Planck-Institut and the Deutsche Gesellschaft für Friedens- und Konfliktforschung. I thank them all, and I thank the reader, for bearing with me on this leg of a long journey.

—A.G.F.

Starnberg, Germany
July 26, 1974
November 7, 1976

Chapter 1

The Sixteenth-Century Expansion

The discovery of America, and that of the passage to the East Indies by the Cape of Good Hope, are the two greatest events recorded in the history of mankind. Their consequences have already been very great; but, in the short period of between two and three centuries which has elapsed since these discoveries were made, it is impossible that the whole extent of their consequences can have been seen. What benefits, or what misfortunes to mankind may hereafter result from those great events, no human wisdom can foresee. By uniting, in some measure, the most distant parts of the world, by enabling them to relieve one another's wants, to increase one another's enjoyments, and to encourage one another's industry, their general tendency would seem to be beneficial. To the natives, however, both of the East and the West Indies, all the commercial benefits which can have resulted from those events have been sunk and lost in the dreadful misfortunes which they have occasioned.

> —Adam Smith, *An Inquiry into the Nature and Causes of the Wealth of Nations* (1776)

The discovery of America, the rounding of the Cape, opened up fresh ground for the rising bourgeoisie. The East-Indian and Chinese markets, the colonization of America, trade with the colonies, the increase in the means of exchange and in commodities generally, gave to commerce, to navigation, to industry, an impulse never

25

> *before known, and thereby to the revolutionary element in*
> *the tottering feudal society, a rapid development* . . .
> —Karl Marx and Friedrich Engels,
> *The Communist Manifesto* (1848)

1. The World to 1500

Hominid beginnings may go back some 15 million years; and according to recent work in Africa the earliest evidence of humanlike creatures dates from about three and a half million years ago. By the fifteenth century, humans numbered perhaps some 500 million, organized by a large variety of modes of production, cultures, and civilizations. These codetermined the socioeconomic formations that would emerge and are still emerging from capitalist transformation, and indeed they helped to determine at which historical time each would enjoy or suffer that transformation.

Africa, where so far as we know people first worked iron, had already witnessed the rise and decline of many great empires. These included the empire of Sudanese Ghana in the tenth century, the empire of Mali between the eleventh and thirteenth centuries, ruled by Muslim converts and still famous for its Timbuktu, the empire of Middle Niger Songhay in the fifteenth and sixteenth centuries, and farther south the empire of Benin, famed for its iron-working and art. Long-distance trade by overland caravan and migrations into West Africa and East Africa had been substantially organized by the Muslims, and Chinese sea-faring galleons had been trading with East Africa. The inhabitants of these parts of Africa, as well as in the region toward the South, ranged from the most primitive tribesmen, such as the Bushmen, to great civilizations, which by the sixteenth century were substantially in decay (Davidson 1959; Rodney 1967; Hargreaves 1967; Amin 1974). For these societies Amin has proposed the term "African mode(s) of production."

For eight centuries Arab civilization had been spreading from the Middle East, not only to North and Sub-Saharan Africa and parts of Southern Europe and the Balkans, but also into South Asia and much of Southeast Asia. Arab culture had flourished and enriched the human heritage more than any other, except perhaps that of China. In China civilization had flourished for about five millenia before the first known European visit, by Marco Polo. The Chinese had expanded their influence into Southeast Asia and had maintained overland contacts with the West through their Mongol conquerors long before the Portuguese arrived in Canton by sea in 1514. In the early fifteenth century, China had dominated ocean trade with Africa, sending out 28,000 men in fleets of over sixty ships, some of them nearly four times as long and seven times as wide as the flagship of Columbus. Yet the people of China, who numbered 60 million in 1400 A.D., remained primarily agricultural and failed to develop their overseas trade, which came to a halt after 1433. As late as 1793, the emperor of China would inform the king of Britain, George III, "As your Ambassador can see for himself, we possess all things. I set no value on objects strange or ingenious, and have no use for your country's manufactures."

The Japanese had accepted but modified Chinese civilization, Confucianism, and Buddhism; but in the thirteenth century they repelled the Mongol invasions, and the Tokugawa regime, established in 1603, resisted the presence of Portuguese and Spanish traders and missionaries, who had established themselves in Japan in the sixteenth century. They expelled more than 10 million inhabitants in 1603 and banned the Iberians in 1624 and again in 1637. By prohibiting Japanese foreign travel abroad after 1636, and permitting only moderate trading with the Dutch and the Chinese, the Tokugawa regime isolated Japan in what was perhaps the only regime outside Europe that can legitimately be termed feudal—until the arrival of Commodore Perry in 1854 and the Meiji Restoration in 1868.

Southeast Asia, and especially the Indonesian-Philippine archipelago, in contrast to Japan, had been the scene of intensive local production and extensive ocean trade long before the Portuguese arrived in Malacca in 1511 (Wertheim 1964; Furnivall 1944, 1948; van Leur 1955; Geertz 1963; Buchanan 1968). This trade was carried on not only by foreign traders such as the Arabs, Chinese, Indians, and others, but also by the inhabitants of Southeast Asia themselves, principally the Siamese and Javanese.

Moghul-conquered India under Akbar was the principal historical source of what Marx came to call the Asiatic mode of production (as distinct from the Germanic, feudal, and of course later capitalist modes of production). The bulk of the population lived in village communities, each of which was a functionally integrated agricultural and handicrafts economy based on the communal ownership of land and on well-defined individual productive and social responsibilities. After the Moghul conquest these communities were forced to pay tribute to the conquering state, a practice characteristic of the earlier "hydraulic societies" in the Middle East and elsewhere. But like these earlier societies, the Moghul state also redistributed (in Polanyi's terminology) locally collected tribute to the tribute-paying communities through the support and organization of public works that were often essential to their existence. The *zamindaris*, traditional landowner-cultivators, were first promoted by the Moghuls to serve as tax-collecting intermediaries between the Moghul rulers and the Indian communities, and later converted by the British into large private landlords. Thus the Moghul conquest of India and the exaction of tribute from Indian producers did not, in contrast to later capitalist development, fundamentally alter the existing mode of production, which remained substantially the same while the new rulers skimmed the cream off the top. Whether the internal degeneration of Moghul rule in the seventeenth century and the "evolution" of Indian society would have developed independently into capitalism has been the subject of much inconclusive debate. In any case, India was to be incorporated into world capitalist development (Marx 1964; Kosambi 1956, 1969; Sen 1962; Hobsbawm 1964a; Godelier 1969a; Bartra 1969).

Russia, or Novgorod, at the beginning of Ivan III's rule in 1462, covered some 430,000 square kilometers. By 1533, it already controlled 2.8 million square kilometers and its population numbered around 10 million people. During the rule of Ivan the Terrible from 1533 to 1584, all of European Russia east of the Urals was brought under Muscovite domain, although the Crimean Tartars would not be subdued until the time of Catherine the Great in the eighteenth century. Yermak began the conquest of Siberia across the Urals, campaigning between 1581 and his death in 1584. Thus, by the end of the sixteenth century, the territory of Russia had doubled, to about 5.4 million square kilometers; but the population did not increase by more than about 2 million. In the same year as Yermak's death (1584), Sir Walter Raleigh landed on the North Carolina coast of North America. Only sixty-four years later, the Russians had reached the Pacific, and one year later, in 1649, they reached the Bering Straits at the far eastern tip of Asia, over 7,000 miles overland from Moscow. Then they drove down into the Amur Valley toward China, from whence they imported tea (*sha* in Russian as in Portuguese) which would become the national drink of Russia no less than of England. In 1622, the Russian population in Siberia was no more than 23,000, and it grew to 105,000 in 1662, out of a total Siberian population of some 400,000. By 1763, a century later, the Russian population in Siberia had quadrupled, to 420,000. In the meantime the European and African populations of North America had risen to over 2 million, but their settlement was confined to the region east of the Appalachians (the American Urals). Not until nearly a century later would the Americans settle on the Pacific, only 3,000 miles away, purchasing Alaska from the Russians who had reached California before them. (All population figures in this paragraph are drawn from Stavrianos 1956a: 156.)

The New World—new to the Europeans at the time of their arrival or "discovery" at the turn of the sixteenth century—presented socioeconomic, cultural, and political formations as varied as those in Africa, or more so. The most recent estimates place the preconquest population of all the Americas at approximately 100 million people, which is double or triple that of earlier estimates (Borah 1962; Cook and Borah 1960). Of these inhabitants only about 1 million, divided into numerous nations and tribes, lived in the present areas of the United States, Canada, and the dry regions of northern Mexico. Possibly less than 1 million inhabited the islands and southern shore of the Caribbean (Sauer 1966; Mintz 1966), and, similarly, probably less than 1 million people lived in all of present-day Brazil and the Amazonic regions of the Andean countries. Still less inhabited the south of present-day Argentina and Chile. With minor exceptions, none of these "Indians" (as Columbus mistakenly called them after having reached what he took to be the sought-after India), scattered over vast lowland territories and divided by countless cultures, had developed any advanced technology or enjoyed any high civilization. Upon contact with the Europeans, their fate would range from extermination, as in the Caribbean; fighting retreat, as in North America and some parts of South America where the existence of open spaces logistically and ecologically permitted it; or temporary isolation where—and as long as—the Europeans or their *mestizo* descendants did not yet covet the Indians' territories. Only in some cases was it possible to press these tribal Indians into temporary labor service for the Europeans, but with little success. In still fewer cases did these Indian tribes offer much technical assistance in agricultural or mining methods to the largely ignorant Europeans.

The large pre-Columbian Indian population was concentrated in three or four relatively small and mostly upland regions and grouped into a few high civilization empires. The Aztec empire, estimated to have counted 25 million subjects in the fifteenth century (Cook and Borah 1960), was centered on Tenochtitlan in the Valley of Mexico, after the Nahua, coming from the north, had conquered it and the surrounding region. Earlier the Toltecs had ruled at nearby Teotihuacan and then declined. In the late fifteenth century, it has been argued that the Aztecs were themselves in decline, possibly threatened by population pressure on their limited resources and area; certainly they were exploiting to the maximum their highly developed agricultural and irrigation technology, advanced science, and far-reaching trade (which did not however use the wheel for transport nor rely on real pack animals) (Katz 1966; Soustelle 1962; Wolf 1955, 1959). The internal problems of the Aztecs were aggravated by external problems with unsubdued or inadequately subdued neighbors, such as the Tlaxcalans, and in turn contributed to them. The alliance of the Tlaxcalans with the Spaniards helped bring about the defeat first of the Aztecs and then of all indigenous people in the area (Gibson 1964). Farther to the south, in the area of present-day Oaxaca, lived the descendants of the former rulers of Monte Alban, the Mixtec and Zapotec peoples, whose political subjection to the Aztecs was still only tenuous, though they were tied to them by trade. In Yucatan and Central America lived the inheritors of part of the technology and culture of the Mayans and Olmecs who had suffered an apparently sudden and still unexplained decline nearly half a millennium earlier (Ribeiro 1969, 1970; Zurita 1941; Phipps 1925).

In South America, from their seat in the Andean Cuzco and their ritual capital of Machu Pichu, the Incas had only recently conquered and subdued an area stretching several thousand miles from the equator well into present-day Chile and Bolivia. Their empire and civilization was still in rapid ascendancy when Pizarro arrived in 1532. In several aspects Inca society was more highly developed than even that of the Aztecs, including agricultural terracing and irrigation, mining and fishing, transportation (using the llama as a pack animal), and communication by courier, which they used to extend their conquest, dominion, and division of labor. Given more time, the Incas might perhaps have incorporated into their empire the adjacent highland peoples of present-day Colombia and Venezuela as well as the Aymara of Peru and the Guarani of Paraguay. But instead they were quickly subdued by the conquering Spaniards, falling victim to surprise, superior military and naval technology, and internal dissension among rival pretenders to the throne (Steward 1946–1950; Baudin 1956).

The mode of production of these highly civilized pre-Columbian societies has sometimes been termed Asiatic. Their social bases were composed of village communities with communal landownership. These were subject to tribute to a higher state or conquering power which in turn provided for and organized much of the infrastructure, although it also relied on state- or throne-owned land and direct exploitation of labor. Hence the application of the term *Asiatic mode of production* is questionable; and certainly, immediately prior to the Spanish conquest, none of these societies were characterized by very long-term stability. Whatever Asiatic mode of production may have existed in the Americas was transformed virtually overnight into something else, but there is no doubt that the preexisting mode of production, technology, and civilization of these indigenous peoples literally formed the base of the mode of production which the conquerors erected on their shoulders (Ribeiro 1969, 1970; Bartra 1969; Frank 1969).

The dawn of the sixteenth century witnessed marked continuity with past developments, and yet during this century the world was to be revolutionized. It would be difficult to maintain that "one world" really existed at the time; but insofar as it did, the Mediterranean was its hub—with the Moslems on one side (or rather on several sides) and some Southern Europeans on the northern shore. Although the Moslems and the Europeans were linked by trade, their commercial cooperation was exceeded by their armed conflict. The Moslems were still in ascendancy economically, culturally, and militarily, as they had been for centuries. They had taken Constantinople in 1453 and would beseige Vienna in 1529, although they had been expelled from Spain in 1492 after seven centuries of rule. Elsewhere in the world, however, three Moslem empires were in ascendancy and experiencing military, commerical, and cultural expansion. The Ottoman Empire dominated the Middle East and had expanded through much of North Africa and the African savannah country south of the Sahara. The Safarid empire ruled in Persia. As early as the eighth century and again in the eleventh century, Moslems had advanced into India. In 1504, the Moslem Moghuls, under the leadership of Babur, captured Kabul in Afghanistan and then went on to establish themselves in Hindu India. Their Indian domain was further extended and consolidated by Babur's grandson, Akbar, who ruled from 1556 to 1605. Though the Moslems had also expanded into the Indonesian archipelago, they were primarily terrestial military powers and overland traders. As such, they had long dominated the spice trade between the Orient and Europe. Though European naval supremacy presented a challenge to the Moslems in the sixteenth century, it was not until the seventeenth century that it would begin to defeat them.

As to Europe, there remains considerable controversy among historians about this period of crisis in the fourteenth and fifteenth centuries. I agree with Pierre Vilar's judgment that it is legitimate "to show how much the recent works of synthesis in France . . . *recognize* the *universal* and *social* character of the crisis and give them a *vague* and *confused* interpretation" (CERM 1971:52). (Emphasis in the original) It is also legitimate to extend these remarks back to the year 1000 A.D. (and earlier) and to the studies undertaken outside of France. Henry Miskimin, himself one of the participants in this controversy, referring to the same two centuries, summarizes the issues in the debate among Blum, Cipolla, Dobb, Kosminsky, Lopez, Miskimin himself, Parain, Pirenne, Vilar, and many others.

> One group of historians, which has acquired a good many new disciples in the last few years, points to declining trade figures reflected in toll and poundage accounts, to the precipitous decline in population, and to falling levels of domestic capital and industry, in order to show a period of depression or recession following the plague. Another group will

point to rising English cloth exports, to increases in the production of Italian silk, or to limited evidence of improved housing in order to find prosperity in the same period. Some will argue that the catastrophic slump in population after 1350 was steep enough to outpace decline in production, that there was a consequent increase in the *per capita* income level, and further that this is the only true measure of depression or recession. The full spectrum holds many more shades of opinion. (Miskimin 1964: 470)

Wallerstein summarizes the diversity of causes to which the European downswing during these two centuries has been attributed.

From about 1150 to 1300, there was an expansion in Europe within the framework of the feudal mode of production, an expansion at once geographic, commercial, and demographic. From about 1300 to 1450, what [had] expanded contracted, again at the three levels of geography, commerce, and demography. . . . There are three main explanations of the crisis. One is that it was the product essentially of cyclical economic trends. The optimal point of expansion given the technology having been reached, there followed a contraction. The second is that it was the product essentially of a secular trend. After a thousand years of surplus appropriation under the feudal mode, a point of diminishing returns had been reached. . . . The third explanation is climatological. The shift in European mereological conditions was such that it lowered soil productivity and increased epidemics simultaneously. (Wallerstein 1974a: 37)

Wallerstein seeks in his own study to combine these explanations. Vilar (1971: 51), on the other hand, after a similar summary of causative interpretations, calls for the development of a Marxist interpretation in terms of the technological limitations imposed by the given forms of productive and social organization and population levels.

Without attempting to resolve these controversies, and still less to offer a more adequate interpretation, I will briefly summarize some of the tendencies, which, despite regional variations, appear to have been remarkably general to Southern, Eastern, and Western Europe as a whole during the five centuries or so preceding the discovery of America.

A discussion of agrarian productive and social relations and the problems of transition from feudalism to capitalism appears later in the chapter. But to summarize briefly, during the eleventh century, feudal relations were still in the process of consolidation. The development of towns and commerce was slow. This development began more seriously in the twelfth century and accelerated particularly after the middle of the century and during the thirteenth century. This was the age of the Crusades against Islamic power and commerce. The first Crusade took place in 1096–1097, the second in 1147–1149, the fourth, also known as the Venetian or Commercial Crusade, in 1202–1204, and the eighth in 1270–1271. During this period it is generally assumed that serfdom in general and labor services in particular began their decline, although there is some evidence that partially contradicts this interpretation, as we will see below.

The apparent demographic and productive decline of the fourteenth century has often been associated with the Black Death of 1348–1349; but it had already begun nearly a half century earlier and was to last for more than another century after the Black Death. Not only did the population decline, but apparently so did prices, manufacturing, and agricultural production (Lopez and Miskimin 1962; Pirenne 1936). In Western Europe, feudal landlords commuted labor services to payments in kind and then commuted payments in kind to payments in money, in response to an unprofitable market demand and faced with the necessity to make concession to peasants in times of labor scarcity. In Eastern Europe, the prospect of land and freedom in unpopulated and depopulated regions attracted German settlers (Blum 1957; Engels 1956). Whether per capita income declined or increased is the subject of controversy, but it is not inconceivable that these measures may have increased the real consumption of some peasant sectors (see section 4 below). Such has been the experience in several later economic depressions; and such increases, as Cipolla et al. (1964) argue, would not disprove but rather confirm the existence of generally depressive conditions, especially outside of agriculture. Similarly consistent with such a depression is Cipolla's observation that the price of precious metals and money increased, concomitantly with the decline of the price level in general.

Even more controversial than the issue of the per capita income are the extent, intensity, and timing of the recovery at the end of the fifteenth century. This recovery seems to have varied from one region to another after about 1450 and to have been delayed until the early decades of the sixteenth century for some regions. Cataluña, for example, was suffering from economic and manufacturing decline at the end of the fifteenth century while Valencia was not—and Castile was already expanding and successfully challenged the Moors in reconquering the Iberian peninsula to the south (Vilar 1964: 325–431).

Finally, and in terms of a hypothesis I shall advance in relation to the depressive periods of the seventeenth century, the post-1762 period, and later depressions until that of the 1930s and the 1970–1980s, we may speculate on how absolutely and relatively depressive the Italian cities were at the turn of the fifteenth–sixteenth centuries and what consequences this may have had in stimulating the Renaissance of Botticelli (1444–1510), Leonardo da Vinci (1452–1519), Raphael (1483–1520), Michelangelo (1475–1564), and the political writings of Machiavelli (1469–1527), who offered his political advice in *The Prince* during the French-Italian wars in 1516.

The turn of the fifteenth century, which witnessed the expulsion of Moors and Jews from Spain in 1492, the discovery of America by the Genoan, Christopher Columbus, on behalf of Spain, and the rounding of the Cape of Good Hope by the Portuguese, Vasco da Gama, in his voyage to India, also marked several continuities in European production and trade. The Moslem conquest of Constantinople in the late fifteenth century and their advance through the Balkans, the recovery of European population growth, the development of agricultural technology and the production of manufactures, and perhaps the rise in the price of precious metals accompanied by the relative decline of the price of other products (Vilar 1969: 74) all lent impulse to the discovery and development of new trade routes and to the search for new sources of precious metals. Throughout the fifteenth century, the Italian city-states, especially Venice, Florence, Milan, and Genoa, had served as intermediaries in the spice trade between the Moslems in the East and the Northern Europeans in the West. Furthermore, they had developed their own manufacturing and had established sugar plantations, based on local and imported slave labor, in Palestine and Mediterranean islands such as Cyprus and Crete (for concise accounts, see Verlinden 1953; Cox 1959). The Spaniards had established similar plantations in the Canary Islands, and the Portuguese—with Genoan capital—in the

Madeira Islands of the Atlantic. Part of this sugar was transported overland to be sold in Northern Europe, and by the end of the fifteenth century Madeira sugar was shipped directly to Antwerp for refinement and resale. After the turn of the sixteenth century, the Portuguese developed sea routes rounding Africa to exploit the oriental trade; the Spaniards sought and found a western cir- cumglobal route, whose commercial value was low except for the importance of the discovery of the New World; the North Euro- peans vainly sought a northwest passage to the Orient via North America, and also a northeast one via Russia; the Russians began to expand into Siberia and to develop more overland trade routes to the Orient; the Germans prospected and developed more silver mines in Europe; and Europeans generally sought gold in West Africa and in *all* of the New World, and later silver in the latter as well. The Europeans then extended sugar plantations in the tropical areas of the New World and fished in its northern waters. At the same time, overland trade to the Orient continued undiminished, and with it the Southern Europeans still held their own for the remainder of the sixteenth century. What were the consequences of these develop- ments in Asia, Africa, and the Americas, as well as in Europe and the world generally? We may examine them in turn.

2. *Overseas Expansion from Europe*

Throughout the sixteenth century and for part of the seventeenth century as well, the new ocean route to the oriental spices was little more than the continuation of the old spice trade by additional means: it did not yet replace the overland route nor the Arabs and Italians who depended on it. But this sea route, as well as others across the Atlantic and elsewhere, served to lay the basis for what would be determinant for several centuries to come: naval suprem- acy, militarily and commercially.

After the Portuguese Henry the Navigator had pioneered the route down the West African coast in the middle of the fifteenth century, and Vasco da Gama had rounded the Cape of Good Hope to reach India in 1498, the Duke of Alberquerque arrived in India in

1503, to establish a Portuguese foothold in Asia. Relying on naval power to take and hold small strategic coastal locations, and without seeking to penetrate inland (for which he lacked the military power and technology), Alberquerque sought to challenge the Arab trade. He first captured two small islands that overlooked the passages to the Red Sea and the Persian Gulf, and then, after an unsuccessful attempt to take Calicut in 1511, he settled for Goa instead (where the Portuguese remained until 1961). In 1513 he captured Malacca in order to control the narrow straits between the Malayan Peninsula and the island of Sumatra, which was the only available connection between the Spice Islands in the Pacific Ocean to the East and the Indian Ocean to the West. In 1515 the Portuguese arrived in Canton, and in 1557 they established a permanent (and still today Portuguese) settlement on the Chinese coast in Macao. By 1542 they had arrived in Japan.

For a century the Portuguese benefited from a total monopoly of the ocean trade *between* Europe and the Orient through the Indian Ocean. (The Spanish established the trans-Pacific "Manila Galleon" trade, with transshipment across Mexico from Acapulco to Veracruz and on across the Atlantic, but the Portuguese were able to derive advantage from that trade by supplying it at its Manila terminus.) But in the intra-Asian ocean trade among India, the Spice Islands, the Malay Peninsula, China, and Japan, the Portuguese were no more than one among many and at best first among many. This trade continued to feed the oriental terminus of the overland caravan trade to Europe, which continued to flourish. Since the Portuguese had nothing of their own to offer, they concentrated on intra-Asian trade (and of course on piracy), supplying Chinese manufactures to Japan and Indian textiles to the Southeast Asians, to earn the necessary resources to buy the spices that they carried to Europe. The Manila galleon trade, during the sixteenth century and until its decline in the seventeenth century, provided an additional opportunity to the Portuguese traders, who were able to exchange Chinese silks destined for Spain and Europe for Mexican silver used in payment for Indian cottons and Chinese silks. Additional supplies of precious metals were acquired in Europe, although except for the German metals, these originally came from mines outside of Europe, in West Africa, the Caribbean, Mexico, and Peru. But the principal assets of the Portuguese in maintaining their trading position were technological advances in naval construction and, perhaps more important still, naval gunnery. Of course these were of no use for conquest or domination anywhere beyond the coasts of Asia.

Perhaps more important than the fact that the Portuguese, and later their Dutch rivals, did not have any terrestial military superiority over the Asians for inland warfare, was the fact that at this stage of mercantile capitalist development such superiority was not yet necessary in Asia. European participation in Asian trade was still no more than the continuation of the long-established Asian and Arab trade in the area, and the type and amount of products exchanged could and did continue to be produced in Asia (though, as we shall see, this did not occur elsewhere in the world) with the *existing* modes of production. This was the case with Indian and Chinese textiles, of which still relatively few entered into external trade, and with pepper, clove, cinnamon, and other spices, the production of which was not particularly labor-intensive (compared to that of sugar, for instance). Therefore, although by the sixteenth century and, indeed, earlier, Asia had participated in world mercantile capitalist development and European capital accumulation, for at least a century or two her peoples were spared the dreadful misfortunes (to use Adam Smith's terminology) that this process visited upon, and required from, many peoples in other parts of the sixteenth-century world. These misfortunes would in one form or another be experienced by their Asian descendants, who were destined to participate in a later stage of world capitalist development and capital accumulation. (Still, the directions of internally generated transformation of Asia's modes of production, particularly in the most immediately affected islands, were unchanged by Asia's trade with Europe: Who knows what level of development these modes of production might have reached, if the peoples of Asia had not later been more intimately integrated into world capitalist development?)

In Africa too, both north and south of the Sahara, the sixteenth century still marked continuity with the past, though it began to lay the basis of the future. The Moghul expansion in India, the Arab expansion in the Spice Islands, and the Ottoman expansion into the Balkans had their counterparts in Africa. In 1517, the Ottoman

Muslims captured Egypt and in 1551 they occupied Tripoli and pushed farther westward. At the same time the expulsion of the Moors from Spain in 1492 brought the Spaniards on their heels across the Straits of Gibraltar into Morocco. After half a century of fighting off the Spaniards, the Moroccans turned south in their turn to conquer the Songhay empire on the other side of the Sahara. The Arab oriental trade, which had a terminus in West Africa, where Indian textiles and Arabian books and horses were exchanged for African gold, was hampered by the Ottoman conquest of Egypt and the Portuguese challenge in the Persian Gulf. Moreover, the Portuguese opened an alternative—or rather an additional—trade route along the Guinea Coast, so that part of the estimated annual West African production of nine tons of gold began increasingly to flow out through the Atlantic ports instead of across the Sahara and to be exchanged for European manufactures and firearms. But this did not materially affect African society in the West or elsewhere, much less transform it, during the sixteenth century; nor did the occasional sale of slaves to Europeans, so long as these slaves were the normal product of the usual inter-African wars, as they had been during the fifteenth century and continued to be during most of the sixteenth century. Only toward the end of the sixteenth century would the New World's demand for slaves begin to turn the capture of slaves into the major business that would transform African society in the seventeenth–nineteenth centuries, people the Americas, enrich the Europeans, and vastly accelerate the process of capital accumulation with the development of the slave and associated triangular trade (Davidson 1961; Amin 1974).

In the sixteenth century then, the level of technological and economic development of the trading partners was still qualitatively equivalent, and trade between the Europeans and Africans was carried on to the mutual benefit and with the mutual respect of both. Innumerable surviving letters and other documentation bear witness to the admiration of many European visitors for the cultural advancement of the African peoples they knew and demonstrates the equality of treatment that the trading partners accorded to each other and to their partners' rulers. A further testimonial from the Elizabethan era is Shakespeare's treatment of Othello.

The year 1492 marks both the economic continuity between the fifteenth and sixteenth centuries and the constellation of political events which generated new directions that would revolutionize the world, creating a single world out of many and transforming the many to create one. In 1469, the crowns of Castile and Aragon in the Iberian Peninsula had joined in marriage to form the nucleus of what would become Spain and its empire. It was this new crown which financed the westward voyage of the Genoan, Christopher Columbus, after he had unsuccessfully offered his services to Portugal. At the same time the Spanish armies completed the centuries-long reconquest of the Iberian Peninsula by expelling the Muslims. They then sought to extend their conquest first in North Africa and later in the New World that Columbus had "discovered."

Columbus' first voyage in 1492 was followed by his second in 1493, his third in 1498, and his fourth in 1502. In 1497, John Cabot also sailed in search of Asia and discovered Newfoundland. On his second voyage in 1498, he advanced down the East Coast of North America as far as Delaware before returning to England. In 1499 and 1500 Alonso de Ojedo and Amerigo Vespucci (whose name was to baptize the New World), sailing in the service of Spain, reached the Amazon. A year later, Vespucci explored more of the Brazilian coast, this time in the service of Portugal. In 1513 Balboa reached and named the Pacific in Panama. In 1519–1522 Magellan passed the straits that now bear his name and led the first expedition all the way around the globe. Later (1534–1541), the French Cartier and Champlain and the British Davis and others sought a northwest passage to the Orient and advanced instead up the St. Lawrence River into the Great Lakes region. Then, attempting a still more northerly detour, Hudson and Baffin explored the regions that bear their names.*

In addition to new trade routes to the Orient, the Europeans sought more money with which to finance the oriental trade as well as intra-European commerce and warfare. The monetary motive

---

* The long-sought northwest passage finally became a technological possibility when a nuclear submarine—originally built for military purposes—passed under the polar icecap (ironically, from West to East). A commercial route in the same direction will be established if the Alaska pipeline runs into difficulties and the politically "safe" Alaskan petroleum is shipped to the East Coast in icebreaker-assisted surface tankers, or more likely in nuclear submarine tankers. Is the northeast passage along the Siberian Coast again a prospect as well?

behind the Spaniards' contact with the American Indians has been emphasized by Adam Smith:

> The pious purpose of converting them to Christianity sanctified the injustice of the project. But the hope of finding treasures of gold there, was the sole motive which prompted them to undertake it. . . . All the other enterprises of the Spaniards in the world subsequent to those of Columbus, seem to have been prompted by the same motive. It was the thirst for gold. (Smith 1937: 528–29)

Moreover, Adam Smith asserted, the English entertained the same hope: in addition to the northwest passage, they sought gold and silver along the way although without success. However, their intention was clearly revealed by the inclusion in Sir Walter Raleigh's charter of a provision reserving to the British Crown the Royal Fifth (after the Spanish *quinto real*) of any gold that might be discovered by his and other companies (Smith 1937: 531). Christopher Columbus had himself been quite explicit in recognizing that "the best thing in the world is gold. It can even send souls to heaven." Hernando Cortez, conqueror of Mexico, confided to his new subjects, "We Spaniards suffer from a disease of the heart, the specific remedy for which is gold." It was not long, however, before the Spaniards discovered a substitute remedy: silver.

The implications of the European search for more money— gold—has been summarized by Friedrich Engels:

> To what extent feudalism was already undermined and inwardly torn by money in the late fifteenth century, is mirrored strikingly in the thirst for gold that reigned at the time in Western Europe. The Portuguese sought *gold* along the African coast, in India, and in the entire Far East; *gold* was the magic word that drove the Spanish across the Atlantic Ocean to America; *gold* was the first thing the white man asked about when he set foot on newly discovered soil. And this craving for distant voyages and adventures in quest of gold, however much it materialized at first in feudal and semi-feudal forms was at root already incompatible with feudalism, whose groundwork rested upon agriculture, and whose conquests were essentially directed at *acquiring land*. Moreover, seafaring was a distinctly *bourgeois* occupation, which has left its anti-feudal imprint also upon all modern navies. In the fifteenth century feudalism was thus in complete decay throughout Western Europe. (Engels 1956: 213) (Italics in the original)

Columbus discovered America—and gold—in the Antilles Islands of the Caribbean in 1492. He and the Spaniards following him subsequently advanced from island to island in their search for more gold and labor to mine it. The Arawak peoples inhabiting the islands had come from the South American mainland and brought with them their principal food staples, bitter yucca and sweet potato. Their agricultural technology and social organization were more than adequate to support in these islands a population ranging from recent estimates of some 100,000 to contemporary estimates of upward of 3 million. Whatever the size of the population, it was well fed, adequately housed, and productive of a variety of handicrafts and artistry. By 1515–1520, the islands were already desolate, and half a century after the Spanish arrival the indigenous population was all but extinct.

Columbus set up his principal base on Hispaniola (Santo Domingo and Haiti). By the time of his third voyage in 1498 and before his fourth in 1502,

> the system of native tribute collected through the chiefs had broken down irrevocably with the destruction of the social structure of the central part of the island. . . . The Indians were, in fact, feeding the Spaniards and providing personal services under a sort of squatter sovereignty that had followed the "pacification" of 1495. The business of producing gold was not working. In his letter to the Sovereign of May, 1499, Columbus considered what had "been the cause why God Our Lord has concealed the gold from us," concluding that it had been on account of the inordinate greed of the people who came to make a quick fortune, disregarding his warnings. A likelier answer is that the easily found pockets of nuggets had been cleaned out, that the Indians knew of no other places to which to take the Spaniards, and that these still knew nothing of placer mining. (Sauer 1966: 98)

The development of placer mining would require for its labor force a further transformation of the mode of production.

In his next voyage, Columbus saw the results of the continued search for gold:

> Columbus was shocked by the change since his last sight of the island, and he was right in saying that the fortunes of Española depended on the natives. Las Casas was of the opinion that between 1494 and 1508 more than three million souls had perished on the island—slain in war, sent to Castile as slaves, or been consumed in the mines and other labors [though of course most of them probably died of Spanish-brought diseases to which they had no immunity]. "Who of those born in future centuries will believe this? I myself who am writing this and

saw it and know most about it can hardly believe that such was possible." . . . By 1519 the Spanish Main was a sorry shell. The natives, whom Columbus belatedly knew to be the wealth of the land, were destroyed. The gold placers of the islands were worked out. The gold treasures which the Indians of Castilla del Oro had acquired had been looted. What most Spaniards wanted was to get out and seek their fortunes in parts as yet untried and unknown. (Sauer 1966: 155, 294)

In 1519 Hernando Cortez defied the orders of the governor of Cuba and set sail for Mexico in a privately financed commercial venture. The indirect profits to Europe would be incalculable.

The Indian populations of Mexico, Central America, and (after Pizarro's expedition to Peru in 1532) the Andean regions quickly fell victim to the Spaniards' surprise tactics treachery, and brutality; to superior Spanish military technology, including naval vessels, horses, and firearms; to the Spanish diseases, against which the Indian populations lacked immunity; and to their own internal dissensions, which prevented them from resisting the conquest in unison. On the other hand, it was precisely the indigenous peoples' highly efficient modes of production that permitted them to support the Spaniards during the early phases of the conquest. (Elsewhere, in regions that lacked a highly civilized indigenous population, both the indigenous Indians and the early English settlers virtually and often literally starved to death.) Moreover, the Indians' own hierarchical social organization served as the principal instrument by which the Spaniards would dominate and colonialize their Indian subjects and by which they would organize the division of labor that would put the indigenous population at their service.

Nonetheless, the consequences for the Indians, Mexican and Peruvian as well as others, were disastrous. Within little more than a century, the Indian population had declined by 90 percent and even 95 percent in Mexico, Peru, and some other regions (Borah 1962). In Mexico, for instance, from a preconquest population of 25 million (or 11 million, according to an earlier estimate by Cook and Simpson 1948), it had declined to a million and a half or less. What is more,

stripped of their elite and urban components, the Indians were relegated to the countryside. Thus the Indians suffered not only exploitation and biological collapse but also deculturation—cultural loss—and in the course of such ill use lost also the feeling of belonging to a social order which made such poor use of its human resources. They became strangers in it, divided from its purposes and agents by an abyss of distrust. The new society could command their labor, but it could not command their loyalty. Nor has this gulf healed in the course of time. The trauma of the Conquest remains an open wound. (Wolf 1955: 213–14)

The indigenous modes of production in Mexico and Peru, although they served as the basis and base of the one the Spaniards erected on top of them, soon proved to be quite inadequate to support the Spanish empire—and through it the process of accumulation of capital and development of the capitalist mode of production in the world—without suffering rapid and substantial, indeed total, transformation. Therein the circumstances of the Spanish colonization of Mexico and Peru differed qualitatively both from the initial mercantile relations between the Europeans and Asians or even between the Europeans and Africans, and from the earlier Aztec and Inca conquests and domination of subject peoples in the same regions of the Americas. In Asia and Africa, the European commercial contact did not—and did not yet need to—transform the existing modes of production in order to produce the goods that entered into external trade and the European-centered process of capital accumulation in the sixteenth century. Similarly, the previous Aztec and Inca conquests, while they subjected the conquered peoples to the payment of tribute, as the Moghuls had done in India, did not require new modes of production to supply the tribute. The placer mining of gold, on the other hand, and still more the deep pit mining of silver in previously unsettled mountainous regions, as well as the exceptionally unhealthy mining of the mercury employed to refine the silver, did require the total transformation of the modes of production, not only in the mining regions themselves but in the entire dependent colonial societies around them. Yet the production of these precious metals was the principal functional contribution of the New World regions to the expansion of trade in the world, the accumulation of capital in the European metropolis, and the development of capitalism.

It may be argued that the Spaniards initially intended to do no more than extend their metropolitan economy overseas, along the lines which J. H. Boeke, erroneously analyzing the Indonesian reality, later called a "dual" society or economy (Boeke 1942, 1953;

Frank in press). Thus in Mexico, during the first stage of colonization lasting from 1520 to 1548, the Spaniards relied first on slavery (until 1533) and then on the *encomienda de servicio* (a system under which rights to the labor of the Indian communities were granted to Spanish landowners, or *encomenderos*) for their labor needs, and on material tribute (of goods traditionally produced in the Indian communities) for their supplies. But after the epidemic of 1545–1548, which wiped out more than a third of the Indian population, and after the discovery of silver in 1548, first in Zacatecas and then in Guanajuato and Pachua, which generated a demand for large supplies of labor in mountainous regions devoid of indigenous settlement, the Spaniards began to waver between their conceptions of an ideal dual economy and the objective requirements of a mode of production capable of generating the required flow of silver. According to Eric Wolf: "All claims to utopia—economic, religious, and political—rested ultimately upon the management and control of but one resource: the indigenous population of the colony. The conquerors wanted Indian labor, the crown Indian subjects, the friars Indian souls" (Wolf 1955: 195).

Thus in 1548 the Spaniards began to replace the *encomienda de servicio* by the *repartimiento* (called *catequil* in Mexico and *mita* in Peru), which required the Indian communities' chiefs to supply the Spanish *juez repartidor* (distributing judge) with a certain number of days of labor per month, variously calculated in accord with fluctuating Spanish needs and Indian supplies of labor. The Spanish official in turn distributed this supply of labor to qualified enterprising labor contractors who were required to pay the laborers a certain minimum wage (approximately one half of the prevailing "free market" wage rate). The use of this labor was subject to certain regulations designed by the Crown to protect its Indian subjects, but these were frequently ignored by the labor contractors. The new system permitted a much more flexible division of labor than the *encomienda*, especially when labor had to be moved to settled mining regions; and it afforded the Crown greater power in its ever-present conflict with the overseas Spaniards who sought to make their fortunes for themselves rather than for their sovereign.

The *repartimiento* was supplemented by the *reducción*, or resettlement of Indians from various partially depopulated communities into reserves (not unlike the later American Indian and Central African reserves) which were strategically located near the mines and which facilitated the political control of the population when indigenous systems of social control were weakened or turned against the Spaniards. The *reducción* became especially common in Peru, where after 1542, the viceroy Toledo faced more serious logistic problems of supplying isolated mining regions with labor than did his colleague in Mexico. Moreover, the forced resettlement of Indians, though it was not extensively used in Mexico compared to its use in Peru, served the additional purpose of permitting Spaniards to concentrate landownership in their own hands.

During the second period of colonization in Mexico, from 1548 to 1575/1578, the Spaniards tried to force the Indians to produce and supply specified quantities of certain products, such as chickens. But the system did not work. At the same time the Spaniards sought to staff their own agricultural enterprises, mostly to produce wheat and animals for their own use, by hired "free" Indian wage labor—but again without success. The resettlement of Indian communities as well as their "natural" decay created "unsettled" lands (*baldío*) in the older agricultural areas. Existing or aspiring Spanish landowners could and did lay claim to these areas, increasingly competing with the Indian communities in the supply of an ever wider range of products for the growing urban and mining market. The mining market, incidentally, had to be supplied with foodstuffs and clothing for its workers as well as all kinds of animal (packmules, hides, tallow for lighting) and vegetable (beams to support mineshafts, wood and charcoal to smelt ores) inputs for the productive process. These inputs either had to be transported at great expense from afar (prices in mining regions were sometimes a hundredfold greater than those in older settled regions) or profitably produced nearby. But the settlement, deforestation, and agricultural overcropping of the mountainous mining regions—which the indigenous societies had avoided as ecologically unsuited for agricultural settlement—quickly eroded the soils and provided the physical basis (besides the many social causes) for the later (and still) depressed area complex of Zacatecas, Guanajuato, Hidalgo, Potosí, and Huancavelica. (This complex, and later Minas Gerais in Brazil, remains depressed to this day, as does West Virginia in the United States, and many similarly exploited regions the world over, for the same reasons.)

A third period in Mexican (under) development may be dated from 1575–1578, when another epidemic wiped out another third to a half of the surviving Indian population, again reducing the supply of labor and increasing its cost. Not long after (accounts range from 1590 to 1610) the Mexican production of silver reached its peak and leveled off. It then began to decline—slowly at first, and sharply after 1630. By 1630 Peruvian silver production had also begun its decline, after having been temporarily favored by the Spanish with greater supplies of scarce but Peruvian mined mercury (quicksilver). The mining enterprise became commercially less attractive as the costs of mining increased. The most accessible veins had been exhausted and further investment was required to dig deeper pits and to pump more water to keep them dry. Labor supplies were declining and money wages were rising. The costs of the ever scarcer mercury required to refine the ores were increasing. Higher taxes were imposed by the Crown to balance lower silver supplies and to finance its European wars. At the same time the prices (measured in silver) of food and of other agricultural products rose astronomically, at least in Mexico, as a result of reduced competition in agriculture from the socially and productively weakened Indian communities, growing urbanization, and an increased stream of Spanish immigrants fleeing from the sixteenth-century Spanish depression. For Spanish entrepreneurs in Mexico, mining became increasingly less profitable compared to large-scale agriculture, so that capital shifted from mining to agriculture, increasing the Spanish demand for labor and land in the agricultural sector. The result was the development of the *latifundium*-agricultural *hacienda* and its debt-tied peon labor, which only later came to be mis-called "feudal" institutions (Frank in press). The ideal of the "dual" society had given way to the objective reality of the transformation of the mode of production in Mexico and Peru, in response to the conquerors' needs to exploit the colonial economy in the process of capital accumulation and in the development of the capitalist mode of production in the world of the sixteenth and early seventeenth centuries.

The most extreme—but also the most important—expression of the first silver age of the Spanish empire was Potosí, the silver mountain where the phrase "worth a Potosí" sometimes "worth a Peru" was coined. This hill, over 3,000 meters above sea level, was discovered by a Bolivian Indian in 1545. Not long after, it was to have consumed the lives of an estimated 8 million of his brothers. The Spanish king and emperor of the Habsburgs, Charles V, designated the town that mushroomed there an imperial city. He inscribed on its shield: "I am rich Potosí, treasure of the world, the king of the mountains, envy of kings." By 1573 the census recorded 120,000 inhabitants, the same number as London and more than Madrid, Paris, or Rome. By 1650 the number had risen to 160,000. In the meantime the privileged among these residents enjoyed thirty-six highly ornamental churches, another thirty-six gambling casinos, fourteen academies of dance, and all the world's luxuries imported from Flanders, Venice, Arabia, India, Ceylon, China, and of course metropolitan Spain. Nearby, the city later named after Sucre was built to permit the enjoyment of the same luxuries at lower and more comfortable altitudes. Today a nostalgic descendant of the imperial Potosí observes: "The city that has given most to the world and that has least." Indeed, even the impoverished population it has today is no more than a third of the number it once had four centuries ago (Galeano 1972: 44–74).

Most other areas of Spanish conquest fell into—or remained in—neglect, as Adam Smith called it. At the farthest extremity of its American empire, in Chile, the modest gold mines had petered out before the end of the sixteenth century, leaving it to export little more than hides and tallow for use in the Peruvian mining regions. Buenos Aires was founded and foundered more than once. For a long time the Spanish interest in the regions that would become the viceroyalty of La Plata and still later Argentina was limited to the inland region, Tucuman and Santa Fé near the Peruvian (today Bolivian) mining centers. German mining expeditions into Venezuela had not prospered. The Spanish Caribbean Islands, which had been the progenitors of the "golden" age and later became the advance base of operations for the conquest of the Mexican and South American mainlands and for the opening of the "silver" age, had become backwater colonies dedicated to little more than yeoman farming and some export of livestock products and tobacco. Havana was also a port of call and assembly for the Spanish fleets that crossed the Atlantic between Cadiz at one end and Veracruz in Mexico and Portobello on the Isthmus of Panama at the other. All goods to and from the Pacific coast and the inland Andean mountain regions of South America had to be transshipped at Portobello. In the seventeenth century even the comings and goings of these fleets would be reduced to one third of their sixteenth-century maximum. North America had not yet attracted much English or French attention. Before the end of the sixteenth century only parts of Brazil had been settled, or peopled, by the Portuguese, who wanted to protect their *de jure* claim (granted by the demarcation line drawn by the pope at the Treaty of Tordesillas in 1494) by *de facto* occupation.

As early as the fifteenth century the Portuguese had had experience in the development of sugar plantations in the Madeira Islands, albeit partly with Genoese and Flemish capital; and they had had access to black slaves by virtue of the African coastal trade. Then declining sugar prices at the turn of the sixteenth century had led to a reduction in Portuguese sugar production. But a renewed though gradual rise in the price of sugar after 1510, which was probably generated in part by the arrival of Spanish gold from the Caribbean (which lowered the price of gold relative to the commodities it could buy), stimulated a renewed increase in Portuguese sugar production after 1520, first in the Atlantic Islands and after 1530 incipiently in new plantations in Northeastern Brazil.

At first the Portuguese tried to use indigenous Indians as a labor supply, but this enterprise never proved very successful, despite the later slave-hunting expeditions of the *bandeirante* Portuguese pioneers in São Paulo who sold their Indian captives to the Northeastern sugar plantations. Sugar production in Brazil did not really take off until well into the second half of the sixteenth century, after Spanish American and German silver had helped substantially to raise sugar prices, and after slaves began to be imported from Africa as a serious business. By the end of the sixteenth century, the price of sugar had risen to six times its 1506 level, and by the middle of the seventeenth century it had reached its maximum of seven times the earlier level. Then the new production of the French and British Antilles brought prices back down to the 1540 level, and Brazilian sugar production dropped sharply. By 1650–1675, sugar prices were down by one half and profits had dropped to one quarter of their former level. Brazil's first boom and economic cycle was over (Simonsen 1962: 96–115; Furtado 1965: cas. 8–12).

Thus the production of sugar in Brazil in the sixteenth century had, in a sense, begun as a continuation of the Portuguese and Spanish enterprises in the Atlantic islands and of the earlier Italian plantations in the Mediterranean islands in the fifteenth century (Cox 1959; Verlinden 1953). But the scale of production, investment in slave labor, capital equipment, and transportation facilities had increased so markedly that the sugar plantation enterprises underwent a qualitative transformation—if not in late sixteenth-century Brazil, then in the Caribbean sugar plantations of the seventeenth–nineteenth centuries (and even the twentieth century) which developed out of the earlier ones—into a new mode of production: the plantation system (see Chapter 3, section 3).

3. Primitive Accumulation in Europe

The increase in the quantity of silver mined and the decrease in its cost of production which occurred during the sixteenth century (before this trend was cyclically reversed during much of the seventeenth century) lowered the price of silver and increased the prices of other commodities that silver could buy. This price inflation began at the mine itself and from there extended in successive waves of decreasing intensity and increasing time lag to the urban centers of the mining regions, to the port of reception, and then to other parts of Spain. From Spain it spread successively to France, Northern and Southern Europe, and finally to the oriental extremes of this chain of interconnected links. Moreover, the farther the silver traveled from the mine, the less in general did it proportionally increase the already existing stock of silver and money, thus generating less inflation by the quantitative increase in the supply of money. English price increases were about half those in France. Vilar (1969) argues that the classical studies from Hume to Hamilton and their followers have overestimated the marginal impact of American silver relative to the stock already existing in Europe and relative to the new production in Germany in the sixteenth century. Hill (1969: 82–83) and others argue that European prices had already begun to recover before the first arrival of American gold, let alone the first arrival of American silver. Nonetheless, there is substantial agreement that the sixteenth-century inflation and its partial generation by American gold and silver helped to concentrate incomes and to lower real wages.

Similarly, it may be argued, the differential—in time and intensity—rates of inflation between regions helped to generate different possibilities for profit in the production and export/import of commodities already entering international trade. The American colonies, of course, offered an attractive market for certain foodstuffs (such as wheat) and manufactures, though they were partly protected by transportation costs. Spain also offered an attractive market for manufacturing exports from other European countries, all the more so since the Spaniards temporarily promoted such imports (some argue that this was in order to combat inflation at home by increasing the supply) and had a plentiful supply of foreign exchange to use in payment. Moreover, the founder of the Habsburg dynasty, King Charles V of Spain (1516–1556) and even his successor, Philip II (1556–1598), were as Habsburg emperors significantly dependent on and responsive to their extra-Hispanic interests. They were beset by Dutch and German foreign advisers who loyally served these non-Spanish interests, and they became increasingly indebted to the Bavarian Fugger financiers and other German and Italian bankers. Contemporary Spanish analysis and commentary testifies overwhelmingly to the extent to which the Spanish understood and opposed the process:

> Spain is like the mouth that receives the food and chews it only to send it immediately to the other organs without retaining more than a passing taste or a few crumbs that accidentally stick to its teeth. . . . The gold and silver are born in the Indies, die in Spain and are buried in Genoa. . . . It is not [having] much money that sustains the states, nor do their [real] riches lie in money. . . . There is no money nor gold or silver in Spain, because it has it; and it is not rich for being it. (Quoted in Vilar 1969: 186–93) (See also Braudel 1972; Carande 1965; and Larraz 1943.)

Or, as Sancho de Monchada summarized simply in 1619, "the poverty of Spain has been the result of the discovery of the West Indies [i.e., Americas]" (quoted in Larraz 1943: 168).

The early sixteenth century was also the time of the formation of the national state, of the Renaissance and the Reformation in Europe. In England the House of Tudor began in 1485; Henry VIII ruled from 1509 to 1547 and Queen Elizabeth from 1558 to 1603. In France Charles VIII (1483–1498), Louis XII (1498–1515), and Francis I (1515–1547) carried war into Italy and after 1520 were in turn opposed by Charles V of Spain and Habsburg, who annexed Flanders and the Netherlands after 1548. History's most famous guidebook to state development, *The Prince*, was written by Machiavelli in 1514. The Italian Renaissance flowered in the age of Leonardo da Vinci (1452–1519), Raphael (1483–1520), Michelangelo (1475–1564) and others. In Germany the expansion of trade during the fifteenth- and sixteenth-century "era of the Fuggers" generated the search for additional supplies of silver and greater flows of peasant-produced surplus value into the hands of landlords and merchants to pay for trade. The German peasantry was increasingly forced into a "second serfdom"—as was the East European peasantry (Kula 1970a,b)—and reacted with the peasant wars under the leadership of Thomas Münzer. Martin Luther also served as a peasant leader at the beginning of these wars, but after nailing his radical ninety-five theses to the Würtenberg church door in 1517, he betrayed the peasants and increasingly sided with the burghers, whose representative he was. The next year (1518), Zwingli began the Reformation in Switzerland and was soon followed by Calvin and then by John Knox in England. "Reformation—Lutheran and Calvinist—is the No. 1 bourgeois revolution, the peasant war being its critical episode," Friedrich Engels (1956: 222) would write. It was the second silver age of the German (and Austrian and Bohemian) mines and the birthtime of the Joachimstalers (or simply, talers), which would compete for supremacy with the Spanish real or peso.

In summary then, we may say that the sixteenth century witnessed the first long, sustained, and widespread quantitative and qualitative development of capitalism in its mercantile stage and the first period of concentrated capital accumulation in Europe. The Rumanian historian, H. H. Stahl, summarizes:

> all of Europe forms no more than a single social system; the laws of the market impose themselves more or less on all countries, however great the differences that separate them. Since commodities get a price on the world market, since the coins of international circulation are subject to the influences of the capitalist variations of the gold market, we witness

the processes of penetration of the laws of the market in all of the regions of the hinterland, which on their own would not have been able to give them birth. (Stahl 1970: 5)

The same process extended far beyond Europe to those regions or "enclaves" which were integrated into the process of world capital accumulation at this stage, especially the New World sources of gold and silver. During this sixteenth-century secular and cyclical upswing, Western Europe experienced a sharp acceleration of the process of capital accumulation based on the concentration of capital through a sharp rise in prices and profits, and, notably, a concomitantly sharp decline in real wages. Although this decline of wages varied, it was quite general throughout Western Europe: "Real wages declined by more than 50%, wherever we take our measurements. . . . The operation was fully paid for by the increased toil, hardships, impoverishment, and dejection of the majority. Contemporaries were often aware that the deterioration was taking place" (Braudel and Spooner 1967: 428).

In Britain the work required to purchase a year's provision of bread increased from ten weeks in 1495 to forty weeks in 1593, and real wages fell more than 50 percent during the course of the century (Mandel 1970, I:148). Much of Eastern Europe was converted into a granary and supplier of wood and other raw materials to meet the demands of West European development. This resulted in the concentration of both landownership and income in the East and of the subjection of the peasants to a "second serfdom," so that their landlords and merchants might prosper from the dependency of Western European development on the supply of raw materials from Eastern Europe. The indigenous population of the New World suffered yet more from its contribution to the process of primitive capital accumulation during the sixteenth century.

4. Productive and Exchange Relations in the
Transition from Feudalism in Eastern
and Western Europe

The productive and social relations in agriculture and the transition between feudalism and capitalism in Western and Eastern

Europe, as well as elsewhere, have been—and indeed promise increasingly to be—the subject of considerable attention and controversy in classical and recent discussion (e.g., Marx 1964; Engels 1956;
Sombart 1922; Weber 1958; Pirenne 1936; Dobb 1963; Dobb,
Sweezy, et al. 1976; Postan, et al. 1965; CERM 1971; RILM 1970). The
following cannot and does not claim to be a summary, much less a
contribution to or resolution of this ongoing debate. Instead I shall
examine some of the events in the agricultural and socioeconomic
history of Europe in the "transition" period from the thirteenth to
the seventeenth centuries in terms of two related working hypotheses. Although oversimplified, these hypotheses will be useful as
guidelines to point to some events in, and interpretations of, this
historical experience, which in the words of Vilar (1969) remain
confused and vague. The hypotheses are: (1) that as I have suggested
in earlier work (Frank 1967), the institutional changes are primarily determined by what is "good business" (Frank 1969: 237);
and (2) that as the historical examination in this book suggests, the
theoretical conflict between explanations in terms of "external"
(Dobb, Sweezy, Takahashi, et al. 1976) and "internal" (Dobb and
others) contradictions and developments can be partly resolved by
the observation that "external" contradictions appear to have more
immediate importance when business is good and internal contradictions have more immediate importance when business is bad; thus in
the uneven and combined development of good and bad business the
"external" and the "internal" factors play a combined dialectical role.

Since I have frequently been accused of offering false or inadequate "external" or "circulationist" causative arguments, against
which the "internal" or "productive" authority of Marx, Dobb, and
Mao is invoked (see, for example, Laclau 1971 and Arrighi 1972,
although Wallerstein [1974b] lumps me along with Sweezy and Mao
against Dobb and Stalin), it may be well to begin with a citation in
line with the first hypothesis, which comes from Dobb.

> But while, no doubt, many factors such as these exercised again a
> contributory influence, it seems evident that the *fundamental considera-
> tion* must have been the abundance or scarcity, the cheapness or dear-
> ness, of hired labour in determining whether or not the lord was willing
> or unwilling to commute labour-services for money-payment, and
> whether this was *a profitable or a profitless* thing for him to do if he was
> forced into it. At any rate, this consideration must have ruled where the

concern of feudal economy was to produce for a market and not simply to provision directly the seigneurial household. (Dobb 1963: 54) (My emphasis)

Douglass North and Robert P. Thomas have recently advanced "An Economic Theory of the Growth of the Western World" along similar lines.

Long-run changes in relative factor and product prices have led to fundamental institutional changes. For instance, changes in the relative value of land and labour altered the profitability of "owning" one versus the other and destroyed the basic *raison d'être* of feudalism. Rising agricultural prices increased the value of land and made it profitable to develop exclusive ownership of land (i.e., develop private property in land). With growing population and a relatively fixed supply of land, labour services became decreasingly valuable, thus providing the basis for the development of a free labour force. When relative prices reversed, the pressures for institutional change worked in the opposite direction. Changes in relative prices also led to an expanded basis for interregional trade and caused other changes . . . . Population pressure undermined the economic basis for the institutional organization of feudalism by reversing the relationship of prices as a result of diminishing returns and by expanding the size of the markets. Increases in population relative to a fixed supply of good land led to agricultural prices rising relative to non-agricultural prices; this in turn increased the value of land and decreased real wages as the output per labourer fell. Growing population, colonization, and consequent different regional factor endowments led to expanding trade. The result was that landlords now found it to their interest to commute labour dues to payments in kind and cash, and to lease the demesne lands in return for rent. On the other side of the scale the rising value of land also produced a basic disequilibrium in the medieval world. Land now offered vastly higher returns if only they could be captured by individuals; a continuous pressure arose to eliminate common-property use of land and to achieve private exclusive ownership. The enclosure movement, undoubtedly the most dramatic of the institutional changes induced by this relative price change, resulted in reorganization of property to permit exclusive ownership. (North and Thomas 1970: 9, 11)

Three sorts of objections might immediately be raised to this approach and these hypotheses. One is that the emphasis on market prices or opportunity costs still appears "circulationist" and overlooks the forces if not the relations of production. But market prices, even with feudal productive relations, and real opportunity costs in fact reflect the relative—perhaps more importantly than the absolute—development of productive forces between different productive sectors, regions, and among different relations of production. The argument is not that these forces and relations are not important or that they should not be studied in their concrete variety, but that, even in the absence of their study by the economic and political actors themselves, they make themselves felt through relative prices and costs in the pursuit of business or profit.

Another objection may be that this interpretation one-sidedly refers to the landlords' decisions without regard to the interests of the peasants and their struggle against the landlords. Rodney Hilton (Dobb, Sweezy, Takahashi, et al. 1976) relying on Marx's argument that the class struggle is the prime mover in the development of all class society, suggests that in feudal society the prime mover was the struggle over rent between the landlords and peasants. But in a feudal society this struggle is subject to the political institutions and power of the ruling class, or parts of it, and is conditioned by the political alliances among the social forces, which are largely determined by their economic interests and the fluctuations of these interests. Thus Engels, for instance, analyzed the Peasant Wars in Germany as a function of economic fluctuations, and thus Chapters 2 and 5 of this book will examine the class struggle in relation to the economic cycle.

A third objection, following Dobb himself (1963: 51), Takahashi, Kosminsky (1956), and others, would be the observation that the apparently identical and simultaneous price, cost, and profit stimuli evoked different reactions from different landlords in different places, and that apparently similar conditions at various times evoked different responses and results. This was particularly the case in the transition from feudalism to capitalism in Western Europe and the development of the "second serfdom" in Eastern Europe. Accordingly, it is necessary to take account of the variety of economic and political circumstances and of their changes in these and other regions.

There is substantial, but not complete (especially by those who are "vague" about their timing of events), agreement with F. L. Carssten's opinion that "it can clearly be shown, however, that the development in East and West [Europe], up to the fifteenth century, took place along parallel lines. . . . The manorial system of the middle ages, the *Grundherrschaft*,* was very similar in most countries of Europe. Yet from this common starting-point entirely different systems developed in East and West" (Carssten 1947: 150, 146). (Among those in agreement are Reginald Betts, Z. S. Pach [both cited in Wallerstein 1974a: 97] and Jerome Blum [1957]. Engels [1956], Dobb [1963], Nichtweiss [1953], and Rosenberg [1943–1944] are among those who seem to detect or emphasize differences as early as the thirteenth and fourteenth centuries.)

But what was the development to which Carssten refers? Jerome Blum argues that in Western Europe

> the twelfth and thirteenth centuries were years of expansion. . . . But the majority of seigneurs, impelled by their growing need for cash resulting from the increased use of money and the higher standard of living, abandoned their own agricultural operations and converted the obligations owed them by their peasants into money payments. . . . In contrast to the twelfth and thirteenth centuries, the fourteenth and fifteenth centuries were times of severe contraction in most of Western Europe. . . . Yet, remarkably enough, the process of emancipation instituted under the stimulus of the preceding boom period, was continued, and in some lands carried to completion, largely because of these hard times of the late Middle Ages. (Blum 1957: 810–11)

Far more remarkable than the "continuation" of emancipation during the last two depressive centuries—on which there is universal agreement and which corresponds to my own "theoretical" expectations and explanations—is Blum's allegation that this process already had begun during the earlier centuries of boom. There is evidence that the earlier tendency went the other way. Postan argues, at least in the case of England, that

> during the 150 years following the commutation of the twelfth century and preceding the wholesale commutation of the fourteenth, many manors stabilized, or even increased, their labour services. In the agrarian history of England these 150 years were a period of *Hochkonjunktur*. . . . On a number of estates for which we have evidence, demesne acreages also grew or at least ceased to contract for a time. (Postan 1937, cited in Kay 1973: 31)

Cristóbal Kay, reviewing estimates from several sources of the distribution of arable land between the manorial enterprises on the

---

* *Grundherrschaft* refers to indirect cultivation by the demesne landlord, through tenants, as distinct from *Gutsherrschaft*, or direct cultivation as an enterprise.

one hand, and the peasant enterprises on the other, finds for England a rough proportion of 40:60 in the eleventh century, which changed in favor of the manors to 50:50 during the "boom" years between 1272 and 1307 (for which data are available) before falling again, and much more drastically, to 25:75 for the post-Black Death depression year of 1378 (Kay 1973: 34–35). Kay's examination of the relative distribution of landholdings and rent receipts between larger and smaller manors produces similar findings (Kay 1973: 35–39), which are consistent with my hypothesis. The evidence offered by Pirenne (1936), Bloch (1961), and others may support the supposition that similar differences between the thirteenth and the fourteenth centuries in the process of transition from feudalism may be found in France.

Blum summarizes the situation in the lands east of the Elbe thus:

> The general pattern that emerges from this survey is a trend toward the loss of their freedom by a large part of the peasantry in these lands of Eastern Europe. But this tendency was reversed—for a time—in Eastern Germany, Poland, Bohemia, Silesia, Hungary, and Lithuania, by the influx of German colonists that began in the twelfth century, and in Russia by the migration from the Dnieper regions into the Oka-Volga triangle. (Blum 1957: 814)

This summary suggests that serfdom was on the *rise* in the East until the twelfth century, while it was on the decline in the West. Why should that be so? The massive migration of Germans eastward across the Elbe has been noted and emphasized by all observers, as has its liberating effects—since the Eastern princes had to offer more land and freedom to attract the settlers. But the timing and causes of this migration are not so clear. It is evident that population to the east of the Elbe was significantly less dense than that to the west. Blum attributes this in part to population growth in the West during the boom period of the fairs and the Crusades. But why should this migration and the attraction of migrants have started in the twelfth century? Blum and others argue that the liberation from serfdom in Eastern Europe was associated at first with the freedom granted to the migrants, a freedom that was then extended to the local peasantry during the thirteenth and fourteenth centuries. It is less clear why such an extension should have occurred at that time. On the other hand, during the fourteenth and fifteenth centuries, the available evidence seems to indicate clearly that the lands east of the Elbe, like those of the west, were going through a long period of depression and contraction. . . . But . . . instead of reducing obligations, as was the general practice in the West where the lords tried to hold their peasants and attract new ones by asking less of them, seigneurs in Bohemia, Silesia, Poland, Brandenburg, Prussia, and Lithuania imposed new and heavier obligations, notably in the form of labour dues and cash payments. . . . steady encroachments were made upon the right of the peasant to come and go as he pleased. . . . By the end of the fifteenth century then, from the Elbe to the Volga, most of the peasantry were well on their way to becoming serfs. During the next century both obligations and restrictions continued to be increased, so that by the end of the sixteenth century the process of enserfment was just about completed. (Blum 1957: 819–22)

In support of his interpretation of the fourteenth and fifteenth centuries, Blum cites Carssten among others; but Carssten's evidence is not clear for this period: "we do not know for certain why so many holdings became deserted in the fourteenth and fifteenth centuries" (Carssten 1947: 159).

Moreover, Blum's interpretation of the evidence would contradict Carssten's claim that until the fifteenth century there was a parallel development between the East and the West.

Other historians place the beginning of the "second serfdom" in Eastern Europe much later, from the second half of the fifteenth century (Engels 1956) and particularly during the sixteenth century. It is universally agreed that the sixteenth century witnessed the renewed enserfment of peasants in the East, in sharp contrast to their liberation in the West; but this later "second" enserfment is also universally associated with, and usually attributed to, the renewed economic expansion of the sixteenth century.

The sixteenth-century enserfment of the peasantry in Eastern Europe (with the exception of Russia, where the renewed economic expansion did not make itself directly felt) is consistent with my hypothesis, for it represented the landlords' response to their increased requirements for labor in order to meet the West European demand for East European agricultural products, principally grains, flax, and hemp. The Western manufacturers and Western-supplied oriental luxuries apparently had already increased by the late decades of the fifteenth century (as had the mining of silver in Germany), but it was significantly increased and consolidated by the price revolution and associated transformations in Western Europe, related to the colonial exploitation of the mining regions of Mexico and Peru.

The Peasant Wars in Germany, led by Thomas Münzer, and the associated Protestant Reformation of Luther, which Engels studied, were the political consequences of this development. The defeat of the Peasant Wars and the success of the Reformation were the results of the alliances that, under the circumstances, were realistically possible.

Kula (1970a), though referring to the entire period from the sixteenth to the eighteenth century, lists six essential causes of the changes experienced by Poland in particular and by Eastern Europe in general: (1) the inflation throughout all of Europe that was the result of the inflow of American precious metals, which increased the prices of staples more than those of luxuries; (2) the relative decline of luxury spice prices as a result of the increased trade with the Orient; (3) the technical progress which led to the decline in the relative prices of some manufactures, such as iron and paper, compared to those of agricultural products; (4) the progress in socioeconomic organization in other manufacturing sectors, such as textiles; (5) urbanization and industrialization; and (6) improvement in the technology of communication, particularly of navigation (Kula 1970a: 504–5). These factors not only increasingly favored the terms of trade for East European agricultural producers with respect to their imports from the West, but they also changed the internal terms of trade between magnates, nobles, and peasants within Poland.

Kula estimates the following terms of trade on commercially sold produce for the province of Carcovia, using 1550 and 1600 as base years.

Terms of trade	1550	1600	1650	1700	1750
of magnates	100	276	385	333	855
of nobles	100	80	144	152	145
of peasants	100	205	169	118	51
of magnates	—	100	139	121	310
of nobles	—	100	180	190	181
of peasants	—	100	82	58	25

By making certain heroic assumptions about the portion of output retained for self-consumption, Kula estimates the index of total income for these groups between 1600 and 1750 as rising from 100 to 220 for magnates and from 100 to 142 for nobles, and as falling from 150 to 92.5 for peasants (Kula 1970a: 502). Thus his analysis implies that the process of enserfment continued throughout the seventeenth century on into the eighteenth century, despite the seventeenth century depression in Western Europe and the associated wars which interrupted trade with the East (see Chapter 2). Although this suggestion would prolong the process of reenserfment well beyond the terminal date assigned by Blum, it would lead one to suppose, as Blum's own interpretation suggests, that enserfment proceeded equally in times of depression and times of economic expansion. This would be hard to believe. Unfortunately, Kula did not publish estimates for the period of enserfment before 1550. Nonetheless, to the extent that the above estimates are reliable, they do throw some further light on the question of this institutional change in expansive and depressive times. If we may assume that enserfment is in some sense inversely proportional to peasant income—and the reduction of labor costs was, after all, an important part of the purpose of enserfing peasants—then we may note that in the depressive half century, 1600–1650, the peasants' loss of income was only less than 20 percent; in the less depressive period from 1650 to 1700, the loss was nearer 30 percent; and in the half century of the eighteenth-century recovery, the peasant loss of income jumped to nearly 60 percent. In the first half century of Kula's table, which was a period of expansion, but also included the beginnings of the seventeenth-century depression, peasants and magnates registered an income increase and nobles a decrease. Of course these numbers cannot be taken too strictly, since the commercialized product, especially for peasants, was relatively minimal (Kula estimates 10 percent); but the *directions* of these changes tend to confirm the hypothesis that the exploitation of the peasants increased during boom times rather than during depressions.

The exploitation of peasants in Western Europe decreased further during the seventeenth-century depression (see Chapter 2). But the question which has interested all the students of this period of history remains: If the boom times—including urbanization and increased market demand for agricultural products—of the sixteenth century accelerated the enserfment of peasants in Eastern Europe, why did these same factors accelerate their liberation from serfdom in Western Europe? Kay analyzes and summarizes part of the answer.

> The market thus played two essentially different roles in Western and Eastern Europe. In Western Europe the growth of the market was mainly internal to the economy and associated with the growth of the towns and cities. This development strengthened the bourgeoisie who, in their political struggle against the feudal landlords, worked towards the liberation of the peasants and also towards increasing at least the standard of living of certain groups of peasants. In Eastern Europe the market stimulus was external to the economy and the adaptation of the Eastern economies to the initial capitalist development of the West strengthened the economic position and, above all, the political power of the landlord class. The East European landlords, in their desire to take advantage of these profitable export opportunities, were driven towards acquiring control not only over production by firmly establishing the *Gutsherrschaft* in its most developed form, but also over the marketing of their grain exports. The landlord class successfully subjugated the middle classes and nascent bourgeoisie of the towns and cities (especially in Prussia and Poland). Thus even though the terms of trade became favourable to the East European countries, their association as primary producers with the capitalist development of the West led to the weakening and subjugation, if not the actual decline, of the bourgeoisie in the towns and cities, and to the enserfdom and drastic reduction of the Peasant Economy through labour rents and the expropriation of land (*Bauernlegen*), resulting in the decline of their general standard of living. This dependence of the bourgeoisie on the *Gutsherrschaft* landlords, and of the latter on Western capitalist development, had as a final consequence the effect of creating one of the first cases of historical underdevelopment. . . . The relationship which emerged between the East European and West European economies, the latter providing raw materials and foodstuffs for the former, is not unlike that to be found in the dependency between underdeveloped and developed countries today. (Kay 1973: 183–84)

It was this same weakness of the incipient bourgeoisie in Germany which, according to Engels' analysis of the roles of Münzer and Luther in the German Peasant Wars, led Luther to abandon Münzer and the peasants, and to ally himself with the landlords in the phase of the war that brought the peasants to defeat. The relative weakness of the bourgeoisie and the towns in East Europe, already before the onset of this association with Western Europe (Wallerstein 1974a: 96), may perhaps be attributed to the earlier Turkish and Mongol invasions of the Eastern regions and the consequent nondevelopment of greater royal as opposed to feudal power.

The underpopulation in Eastern Europe, both absolute and relative to the West, would—as in the New World as well—occasion new forms, or renewed forms with new contents, of forced labor servitude in response to the opportunities of demands of profitable good business.

In Western Europe, in the meantime, the sixteenth century economic growth and the increasing demand for agricultural products offered the local peasantry in many parts the opportunity to participate in the direct market provision of the supply and in the income to be derived from this provision. This the Western overseas demand in Eastern Europe did not do. However, circumstances varied from one country and region in the West to another. In France, where towns and internal commerce were more developed but where neither *Gutsherrschaft* nor the development of a livestock economy were apparently feasible, the struggle for the rent from the land tended toward sharecropping. In Spain and England, during the enclosures movement, common grazing lands were enclosed and/or crop lands were given over to sheep; this gave rise to the common saying that sheep ate men, who could not survive without crops. Sheep would have eaten a lot more men if Eastern Europe had not risen to the occasion and satisfied the resulting increase in the demand for grains, or if the mining regions of the New World had not provided some of the means to pay for the grains. The precious metals from the New World enabled the Western European countries to settle directly or indirectly the deficit in the trade balance with the Orient, which provided some of the goods (spices) to pay for East European imports. As it was, some of the displaced peasants—in a relative labor-surplus European economy—were able to move into the towns, thus giving rise to the expression that "town air made free." But most of them could be harnessed through the putting-out system into spinning and weaving the wool in the countryside itself, even though their products were increasingly sold in the towns and abroad, including Eastern Europe and the New World.

In summary then, I would argue that during the booming six-teenth century when business was good, "external" and "circula-tory" opportunities and demands stimulated institutional transforma-tions in both Eastern and Western Europe, as well as in parts of the New World. Such opportunities had probably had a similar impact during the previous long expansionary period of the twelfth and thirteenth centuries, when Europe's relations with the Muslims had changed, particularly in the Mediterranean regions. On the other hand, these expansions were brought to a halt, perhaps by the increasing limitations of the productive forces relative to the rela-tions of production—or, in other words, by decreasing returns to the scale of production—which gave rise to the depressions or reces-sions, or, perhaps more accurately, retrenchments of the fourteenth and fifteenth centuries, and then again of the seventeenth century. During these periods of depression, "internal" productive or produc-tivity transformations and qualitative political and social transforma-tions of the relations of production had to take priority; in situations where these changes failed to occur, or were inadequate, the region or society would be condemned to historical oblivion, if only because of the backwardness of the modes of production relative to those in societies, such as England, that did undergo such qualitative changes.

Thus England flourished in the seventeenth century relative to the rest of Europe, and especially relative to the decline of Spain and Italy (see Chapter 2). In the uneven and combined cyclical historical development, the "external," "circulatory" determinants are dialecti-cally related to the "internal," "productive" ones, even beyond the tautological observation that both or all of these determinants are obviously internal to the social system we are studying. These two hypotheses form the guiding principles in the selection of historical events and interpretations presented in the following chapters: (1) institutional changes are primarily determined by what is "good business"; and (2) external contradictions and developments have more immediate importance when "business is good," and internal contradictions and developments have more immediate importance when "business is bad."

Chapter 2

The Seventeenth-Century Depression

It is now commonly admitted that there was, for several decades in the seventeenth century, a period of major economic and social recession, crisis and secular readjustment, which contrasts strikingly with the periods of economic expansion which preceded it and followed it. Its effects were not confined to any single country, but with a few marginal exceptions these can be traced throughout the entire range of the economic area dominated by, and from, Western Europe, from the Americas to the China Seas; nor were they confined to the economic field.
—Eric Hobsbawm (1960)

Most of the seventeenth century was marked by a worldwide depression: the "decline of Spain," the decline of Italy and of the Ottoman Empire, the Thirty Years War in Germany. These developments, long treated as isolated phenomena and variously attributed to one or another specific and often noneconomic cause, are now being increasingly recognized by modern historiography to have been the mutually related processes of a single global crisis (Hobsbawm 1960). What is more, the crises and depression of the seventeenth century may—and should—be traced and related to the earlier economic expansion: the development of capital accumulation in the sixteenth century. It is clear that the depression of the seventeenth century followed the growth of the sixteenth century and brought the latter temporarily to a halt, but it has not yet generally been accepted that the general crisis of the seventeenth century must be interpreted as a necessary economic and political development—the consequence of the economic limitations of growth and accumulation in the previous sixteenth-century upswing. And still more important, the crisis of the seventeenth century must be studied as the critical resolution of development limitations, a resolution which was the necessary requirement for, and the basis of, the development of capitalism and the accumulation of capital in the stage that followed, namely the eighteenth century. This task is still only in the initial stages of fulfillment. Although it will not be possible to meet these requirements of scientific historiography and political economic (as well as sociocultural) analysis here, the following review of the seventeenth century is undertaken with these objectives in mind.

The crisis of depression and decline was evident in the Mediterranean area, which had been the principal center of economic activity since the fifteenth century. The Ottoman Empire, the Northern Italian cities, and Spain all declined, never again to recover their leadership. The other hub of economic activity, the Baltic area, also suffered decline; in Poland, the cities of the Hanseatic League and other German regions, and Denmark. In addition, the France of Richelieu was in crisis, as was the England which experienced the Cromwellian revolution of 1640 and the Glorious Revolution of 1688. Only Belgium and Holland—the latter in its "golden" century—seem to have partially escaped the general depression. The "European periphery" in Asia, Africa, and Latin America—and notably in the "new" areas of Siberia, North America, and the Caribbean—experienced the seventeenth-century world depression variously and differently, as we shall examine below. Braudel and Spooner (1967: 404–5) date the beginning of the declines or depressions from the 1580s in Spain (others date the decline from 1575–1580); from 1589–1592 in France; from 1620 in Germany; and from 1640 in England and Holland. But in selecting these dates they are primarily following the history of price movements, which were influenced by the "inflationary" consequences of the Thirty Years War from 1618 to 1648.* Hence, I argue that it is more accurate to date the general depression in England, for example, from 1615 (Supple 1969) and most certainly from the cyclical depression of

---

* Braudel, in the first edition (for example, 1953, II: 544–47) dates the economic decline of the Mediterranean from 1610–1620.

1620–1624. The decline of Italy may be dated from the beginning of the seventeenth century (Cipolla 1970) and the decline of Ottoman Turkey perhaps even somewhat earlier (Lewis 1970).

It may be observed that, in general, the downswing of the seventeenth-century depression that swept across these areas followed the same sequence and rhythm as had the upswing of sixteenth-century expansive development. This sequence is especially evident in the wave of the sixteenth-century price revolution, as explained in Chapter 1. This observation is only one of several grounds for agreeing with Hobsbawm, Vilar, and others that the seventeenth-century depression had a *common economic cause* and for rejecting explanations which attribute the declines of individual regions to specific agricultural failures, political decay or crises, or war—especially the Thirty Years War. Such explanations are more properly to be regarded first as consequences and then as contributing aggravations of the general economic crisis (Hobsbawm 1960; 1965: 14).

The decline in prices, or, more accurately, the drastic decline in their rates of inflationary increase, which the price historians have observed and which Braudel reviews in the *Cambridge Economic History of Europe*, is only the most visible manifestation of the crisis and depression. The analysis of prices should not be limited to monetarist quantity theory, which regards changes in the price level as simple results or reflections of changes in the quantity of money due to fortuitous fluctuations (in this case decreases) in the production of silver and gold. Along with the decline in prices, there was undoubtedly a decline in rates of profit. Even the British and Dutch East India companies, chartered in 1601 (more precisely, December 31, 1600) and 1602 respectively, were notably unprofitable during most years of their operation until the last part of the seventeenth century.

Foreign trade either declined or expanded only slowly. The trade of the Ottoman Levant and its Italian cities atrophied disastrously. Shipping between Spain and its American possessions declined to one-third of its sixteenth-century maximum. Baltic trade was sharply reduced after 1620. Even the oriental trade, despite Holland's "golden" century, declined from 1620 to 1650 and fell off drastically between 1650 and 1680 (Vilar 1969: 235). British exports, especially of textiles, fell off after 1620 (Supple 1969). Internal production also declined, either absolutely or in its rate of growth, although perhaps less than external trade. This was especially true of the production of manufactured goods, as we shall see below. These and other economic problems were reflected in—and then aggravated or accelerated by—political crises, of which we may regard the two English revolutions and the Thirty Years War as only the most notorious. The financial reforms of Colbert in France were an unsuccessful attempt to stem the tide. Moreover, both the economic and political crises were reflected in the cultural sphere, which experienced a simultaneous flowering or renaissance. Geographical expansionism also increased. Recovery, in turn, from the seventeenth-century depression may be dated roughly from the 1690s—for Britain perhaps from the year following the Glorious Revolution of 1688–1689—although this date varies from country to country, as we shall observe. (In emphasizing the identification of this long seventeenth-century depression I do not deny the importance of some intervening temporary cyclical upturns.)

1. The Decline of the Mediterranean

We may begin a review of the seventeenth-century depression in particular regions with those economies whose decline effectively eliminated them from the competitive race for economic and political supremacy and development: the Turks, the Italians, the Spaniards, and perhaps the Portuguese, the East Europeans, and in a way the Germans. Although these productive and commercial centers all participated in the general or common cyclical downturn of the seventeenth century, their individual declines were for all intents and purposes permanent (at least until the late nineteenth and twentieth centuries) and apparently secular. In other words, these economic centers did not individually achieve an adequate domestic and international adjustment to the limitations of sixteenth-century development and its seventeenth-century crisis-challenge; but their economic and military declines and elimination did contribute to the crisis-adjustment of the world mercantile capitalist system and to the process of capital accumulation as a whole. Moreover, the decline of these centers was an integral factor in the successful adjustment of other centers of economic activity to the capitalist system and accumulation process, notably England and to a lesser degree Flanders and France. The elimination of France from—or at least retardation in—the process of capital accumulation would be the subject of a later cycle.*

The expansion of the Ottoman Empire of the sixteenth century was halted at the end of that same century. Western historians have usually attributed the empire's subsequent decline to both external and internal political causes. While this is useful as far as it goes, it underlines the need for a further analysis, to uncover the more profound "internal" causes which led to a change in the essential role or function the Turks played, along with the Arabs, in the incipient process of capital accumulation on a world scale and mercantile capitalist development. Bernard Lewis marks the decline of Ottoman power by the treaties of 1606, 1683, and 1718. These three treaties, more than causing the decline, consecrated it, and expressed the ever decreasing bargaining power of the Turks relative to their rivals.

Long before, at the Battle of Lepanto in 1571, the Ottoman advance had been stopped at the gates of Vienna. By 1580, an Ottoman geographer warned Murad III of the dangers to Islamic trade—and faith—that increasingly would result from the European establishment in Asia and their control of the sea routes to the west. He advised the construction of a canal at Suez, the capture of the oriental ports held by the Portuguese, and the expulsion of "the infidels." By 1625 another Ottoman observer complained of the increasing competition from the Europeans in the oriental trade and of the supposedly consequent increasing scarcity of gold and silver in the lands of Islam. He advised the latter to capture the shores of Yemen (where the Portuguese had established forts to protect their oriental trade): "otherwise before very long, the Europeans will rule over the lands of Islam" (Lewis 1970: 222). European commerce was seen as unfair competition because it had access to and used new sources of gold and silver (from the New World) with which the

---

* Hobsbawm (1960) develops a similar argument.

Turks and Arabs could not compete (the less so insofar as the Europeans also diverted the traditional trans-Islamic flow of sub-Saharan African gold). The Turks, accordingly, were forced into increasing debasement and devaluation of their currency. Both their agriculture and their industry declined, in part due to state economic and fiscal policies in the face of the emergency and in part due to the increasing costs of maintaining a military machine that was fighting a losing battle with ever more expensive and professionally manned artillery and firearms (Lewis 1970).

Northern Italy, which had survived and even continued to prosper from the sixteenth-century expansion of trade via the Atlantic and the mercantile capitalist development of Spain and Northern Europe, definitely and definitively declined during the seventeenth century. This was the case at least of the industry and trade of Venice, Como, Milan, Cremone, Florence, Genoa, and even of Naples in Southern Italy. Some minor manufacturing regions, on the other hand, such as the peripheral areas of the colonized world—e.g., the Spanish empire in America—were able to derive temporary and partial benefit from the general decline by increasing their manufacturing production. They were unable, however, to firmly establish themselves. The prosperity of the Italian cities had been derived from (a) their privileged participation in the oriental trade with Northern Europe; (b) their earnings in financial and transportation services associated with this trade and part of the sixteenth-century European expansion; (c) in some cases, Mediterranean sugar plantation profits; and especially (d) the manufacture and export of high quality and high cost textiles. All of these sources of prosperity suffered during the seventeenth-century depression, either from reduced trade, service, and plantation earnings due to the sixteenth-century development of competitive alternatives elsewhere, or from cyclically depressed prices, demand, and profits. Mostly, however, it was a combination of both, in which the Italians and their competitors suffered cyclically. But some of their competitors, taking advantage of new productive opportunities, were able to survive and recover, while the Italians and some other economies declined and were eliminated.

Italian textiles suffered drastic restrictions of their export markets as a result of local competition in England, France, and the Low Countries; and they apparently suffered from these competitors' penetration into the "third" or "neutral" markets of Germany, Spain, Portugal, and Africa. Italian textiles were higher priced and more luxurious (like the "old draperies" of England which were also increasingly displaced) than the coarser and cheaper Northern European textiles (and English "new draperies"). Moreover, high-cost Italian producers were protected by strong guilds which resisted the adoption of new productive methods; these were more easily introduced among their newer competitors in Northern Europe. Taxes were especially excessive as a component of costs, perhaps because of proportionately greater military obligations of the Italian city-states. Moreover, since the sixteenth-century inflation had advanced faster and farther in Italy (as well as in Spain) compared to Northern Europe, Italian exports had probably become relatively more uncompetitive in Northern Europe for that reason as well. During the seventeenth century, the Italians, like the Spanish, increasingly resorted to debasement and devaluation of the coinage, perhaps to a greater degree than their northern rivals; but this policy only offered temporary relief at the cost of still greater long-term damage to the economy's competitive position in the international market. By the end of the seventeenth century, the erstwhile textile kings in Italy were importing manufactures from England, France, and Belgium, exporting semiprocessed raw materials in return, and relying increasingly on foreign, especially English, shipping (Cipolla 1965). Italian capital, when it was invested, increasingly flowed abroad, where profits were more attractive than at home. Financial supremacy in the meantime had passed to Amsterdam.

The decline of Spain in the seventeenth century has given rise to much analysis and controversy (List 1856; Hamilton 1929; Vilar 1964, 1969; Larraz 1943; Chaunu 1974; Vicens Vives 1962; Reglá 1961; etc., as well as contemporaries cited by them, especially Sancho de Moncada, Martinez de la Mata, Cellorigo, etc.). But there is general agreement among all of these writers that during the seventeenth century Spanish domestic economic development was reversed and that internationally Spain was all but eliminated as an autonomous contestant in the struggle for economic (and political) supremacy and benefit within the mercantile capitalist system and the process of world capital accumulation. What is more, the milking of the Spanish economy by her competitors and enemies, already begun during Spain's golden (or silver) century, was intensified to the point of all but milking Spain dry. Returning from Italy, a Spaniard reported in 1654 that "a witty cartoon has now appeared in Rome: a very fat cow with a large udder called Spain; around it many sucking calfs called England, Flanders, Holland, France, Germany, Italy and others of our enemies" (cited in Reglá 1961: 338). According to Larraz (cited in Reglá 1961: 346) the inward- and outward-bound shipping between Spain and its American colonies declined from about fifty-five ships and 20,000 tons annually each in 1600–1604 to twenty-seven ships and 9,000 tons in 1640–1650 and to eight ships and about 2,500 tons each in 1701–1710. Moreover, according to a contemporary French source, of all the merchandise arriving in Cadiz at the end of the seventeenth century, 25 percent was consigned to French merchants, 22 percent to Genovese, 20 percent to Dutch, 10 percent to English, 10 percent to Flemish, 8 percent to German, and only 5 percent to Spanish receivers (Reglá 1961: 346). Simultaneously, Spanish merchant shipping was replaced by that of her European rivals.

Foreign control of the Spanish economy and trade, the anti-nationalist Habsburg economic policy, the price differential between Spain and the rest of Europe due to its greater inflation and devaluation (in part through copper vellon coinage) and of course the competitive disadvantage of Spanish industry compared to that of France, the Low Countries, and increasingly England, spelled the virtual destruction of Spanish industry in the seventeenth century. The only exception was a temporary Catalan revival associated with wool exports. The shutdown of textile establishments in Castile and elsewhere gave rise to numerous complaints and, with the exception of temporary relief, unsuccessful attempts to save them. This shutdown also was reflected in the decline of population in the principal old textile centers:

City	Number of Heads of Families (Vecinos)			
	1530	*1594*	*1646*	*1694*
Toledo	5,898	10,933	5,000	5,000
Segovia	2,850	5,548	—	1,625
Salamanca	2,459	4,953	2,965	2,416
Valladolid	6,750	8,112	3,000	3,637

SOURCES: Larraz 1943; Vicens Vives 1962: 139.

These data for *vecinos* correspond to estimated total populations of 55,000 in Toledo, 27,000 in Segovia, 25,000 in Salamanca in 1594 (Reglá 1961: 15). Although total population in these provinces also declined during the seventeenth century, the population decline in the manufacturing cities was still greater, and possibly greater than that of *vecinos* (Reglá 1961: 254).

The decline of Spain is summarized by other testimony. Thus, the German nationalist, Friedrich List, observed, looking back from the mid-nineteenth century:

> Valencia, Segovia, Toledo, and many other cities of Castile were distinguished by their manufactures of wool. Seville alone numbered sixteen thousand looms, and the woollen manufactures of Segovia employed thirteen thousand workmen in 1552. Other branches of industry . . . were developed in the same proportion. (List 1856: 13)

Yet only a half century later Sancho de Moncada observed in his *Restauración Política de España 1619* (1746 edition) that foreign manufactures "have occasioned the neglect of all the trade and commerce of Spain, whose decline had been experienced in Toledo, Burgos, Medina, Sevilla and other mercantile places" (quoted in Larraz 1943: 166). During the remainder of the seventeenth century, the decline of Spain was to be still greater. It is significant that during much of this time the kings of Spain were also the Habsburg emperors, and that the interests of Charles V and his Northern European bankers lay elsewhere. Larraz writes:

> The interpretation of the foregoing data is quite clear. . . . The intervention in Europe made the Treasury of Castile spend, through contracts and transfers of foreign bankers—principally Genovese—all the money that was consigned to the Treasury from the [Spanish American] Indies and also a goodly part of what was consigned to private individuals, which was obtained through taxation and, in some cases, through expropriation. Thus ended the Castilian golden century. . . . Sancho de Moncada said in 1619 that nine parts in ten of the trade with the [Latin American] Indies was by foreigners, "so that the Indies are for them and the title is for your Majesty." A few years later, in 1624, Struzz testified to the reality of the commerce with the Indies. With total official tolerance, "the largest part of the merchandise that the fleets carry is foreign property under names of Spaniards." . . . The trade coming from Sevilla and Cadiz . . . fell almost entirely into foreign hands. The testimony from all sources, from Spaniards and non-Spaniards, support the above statement throughout the seventeenth century. (Larraz 1943: 79, 89–90, 88–89)

Similarly Adam Smith observed that "the colonies of Spain and Portugal, for example, give more real encouragement to the industry of other countries than to that of Spain and Portugal" (Smith 1937: 591). (The "decline of Spain," as Hamilton and others have called it, is of course extremely instructive for any analysis of underdevelopment; but the latter is beyond the scope of this book.)

Along with Germany and other regions bordering on the Baltic Sea, Eastern Europe—Poland and Danzig—had been an important exporter of foodstuffs and raw materials to Western Europe and perhaps its most important customer for imports of textiles and other manufactures during the sixteenth century. In the 1620s the Baltic market for northwest European exports collapsed, initiating the general crisis (Hobsbawm 1960; 1965: 10). Nonetheless, East European production of foodstuffs for exports continued and grew during the seventeenth century, and enjoyed favorable terms of trade (Kula 1970a: 153). In Eastern Europe, production for the export market continued to generate the second serfdom of the peasantry and the increased wealth of the largest landowners and merchants. Real income (money and in kind) of the magnates increased from an index of 100 to one of 220 between 1600 and 1750, while that of nobles increased from 100 to 142 and that of peasants decreased from 100 to 92.5. The relative money incomes changed much more drastically still. This restricted the internal market both for domestically produced manufactures and for certain imported ones, consolidating the dependence of Eastern Europe as a raw materials producer and supplier to Western Europe (Kula 1970a: 146–54). In other words, the seventeenth-century crisis apparently also eliminated Eastern Europe as a potential competitor of the West in the contest for economic supremacy, capital accumulation, and development.

2. Depression and Transformation in Northwest Europe

In France, the seventeenth century produced Richelieu, Colbert, and Louis XIV, as well as the Frondiste uprisings during the mid-century. These uprisings were both the result of, and a revolt against, the economic conditions generated by the long depression and the often successful attempts by the state to shift its burden onto the poor. Stagnation and decline befell the French economy in general and also its industrial production after 1630, simultaneously with the decline of the money supply and prices. Unemployment and pauperism increased, generating the Frondiste uprisings. Thus, the economic policies of Colbert (despite the fact that his name has become a synonym for mercantilist policy, not unlike that of the contemporary mercantilists elsewhere in Europe) and those of Richelieu before him represented not so much the execution of autonomously generated mercantilist ideas or theories (and still less "erroneous" "bullionist" ones) as they reflected the necessary and logical response to the exigiencies of the seventeenth-century depression. "Colbert's policy of industrialisation was really nothing but a desperate effort to counteract this declining trend; it was undertaken in the highly unfavourable conditions of deflation, falling prices, incomes and consumption, and ended in semi-failure" (Crouzet 1967: 141–42).

Colbert also sought to allay France's internal economic problems by launching a vast commercial offensive overseas (requiring military support, however), especially in the New World. One of his instruments was the founcing of the French West Indies Company in 1664. But this commercial foreign policy also had only limited success, at least during Colbert's own lifetime, because of the economic circumstances of the times. Moreover, Colbert's economic policies, especially overseas, often had to compete with the interests and ambitions of France in continental Europe, represented by Louvois, the minister of war and Colbert's rival, who sought to devote French resources to the prosecution of its incessant European land wars and to the expansion and consolidation of its position on the European continent. By and large this terrestial military and economic posture overshadowed and won out over the naval and overseas commercial one. The former dominated French policy until France was defeated by England in the Seven Years War. The outcome of this war, the Peace of Paris in 1763, established British dominance on a world scale. This dominance was based on Britain's naval power and colonial supremacy at a time when its technology and industry was not yet definitively superior to that of France. Perhaps this outcome and the respective policies leading up to it had been geopolitically predetermined by the respective continental and insular locations and interests of the two great rival powers.

England entered the seventeenth century as a second-rate power, both economically and politically speaking, and emerged from the seventeenth-century crisis as a first-rate power, even though its total supremacy would not be finally established until the Peace of Paris in 1763 and reconfirmed at the Council of Vienna in 1815, after Napoleon's defeat at Waterloo. Although the seventeenth-century depression initially or superficially weakened Britain, as it did its European rivals, the British economy, more than any other, made the economic adjustments that would permit further capital accumulation and capitalist development in the eighteenth century and after. Most of its rivals, meanwhile, were economically and/or militarily and politically eliminated during the seventeenth century. In 1588 Britain had defeated the Spanish Armada, while the Dutch were regaining their political independence from Spanish rule. Britain also used to good advantage the Spanish annexation of Portugal in 1580 and Portugal's renewed independence in 1640. In return for the offer of political protection to Portugal, Britain gained commercial privileges in the treaties of 1642, 1654, and 1661 and finally achieved complete economic supremacy over, and domination of, Portugal after the Treaty of Methuen of 1703. This treaty definitively eliminated Portugal's manufactures and converted it into a purveyor of its own primary products as well as gold from its Brazilian colony to Britain. Moreover, Portugal became a purchaser of British manufactures for both its own and Brazilian consumption.

The economic elimination of Italy was reviewed above. Rivalry with France continued through several wars, though it would not finally be settled in England's favor until the Seven Years War of 1756–1763. Germany, whose development had been substantially abreast of England's during the sixteenth century, was eliminated by the Thirty Years War of 1618–1648, not to recover until the late nineteenth century. The Anglo-Dutch rivalry, despite Holland's golden age of the seventeenth century, was tilted in England's favor by the English Navigation Acts of 1650–1651, etc., and was politically settled in England's favor by the wars from 1672 to 1696. Holland's economic decline did not become definite, however, until after England also had emerged victorious from the War of the

Spanish Succession against France between 1701 and 1713, and the Treaty of Utrecht. In the meantime, domestically, England had experienced the bourgeois revolution of 1640 and the Glorious Revolution of 1689. The latter in particular increased the political power of the manufacturing interests relative to the interests of landed and commercial groups, who were disadvantaged after 1700.

Underlying these political moments and movements was a substantial economic transformation of the English economy, domestically and internationally, generated by the seventeenth-century depression in the mercantile capitalist system as a whole and in Britain itself. During the sixteenth century, from 1500 to 1602, the wage index in England had risen from 95 to 124, while the price index had risen from 95 to 243. The index of real wages of British masons had fallen from 115 in 1475–1480 to 46 in 1600 and 38 in 1610–1620, so that to buy one year's consumption of bread a British worker had to work ten weeks in 1495 and forty weeks in 1593 (Mandel 1970, I: 107, 148). During most of the seventeenth century, these price and wage trends would be generally reversed, with the index of real wages rising again to 55 in 1700 and that of prices rising only slowly over the long period and falling during several shorter ones (Mandel 1970, I: 108; Clough 1968). During the first decade of the seventeenth century and until 1614, prices and apparently profits were still rising in England. But after 1615 and especially after 1620, the former ceased their rapid rise and the latter definitely fell sharply. The export of shortcloths, which around 1600 had been approximately 100,000 (notional) shortcloths and in 1614 had risen to a maximum of 127,000, declined to 75,000 in 1622, and then hovered between 80,000 and 90,000 during the next two decades to 1640 in all years but two (Supple 1969: 258). (Minchinton [1969: 9] gives a 75 percent increase in British exports from 1600 to 1640, which he calls a relatively low annual rate of increase of 1 5 percent.)

What the production, as distinct from export, of these manufactures was is difficult to say, but if it grew, t certainly did not do so rapidly, in comparison to earlier and later periods (Supple 1969; Hobsbawm 1960). Some indication of growth of some production may be the triplication of coastal ships between 1628 and 1683 with a tonnage increase until 1660 of approximately 1,100 tons per year (Hobsbawm 1960; 1965: 48). Nonetheless, economic growth, all authorities agree, was certainly stagnating in Britain during this major part of the seventeenth century. Imports exceeded exports, and the balance of payments was generally passive in Britain. It was this cyclical problem which was at the root of the "bullionist" worries and recommendations of the British mercantilists of the time, especially of Thomas Munn's famous tract, *England's Treasure by Fforraign Trade*, which he wrote as a governor of the East India Company but in the aftermath of the downturn of the 1620s and in response to that crisis (Supple 1969: 212).

These depressive circumstances either generated or facilitated costly economic adjustment in Britain, which were to place its economy in a competitively advantageous position against her continental rivals. The times obliged the increasing replacement of the finer, short wool textiles ("old draperies"), whose principal export market had been the Baltic region, by the coarser long wool ones ("new draperies"), which would penetrate the South European, Portuguese, and new American markets. The progressive elimination of the former was accompanied (or facilitated) by the natural concentration of capital during hard times, the gradual elimination of the artisans who produced the older textiles by older methods, and their progressive replacement through the putting-out system. This involved a new "division of labor" between the merchant capitalists, who were favored by the process, and the peasants, whose reliance on agriculture was undermined as the symbiotic relation between artisan manufacture and peasant agriculture was being destroyed.

This process, widely associated with the transition from feudalism to capitalism, was singularly accelerated by the seventeenth-century depression in England—so much so that it may be argued, following Hobsbawm and many others, that it was precisely the seventeenth-century *depression*, rather than simply a long-term secular trend of development, which critically accelerated the changes in the division of labor, both domestically in England and elsewhere as well as internationally. These changes in turn permitted the development of capitalism to continue and then to "take off," propelled by factory and uniform interchangeable parts production.

Yet none of this transformation in the mode of production, development of the division of labor, and accumulation of capital was or could be limited to the narrow confines of any single national economy. Its stage was the developing world economy, and its actors were all of the participating subeconomies, including especially the colonized and also the newly settled regions. Most specifically, for Britain, this transformation involved: (1) increased reliance on and support from the state for the manufacturing and commercial interests, after the revolutions of 1640 and 1688; (2) the protection of the Navigation Acts of 1650–1651 against Dutch competition and of the Portuguese treaties, which (a) opened a captive market for British textiles in a weak country, (b) obviated the purchase of French wine with scarce bullion or foreign exchange, and (c) paved the way for the increasing prohibition of all imports from France (Sideri 1970); and (3) a new colonial policy in Asia, Africa, and the Americas (see section 3 below).

The relationships between economic depression, commercial and industrial policy, revolution, the state, and war were particularly important and evident in British rivalry with the Dutch. In the first half of the seventeenth century, the Dutch had five to six times more total shipping tonnage than the British, and thirteen times more tonnage engaged in the vital Baltic trade; moreover, even half the cargoes that arrived in Britain from the Baltic arrived in Dutch bottoms. This was because the Dutch ships had a cost advantage over the British, particularly in the carriage of relatively low-unit-value bulk cargoes (Wilson 1957: 42–46). Thus the Dutch carried nearly three-quarters of East European and Scandinavian grain and timber westward through the Baltic, a similar proportion of French and Portuguese salt eastward, and between one-third and one-half of Swedish metals (Wilson 1957: 41–46). This trade had developed during the sixteenth century, along with East European exports of flax and hemp and the Baltic regions' imports of salted fish and especially textiles from the West. The British Merchant Adventurers and other trading companies exported textiles, which accounted for 80 percent of British exports at the beginning of the seventeenth century; but much of this was semifinished "white" cloth, which was dyed and finished in Holland before its reexport eastward by the Dutch, who thereby earned the value added by their labor, transport, and merchandizing (Jones 1966: 38; Wilson 1957: 27–28). Only the British Eastland Company exported finished cloth, but at a higher price than the Dutch. Thus the Dutch exports accounted for over half the textile trade to the Baltic regions (Wilson 1957: 41). Both the Dutch and English suffered from a balance of trade deficit, especially the English, which was filled by the supplementary shipment of bullion—hence one importance of the "Spanish connection," which was the ultimate source of this vital element.* Wilson summarizes:

> the burden of England's tale of complaint [as] the resentments which English merchants and politicians felt against what they deemed to be England's subservience to the Dutch economic system. Why was treasure draining away from England? Why was trade hampered and strangled by a physical scarcity of coin? The answer was plain. So long as the Dutch sucked England dry of her stocks of raw materials, there could be no development of England's manufacturing capacity, no opportunity for English merchants to benefit by the most profitable stages of the economic process. So long as English purchasers could be tempted in an uncontrolled market by succulent Dutch imports and so long as English importers were undersold by competition of Dutch rivals in an open market, it was impossible to correct the disequilibrium in the balance of trade. (Wilson 1957: 144–45)

An early British attempt to remedy this situation was the so-called Cockayne project, named after a London alderman who was also a member of the Eastland Company, which exported finished cloth. He had already unsuccessfully sought to enforce the finishing of all colored export cloth in 1606. But in 1613 he sought and procured the enforced dyeing and finishing of all exported cloth through the

---

* On the other hand, this connection may have had an even greater importance by the seventeenth century in enabling multilateral settlements of this deficit in the balance of trade with the eastern regions. Thus Sperling and Price argue that in fact little bullion was actually shipped to the East, at least from England, except to Russia and of course to the Orient, and that the deficit was paid through indirect shipments from Holland or Hamburg and through letters of credit on these places, often on merchants from Southern Europe (see Sperling 1969: 461 for quotation from Price). A contemporary, though somewhat later (1704) observer, seems to confirm the same:

> & to what concerns the correspondence by letters & bills of Exchange . . . for whoever had sent goods to Danttzig, Hamburgh, Sweden and Danemark, Moscovey or Germany to France and Spaigne, and had account from these places that sd. goods were disposed of, and the money come in for them, they send there bills to Holland upon these places & had ready money for the bills wch always indepted these Nations (to wit France and Spaigne) very much to Holland . . . (Quoted in Sperling 1969: 461)

revocation of the Merchant Adventurers' charter to export unfinished white cloth. The Cockayne project was a dismal failure and was abrogated after 1617 with the reinstatement of the Merchant Adventurers' former privileges, for two related reasons: British manufacturing was not yet economically prepared to supplant the Dutch processing of its cloth, and its short-lived attempt to do so coincided with an economic recession in which demand, prices, and profits declined. Supple notes the "basic and immediate issue":

> This was the general decline in the prosperity of *all* types of old drapery.
> . . . Thus the deciding factor in the collapse of the Cockayne project
> was a fall in demand, on the part not so much of European consumers
> as of those merchants who had secured control of the cloth trade. . . .
> The two eventful years 1615 and 1616 achieved no favorable results and
> taught some harsh lessons. They demonstrated, for instance, that the
> international division of labor by which the Dutch dyed and dressed
> England's semi-manufactured textiles was not an arbitrary phenome-
> non sustained by artificial survivals of company regulations. On the
> contrary, by the early seventeenth century it reflected economic
> realities against which England might tilt only at her peril. It was now
> uneconomic for English industry to attempt to add another process to
> the manufacture of the old draperies. The achievement of this direction
> was pitifully inadequate and as late as 1632 some 75 per cent of the
> shipments to the Low Countries and Germany were still of unfinished
> cloth. (Supple 1969: 45, 49–50)

Under the circumstances, another remedy was sought in the protection of British shipping. In 1615 the Levant Company had received a proclamation, which extended its monopoly from trade to and from the ports it served to the import trade of all commodities from these foreign ports. In the wake of the 1620 depression, and despite the attempts by opponents to blame the *monopoly* of the trading companies for the decline in trade, the Eastland Company was granted a similar proclamation extending its monopoly privileges in 1622. The official purpose was "to maintain and in-crease the trade of our merchants and the strength of our navy . . ." (Hinton 1959: 31). In the following two decades, British imports rose considerably, but exports increased to a lesser degree and frequently remained below the 1614 high point (Supple 1969). In the meantime, fishing for herring, to be salted and sold to Eastern and Southern Europe, became an important bone of contention between

Britain and Holland. This was reflected in the controversy between the English John Selden's *Mare Clausum*, which sought to protect British shipping and fishing by claiming sovereignty over part of the sea, and the Dutch Grotius' *Mare Liberum*, which argued for freedom of the seas to further Dutch interests and protect its neutral shipping in times of Anglo-French and Spanish wars.

The mid-century years witnessed a serious economic depression, which led to the Navigation Acts of 1651 and the first Anglo-Dutch war of 1652 (Jones 1966: 47–49; Wilson 1957, chs. 4 and 5; Hinton 1959, chs. 7 and 8). English shipping from the Baltic declined rapidly and drastically: 1647, 130 ships; 1648, 93; 1649, 64; 1650, 22. The volume of cloth exports declined from 20,000 pieces to 11,000 during the same years; and increasingly much of this export—in 1649 more than half—was exported in foreign bottoms (Hinton 1959: 84–85).

> In the new depression which settled on the English economy in 1649, these ideas of restricting foreign economic activity—especially Dutch—which were common to the crises of the previous half-century, were again revived. In that year the Council of State referred to Parliament the desire for a stricter regulation of foreign imports expressed by the East India, the Levant, and the Eastland Companies. (Wilson 1957: 54)

These and other companies asked for protection against imports by foreigners, and the shipowners, through their spokesmen in the foreign Ministry, asked for a general monopoly on all import and export shipping. Only the Merchant Adventurers, whose business was principally exporting, were opposed to some such measure (Wilson 1957: 55–56). The resulting act sought to reconcile these and other private interests and to advance the "national" interest. Passed in October and enacted in December 1651, it was entitled "An Act for the encouragement of shipping and navigation." Hinton summarizes:

> Its provisions did encourage, and were designed to encourage, trade; but trade supported navigation. Its core was contained in two simple provisions: (i) goods were to be imported only from the place of their growth or production, and (ii) goods were to be imported only in English ships or in ships of the place where they were grown or produced. The first condition cut out the Dutch entrepot, the second cut out Dutch ships. . . . The Navigation Act could not increase, and

was not intended to increase, the volume of trade. It could rescue, and was only intended to rescue, it from the hands of the Dutch. (Hinton 1959: 89, 93)

As Wilson comments, this 1651 act 'harnessed the products of colonies firmly to the mother country, and thereby created by legislative act an entrepot system which pleased those who had preached that England should follow Holland's way to wealth" (Wilson 1957: 57).

The rump parliament that passed this act—as well as one in 1650 forbidding the British colonies to trade with the Dutch—was the one that had emerged from the civil war of the 1640s, and more nearly represented manufacturing, commercial, shipping, and naval interests. These same interests, spurred on by the depression, successfully pressed for war against the Dutch, despite the personal opposition of Cromwell. Cromwell was opposed to war with the Dutch because he wanted to include them in a Protestant federation against the Catholic French and Spaniards (Jones 1966: 46; Wilson 1957, 61). Strategically, the British were in a more favorable position than the Dutch, especially since their principal aim was only "defensive" (that is, to interfere with Dutch trade), while the Dutch had to attempt to destroy British shipping. The effects of the war, the Navigation Act, and the accompanying recovery of the 1650s on British shipping were immediate and dramatic. For instance, during the entire half century between 1600 and 1650, the number of British naval ships built and rebuilt had been fifty-eight, of which nineteen were in the first two decades; yet in the single decade 1651–1660, the corresponding number was fifty-one, of which nine were over 1,000 tons as against only four in the preceding half decade (Hinton 1959: 96).

The renewed recession of 1660, probably more than the restoration of the Stuart kings in the same year, also provided the impetus for the second Navigation Act. "The speed with which the new Navigation Act was passed in 1660 demonstrated the seriousness of the slump and the determination of the restored monarchy to act with the same energy and methods as the Rump in 1651–52" (Jones 1966: 56). Taking account of provisions of the earlier act, which because of their very generality had proved difficult to enforce, the new act enumerated the specific commodities, both of European and colonial origin, which could only be imported into Britain or her possessions and in ships belonging to Britain or the place of origin of the goods. The bulk cargoes, in which the Dutch had a cost advantage, were now particularly reserved for British shipping, thus stimulating the building of tonnage. In 1662 restrictions were added against British acquisition of foreign-built (again Dutch) ships. In 1663 the Staple Act ordered the British colonies to purchase most commodities only from Britain itself. This provision, however, proved difficult to enforce, and therefore added the protection of exports to the protection of imports and shipping. By 1664 renewed hostilities with the Dutch erupted at the Dutch slaving posts in West Africa and in New Netherlands. These hostilities resulted in the British capture of New Amsterdam (now New York) in North America.

By 1665 the second Anglo-Dutch war was formally declared and fought in the West Indies and Europe. Hinton observes that "Cromwell's Dutch war was a war of preservation. Charles II's was a war of aggression. Cromwell wished to defend himself against the Dutch. Charles wished to make himself their master" (Hinton 1959: 145). This reflected perhaps both the relative economic development of the two powers in previous years and the possibly less unfavorable economic conditions of the mid-sixties compared to the late forties of the seventeenth century. (A similar difference between offensive and defensive wars occurred in the eighteenth century, when Britain fought a more defensive one against France during the depression of the 1740s and a more offensive one in the Seven Years War of the prosperous 1750s. At that point, however, the recession of 1761 resulted in a change of government and policy which gave up at the peace conference table much of what had been won on the battlefield.) The second Anglo-Dutch war was more nearly won by the Dutch, who however, moderated their demands against the British at the peace table, because they were concerned in part by the emerging threat of war with France. One of these Dutch concessions was the surrender of New Netherlands to England, thus consolidating England's hold on a continuous territory along the East Coast of North America from Boston to Charleston. Still a third Anglo-Dutch war was to break out in 1672.

Three observations serve as conclusions:

> The Cockayne plan, the fishery projects, the Navigation Acts, the trading companies—all illustrate the essentially *dual* objectives of Eng-

lish mercantilism. Through the endless sessions of committees and the long battles of pamphleteers, the search went on for a policy that would reconcile the interests of profit and power. (Wilson 1957: 153)

In the first half of the seventeenth century, trade did not follow the flag. The flag followed trade. (Hinton 1959: 66)

This expansion well deserves the name of commercial revolution which is sometimes bestowed on it It did not come about by accident. It was not the effect of beneficent economic competition. It was the result of deliberate policy consciously pursued by successive governments, and at last pursued successfully. The decisive turn of events can be identified in 1649: the weakness of the state made strength essential, the revolution gave money to build a navy, and the energy of the revolutionaries carried them to success. In general, it appears that the most potent item of economic policy was war. (Hinton 1959: 163)

The seventeenth century is often called the golden century of Dutch capitalism. But this interpretation should be qualified by placing Dutch development in the total context of the seventeenth-century depression and by taking account of its particular limitations. To begin with, the first notable rise of Holland, and particularly of Amsterdam as a financial center (after it replaced Antwerp when the latter was captured by the Spaniards in 1585) occurred at the very beginning of the seventeenth century—and indeed still during the sixteenth century—before the depression had gotten well under way in much of Europe and the world. The founding of the Dutch East India Company in 1602, of the exchange bank in 1609, and of the lending bank in 1614 in Amsterdam, the founding of the new stock exchange in 1608, and generally the large increase in population (by migration), trade, and wealth were concentrated in the relatively brief last decade of the sixteenth and first two decades of the seventeenth century, which were still part of the sixteenth-century upswing (Barbour 1963). Thereafter, Dutch trade in Europe could and did take advantage of the Thirty Years War to register speculative profits from foodstuffs and military equipment at the expense of the belligerents. But these profits were not based on any significant increase of Dutch production—although the production of textiles and metallurgy for arms did increase in Flanders—nor were they accompanied any longer by any substantial increase in overseas trade and much less in new Dutch sponsored colonial production to feed such trade. Dutch trade did not really pick up and become golden again until the last quarter or even the end of the seventeenth century—when Europe and the world were pulling out of the depression. Even this, however, was no more than an Indian summer, which did not last beyond about 1720, when capitalist development in general was overtaken by another downswing which all but eliminated the Dutch as well. The Dutch decline thereafter cannot be attributed simply to a small population base (shared, for instance, by the Swiss) but to a small productive base, or the failure to develop a productive base for further capitalist development. Hobsbawm (1960) terms Dutch development of the seventeenth century "in a certain sense an economy of 'feudal business', a Florence, Antwerp, or Augsburg on a semi-national scale." But Florence had developed a larger productive base, relative to its time of ascendancy, than Amsterdam ever did.

Instead, after 1618, beginning especially with Jan Coen, sometimes called after his Portuguese precursor, the "Dutch Albuquerque," the Dutch dedicated themselves in their overseas operations to displace others—especially the Portuguese—from existing trade and to monopolize it for themselves. For half a century, more than expanding colonial production and commerce, the Dutch sought to take advantage of, and to accelerate, the decline of Portuguese power in Brazil and especially in the Orient. The Dutch also sought to take advantage of the decline of Arab power in the East. The following measures were all designed to replace the Portuguese and Arabs in the Orient trade: (1) the establishment of a permanent base at Batavia; (2) the unsuccessful attempt to capture Goa and its subsequent blockade for several years; (3) the establishment of a base at the Cape of Good Hope (the germ of what would become the Boers in later centuries); and (4) the expulsion of the Portuguese from Ceylon and some other islands. These measures proved effective and established a Dutch trade monopoly, but without necessarily increasing the size of that trade or the quantity of the East Indies production of spices. Indeed, because of the overproduction of cloves and nutmeg (the islands of Ambon produced more of the former and those of Banda more of the latter than the whole world would buy), the Dutch enforced the destruction of plantations or spice harvests that might benefit the commerce of their competitors to the detriment of their own monopoly (van Leur 1955: 240).

During this period, the Dutch showed little interest in India or in India's production of textiles, leaving the business to their increasingly strong English and French rivals. Thus seventeenth-century Dutch ascendancy in the oriental spice trade was little more than monopoly concentration in the overseas commerce. (Monopoly concentration, whether in overseas trade or in intra-European trade, is normal during a long general economic downswing. The Dutch would be eliminated in their turn in the next downswing.) As for intra-Asian trade, the Dutch share remained "of a very modest size." In 1622 the Dutch share was approximately 12,000 to 14,000 tons (out of a total of about 24,000 tons in the Dutch oriental trade as a whole) compared with Indonesian shipping of 50,000 tons, Chinese and Siamese shipping of 18,000 tons, Cormomandel shipping of 10,000 tons, etc. (van Leur 1955: 235). Though there was a temporary increase of outward bound East India fleets between 1650 and 1670, a substantial increase did not come until after the turn of the eighteenth century (Boxer 1962: 247). But by that time the composition of Dutch overseas trade had shifted qualitatively from about 15 percent textiles and 70 percent spices purchased in Asia between 1620–1650 to 55 percent textiles and little more than 20 percent spices in 1700 (Mauro 1964, 132).

3. Asia, Africa, and the Americas

Referring to the mid-seventeenth century, J. C. van Leur argues:

a distinction must be made between the economic and the political element in the development of Dutch power in Indonesia. Dutch political influence depended on arms power: the Company's technology in the arts of war appears to have been super or to that of the Indonesians, both on water and on land. In that region the defensive power of the Orient seems to have become weaker comparatively. . . . The heart of the whole matter lies in the military aspect—the progress of Dutch power must be attributed not to more diplomatic insight, to greater courage and greater impetuosity, to greater economic reserves, but to sturdier rigging and the greater mobility of armed troops. The modern idea that the political domination in colonial lands is based on the preponderance of a more highly developed economic system, is in fact even the instrument of it, needs here to be discarded. The pattern of the seventeenth century belongs in another configuration as far as economics is concerned. The Dutch Company's profits—which were not sufficient for financing its outposts in the Indies, its servants, and its ship personnel and for keeping the rotating commercial capital up to the mark—and the goods for the Company's return fleets were both obtained from Asian trade, for a small part under pressure but for the largest part in free commercial exchange. Coined money, mostly silver, had to be shipped from Europe to Asia every year. And . . . there was no question of a European preponderance in trade, either in volume or in organization. . . . I have already indicated regarding the seventeenth century that the history of Indonesia definitely cannot be made equivalent to the history of the Company, that it is incorrect to make a break in describing the course of history upon the arrival of the first scattered seafarers, merchants, and privateers from northwest Europe and change over to the point of view of the small, oppressed European fortress, the stuffy trading-house, and the armed ship riding at anchor. (van Leur 1955: 188–89, 270)

In his *Introduction to the History of South-East Asia*, B.R. Pearn summarizes the effects of the European impact: "It is evident that the Portuguese, Spaniards, Dutch, French and English achieved very little in South-East Asia in the sixteenth and seventeenth centuries, except in limited areas. . . . On the mainland, the Europeans had still less influence. . . . In general, at this time European influence touched only the fringe of South-East Asia" (Pearn 1963: 80). The same may be said, with still more reason, of Asia as a whole. Moreover, during the sixteenth-century expansion of the European centered mrercantile capitalist system and its development, the principal impact such as it was (excepting perhaps in the Spanish Philippines) had been the arrival of the Europeans as competitors of the Muslims in the East-West trade and as competitors with many others in the intra-Asian trade. During most of the seventeenth century the total European impact hardly increased in most of the area, as is suggested by the brief review of the trade by the Dutch, who after all then accounted for the principal European presence in Asia.

Meanwhile, the Spanish Manila Galleon trade virtually disappeared with the drastic decline of silver production in its Mexican link of the trading chain. The seventeenth-century depression in

Europe, the drying up of the flow of the Spanish American silver that had financed or lubricated much of this East-West trade during the previous century, and the failure of the dominant Dutch to produce exportable goods (which, moreover, they would not have been able effectively to sell in Asia at the time) all contributed to the virtual maintenance of the status quo as far as European penetration of and impact on Asia was concerned. Asian developments independent of this marginal European impact have received insufficient attention by other historians. Their examination in this study is hardly possible.

Much the same is the case for the Middle East. The seventeenth century merits hardly a page in H.A.R. Gibb's (1955) classic historical survey of Mohammedanism and no more in Anthony Nutting's (1964) study of the Arabs. Other developments—or their opposite—in the Middle East are briefly examined in section 1 of this chapter.

Nonetheless, some Indian sources and a Soviet one afford an overview of the historical development of trade in India during the seventeenth century. (Certain theoretical problems regarding the prevailing mode of production and its transformation are treated separately in Chapter 4, section 2.) Ishwar Prakesh writes:

> In India, the 17th. century was an era of stabilization. The industrial organization of the country during this period was sound, and articles of merchandise were made in such abundance that the country was as a whole not only self-sufficient but had a huge surplus which was exported to different regions of the world. . . . The merchant class was the most influential class which had an effective control over commerce and industry of the country. . . . Next to textiles, the other flourishing industry was metals [followed by] weapons . . . paper . . . leather . . . wood-ware . . . ship-building . . . All the different patterns of industrial organisation, evolved from Indian urban handicrafts during the 17th. century, existed side by side. The notable change that had occurred during this period was the widening of markets for all industries, especially the textiles, the material outcome of which was a prosperous class of merchants in the country. Indian and foreign merchants both became important instruments for the penetration of capital into industrial production and the growth of a well-organized textile industry. . . . In the history of the Mughal Empire this was the peak period in industrial production. (In Ganguli, ed. 1964: 44–52)

Tapan Raychaudhuri adds:

> It is a safe assumption that the 17th. century witnessed a substantial increase in the volume of India's exports. The total investments of the European companies increased steadily throughout the period and there was also an expansion of Indian participation in the overseas trade. . . . By the latter half of the 17th. century . . . in several parts of Southeast Asia, Indian competition became a growing threat to European commerce. (In Ganguli, ed. 1964: 69, 73–74)

It would be useful to achieve greater accuracy about the precise dating of these developments and to distinguish with greater certainty to what extent they were Indian and/or European generated. Dutch trade in India, after pushing aside the Portuguese, "reached its highest point in the 1640's and 1670's" (Chicherov 1971: 115). It declined because of the weakness of the Dutch bourgeoisie, due to growing British and Indian competition and the intra-Indian wars which threatened its supplies (Chicherov 1971: 116). "In the 1630's and 1640's English trade in India declined due to competition from other European merchants and the famine in Gujarat and on the Coromandel Coast, as well as to the shortage of capital and the civil war in England" (Chicherov 1971: 123). These conditions, we may presume were associated in turn with the general commercial depression. Only after mid-century did English trade in India again begin to increase, from exports of 100,000 rupees from Bengal and Golconda in 1649–1653 to 300,000 rupees in 1658–1660. Then, after 1670, the English East India Company increased its allotments for purchases in Bengal from £30–£40 thousand a year in 1669–1672, to £90–£100 thousand in 1676–1678, and £230 thousand annually in 1681–1682, purchasing increasingly Indian textiles rather than spices, etc., that the Dutch had sought earlier on (Chicherov 1971: 124). First, the English sought to protect their own growing silk and textile manufactures by repeated increases of duties against Indian imports in 1660, 1685, and 1690, until in 1701 the importation of Bengal silk was forbidden altogether and that of Indian cotton textiles was prohibited subsequently. Henceforth, the British purchases in India were for re-export to Europe, Africa, and the Americas.

During most of the seventeenth century neither West African relations with Europe nor their local consequences took a qualitatively different turn from those of the sixteenth century. The relative importance of the trans-Saharan routes, which were disturbed by war in the West and replaced by oceanic routes on the coast, shifted increasingly from western to central and eastern ones. In West Africa, as in South and South East Asia, the seventeenth century witnessed rather more rivalry among European powers for supremacy in the limited trade than significant expansion of the same. Only toward the latter part of the seventeenth century, and in relation to the (under)development of the West Indies, did these trends take a different turn. In the meantime, the empire of Mali suffered further decline and the empire of Songhay was destroyed by the Moroccans, while the Fulani advanced into Hausa Bornu and the Akwamu took control of most of present-day Ghana. But the Ashanti would not really begin their expansion until after 1700, constructing their empire on the back of the slave trade of the eighteenth and nineteenth centuries (as we shall see in the following chapter, section 4).

Before the later seventeenth century, only the slave trade to Brazil was of any significance. Simonsen estimates an importation during all of that century and the preceding one of 350,000 slaves from Africa compared to the 1,000,000 more that would be imported to Brazil alone between 1700 and 1850 (Simonsen 1962: 134). And only in Brazil can colonial production be said to have flourished before the late seventeenth century. Yet even there, the Portuguese occupation from 1629 to 1651 apparently did not substantially increase production except briefly between 1638–1645 (Simonsen 1962: 113, 118–20). After the expulsion of the Dutch, Brazilian sugar production increased again, only to begin its decline after 1660 and permanently to lose its dominance of the world market after the latter part of the seventeenth century. The "development" of the West Indies had begun.

The seventeenth-century depression was most pronounced in the regions—or sectors of the world economy—that had most severely or intimately participated in the sixteenth-century expansion. These included Spain and her colonial American suppliers of silver, although the consequences of the depression differed between the metropolis and its colonies. The production of silver began to fall off by 1600 in Mexico and soon afterward in Potosí. New mines, however, maintained Peruvian production for a while longer. But after 1630 the Peruvian production—and Spanish American production of silver and gold as a whole—fell off quickly and sharply. Spanish (regal and private) imports of precious metals from America, which had reached 36 million pesos in the quinquennium 1591–1595, declined to 30 million by 1616–1620 and to 25 million in 1626–1630, dropped to 17 million between 1631–1635, and then dropped to a minimum of only 3 million during the decade after 1650 (Vilar 1969: 164, after Hamilton). By mid-seventeenth century shipments or at least Spanish receipts of gold were down to no more than 50 kilos per year and those of silver (which had reached a maximum of about 300,000 kilos yearly) had declined to no more than 45,000 kilos (Vilar 1969: 223–24). At the same time, the Spanish fleets, which had counted 20,000 tons annually at the turn of the seventeenth century had dwindled to 9,000 tons a year by mid-seventeenth century (Larraz 1943: Reglá 1961: 330). As Borah has noted, New Spain's century of depression during the seventeenth century and

> the economic difficulties besetting the cities of New Spain were hardly unique in the Spanish empire. They were almost certainly paralleled by similar developments in the major Spanish colonies in the New World, for Guatemala, the Audiencia of Quito, Upper and Lower Peru, New Granada, and Tierra Firme suffered similar catastrophic reductions in the number of natives. (Borah 1951: 29)

Borah interprets the movement of the Mexican colonial economy in terms of demographic findings" (Borah 1951: 1). These are no doubt important, and they do show important population declines in many parts of the Spanish empire (Céspedes del Castillo 1947: 497 ff.).

But over and above the declines in population and in the production and export of precious metals, the seventeenth-century depression also manifested itself in other significant aspects of economic and social life in the Spanish colonies. Céspedes del Castillo calls the seventeenth century in the Spanish Americas "the forgotten century (1574–1699)" and adds that "in this quiet and relatively forgotten century, society is gradually but profoundly transformed" (Céspedes 1947: 494, 496). One of the transformations he notes is the development and consolidation of the agricultural *latifundium* and the *hacienda* as its institutional form.* This development of the hacienda and the growth of the latifundium are not simply an involution into the quiet of rural life as mining fell off. They represented the development of an alternative economic or productive base during the long seventeenth-century depression; and they were intimately related or tied to the development of a trading and manufacturing economy, relatively independent of Spain, but nonetheless dependent on trade with the Spanish American colonies. Although Spain prohibited direct intercolonial trade between Mexico and Peru in 1604 and again in 1631, and reiterated this prohibition to others of its American colonies, this intracolonial trade did exist and it grew precisely while trade with Spain fell off.

If Spain was intent but increasingly powerless to restrain contraband trade between her colonies and the Dutch, English, and French rival interlopers, who increasingly took over Spanish Caribbean islands by mid-sixteenth century, this was only the reflection of the development of commercial—and productive—relations among the colonies of the Spanish empire. This colonial development—during the depression in the metropolis and in colonial trade with the latter—involved increasing development of local manufacturing and the exchange of these manufactured goods among the colonies. The results, at mid-seventeenth century, at the southern-most extremity of the Spanish empire are summarized by a contemporary observer in Chile:

> What human industry achieves in that country is principally cattle and livestock products, tallow, sheepskins, and local textiles. These products are shipped to Lima, which keeps what it needs . . . the rest is distributed throughout Peru, the textiles going to Potosí and the mines and cities in that region which depend solely on Chilean supplies of clothing, Panama, Cartagena, and all those parts of Tierra Firme; clothing is also sent to Tucumán and Buenos Aires and from there to Brazil. The second type of commodity consists of rigging to supply the ships of the South Sea and of matches for firearms, exported from Chile to all of the armies and garrisons situated along the Peruvian and Tierra Firme coasts. . . . the third class of merchandise is the mules which are

---

* The classic study of this transformation in Mexico is that of Chevalier (1963), some of whose findings are summarized and partially reinterpreted in Frank (in press).

shipped by way of the unhabited region of Atacama to Potosí. (Ovalle, quoted by Ramirez 1967: 31–32, and Frank 1969: 35–36)

Thus the seventeenth-century depression certainly affected the process of capital accumulation and the transformation of the modes of production that accompanied it in both the European metropolis and the Spanish American colonies; but just as certainly the directions of this transformation were quite different for the colonies than for the metropolis.

More noteworthy European economic enterprise during the seventeenth century was dedicated to the expansion of the North Atlantic fisheries, offshore from Newfoundland and Nova Scotia, and to a lesser extent to the penetration of the fur trade in the St. Lawrence region. Both had begun already during the sixteenth century as European fishing moved westward from the Baltic and North Seas. Salted and dried codfish had a market in Southern Europe and was an important staple for ship's crews on the Middle Atlantic crossing. Nonetheless, after the 1580s, fishing by Portugal (annexed by Spain) and Spain itself declined in the North Atlantic. In fishing and its related shore supports, as in other activities, the seventeenth century was then marked by increasing rivalry for monopoly control between England, France, and Holland. At mid-seventeenth century, the Caribbean settlers and later the plantation slaves began to provide what would come to be the principal market for North Atlantic fish. For a long time, however, fishing stimulated only modest settlement in North America. Though the English established some settlements for drying fish, their development was opposed by port interests at home; the French, for their part, had sources of salt which permitted them to cure the fish on shipboard. For the fur trade, European settlement appeared as an obstacle that interfered with the trapping of animals, which was largely left to the Hurons by the French and to the Iroquois by the Dutch, until in 1650 the Iroquois attacked the Hurons to obtain monopoly control of the trade for themselves and their buyers.

Toward the latter part of the seventeenth century, and spurred on partially by the international competition for control, the fishing industry nonetheless increasingly demanded and achieved participation in the benefits of the North Atlantic fisheries and in the trade of their product with the growing Caribbean market. Therein the settlers in New England were importantly favored—and encouraged—in comparison with those of New France. The former could, by virtue of location and seasonal timing, make two trips per winter to the West Indies, including the French West Indies, while the French settlers could scarcely make one ill-timed trip a year. Herein then, was the early base of the triangular trade that would develop between England, New England, and the Caribbean. The French were never able to establish an equivalent triangular trade between France, New France, and the French Caribbean possessions, whose rum, moreover, competed with French wine and therefore found little welcome there (Easterbrook and Aitken 1967: chs. 2–4).

The half century of relatively most severe depression (1620–1670 approximately) also witnessed the incipient expansion of Europeans into new frontier regions (without the commitment of heavy investment for development) and strong rivalry among competing powers. In this competition, each sought to take advantage of, and accelerate, the decline of the previously established Spanish and Portuguese hegemony and, insofar as possible, to establish a monopoly position of their own. The Dutch, who took the offensive against the Portuguese in Dutch East India, under the leadership of Jan Coen and his successors after 1618, also advanced in the West. The Dutch West India Company, founded in 1621, promoted the settlement of several parts of North America and the Caribbean, among them New Amsterdam on the island of Manhattan in 1626. Simultaneously, the Dutch began their incursions against the Portuguese in Brazil, which they were able to occupy after several years of fighting, from 1629–1651. The British, whose Sir Walter Raleigh had landed in Roanoke, Virginia, in 1584 and founded the Jamestown colony in 1607, dispatched the Mayflower in 1620 and arrived (by mistake) to found the Pilgrim colony on Cape Cod in Massachusetts. Then during the years of greatest economic decline in Britain, the decade of the 1630s, came the first big wave of English immigrants to North America, 16,000 of them arriving in the Massachusetts Bay colony alone. Maryland was settled in 1632 and Rhode Island in 1636. But English settlers began to arrive as well in the Caribbean, first in 1624 in St. Kitts, which was taken with little resistance from the Spaniards (soon after, the French sought to take it from the British), and then in Barbados, which so far as is known had not been settled by Europeans between 1492 and the English arrival in 1627. By 1643 the tiny island had 37,000 inhabitants of English origin, the maximum it was to have for centuries to come. These English settlers were later replaced by African slaves to produce sugar (Harlow 1926; also see Frank 1974; 1976). After Cromwell's triumph over the royalists he sought to capture most of the Caribbean for the British, taking Jamaica in 1655 and using it as a base of operations intended to incorporate the Spanish American mainland in Mexico and South America into the British Empire. This strategy was similar to that executed by the Spaniards, a century and a half before, in acquiring their own empire.

4. The European Response

The French, who (except for Holland) were perhaps least affected by the early seventeenth-century depression, at first lagged behind on the North American and Caribbean frontiers. They were more concerned with domestic and European consolidation, as they would continue to be for a century or more to come—until British control of the seas and overseas colonies would definitely defeat them. The settlement of New France in Quebec lagged substantially behind that of New England, and that of French Martinique behind that of British Barbados. But when France was beset by increasing economic difficulties during the third quarter of the seventeenth century, Colbert also stepped up the French offensive in the Caribbean. The French West Indies Company was founded in 1664, and after little success, fused into the French West African Company in 1672, which obtained a French monopoly for the slave trade to the Antilles in 1679. St. Dominique became French in 1697. Despite its late start, St. Dominique would overtake all other colonies in the production of sugar sweet wealth—but not until the eighteenth century. In the meantime, the Spanish colonies in the Caribbean, when they were not taken over by Spain's European rivals, languished (by "colonial" standards, that is) or continued their slow development as yeoman farmer-settler colonies (see Frank 1974; 1978).

In summary, then, while the seventeenth-century downswing lasted, European mercantile capitalism expanded on its New World frontier, but without significant productive impulse or investment or commercial success—and with frequent commercial failures of the colonizing and/or trading companies. Commercially perhaps the greatest significance of this seventeenth-century migration was the market it afforded for European manufacturing exports during the early years of the next upswing at the end of the seventeenth century. This market in the colonies thereby may have facilitated this upswing by taking up the slack of Brazilian imports after the decline of its sugar cycle and before the beginnings of the Brazilian gold rush around 1700. Insofar as there was a great deal of real investment during this period, it was achieved not so much by the placement of capital as by the settlement of European migrants who with their blood and sweat cleared the ground for the primitive accumulation of capital that would follow. And follow it did— during the next major cyclical upswing of the eighteenth century, although its initial stages had already begun at the end of the seventeenth century.

In summarizing seventeenth-century developments, we may also briefly return to the earlier discussion of the argument by Dobb, Sweezy, Takahashi, et al. in *The Transition from Feudalism to Capitalism*, which turns on Marx's distinction between two processes of the transition: "the producer becomes merchant and capitalist . . . or else the merchant establishes direct sway over production" (Marx 1962; III: 329). It was suggested in Chapter 1, section 4 that these two processes of transition and these two sources of accumulation were both important and mutually related, but that perhaps the second, "external" one predominated during cyclical upswings and the first, "internal" one during cyclical downswings. During cyclical upswings, such as those which were relatively predominant in the sixteenth century, merchant capital also achieved a relative predominance, and contributed significantly through overseas trade (and, of course, pillage) to metropolitan capital accumulation by the provision of "external" capital forceably extracted from the colonial world. But during cyclical downswings, such as predominated particularly during much of the seventeenth century, capitalist *development* (albeit perhaps not visible growth) was promoted predominantly through changes in the mode of production. During the seventeenth century, while overseas trade stagnated and the extraction of surplus from the colonial world failed to sustain its earlier notable rate of growth, the previous expansion and accumulation of capital underwent a crisis of adjustment, in which the centralization of existing capital replaced the generation of new capital through concentration. Thus, while trade and profits declined and wages even rose during much of the seventeenth century, the expansive developmental and accumulative process of the sixteenth century underwent a long period of readjustment which involved a process of international centralization of capital. This process, centered in Northern Europe and particularly in England, eliminated the weaker Italian and Spanish economies. At the same time a similar process of centralization eliminated the competition of weaker merchant and landed owners of capital. Their frequent antiprogressive alliance (emphasized by Dobb) may perhaps be regarded as a defensive alliance.

Simultaneously in England, the new draperies produced through the putting-out system gradually replaced the traditional old draperies. Marx, in the chapter, "Historical Facts about Merchant's Capital," analyzes this development as the merchant's direct sway over production, which "cannot by itself contribute to the overthrow of the old mode of production, but tends rather to preserve and retain it as its precondition." At the same time, however, "this serves historically as a stepping-stone" in that "the merchant turns the small masters into his middlemen, or buys directly from the independent producer," and thus becomes a stage in a "three-fold transition" to the capitalist mode in which "the industrialist becomes merchant and produces directly for the wholesale market" (Marx 1962; III: 329–30). It is this productive transformation in England, generated and enforced (or, at least, stimulated) by the seventeenth-century depression, that gave England the competitive advantage over her European rivals in the subsequent eighteenth-century expansive development. England already had gained a competitive advantage in the textile and other manufactured exports to the new colonies in the Caribbean and North America, after migration and settlement during the initially depressive times of the seventeenth century had created a new market for European exports. Thus this seventeenth-century transition is also reflected in a changed commodity composition of international trade, from the spice and luxury trade of the sixteenth century to the sugar (for increasingly more widespread popular consumption) and new textile trade of the eighteenth century. Nonetheless, for England—and, of course, for Holland, which never developed a substantial industry of its own—re-exports accounted for a significant part of increased exports toward the end of the seventeenth century. These amounted to some 30 percent of English exports in the 1660s (Minchinton 1969: 26) and by the 1690s, when Britain was again engaged in wars, Indian textiles produced in Bengal reached a high point in this trade (Glamann 1971: 86).

In this review, the seventeenth-century depression appears as a continuous economic decline. But around this general downward trend there were of course important lesser cyclical movements. These movements were not entirely coincident among countries and—especially in regard to price fluctuations—were often influenced by, and influential for the many wars and revolutions of the century. Further research is necessary to study these developments in their true multiple cyclical reality.

The relative tranquillity of the seventeenth century in Asia, Africa, and Latin America—the "quiet century" in Spanish America—and the incessant wars and frequent revolutions and popular revolts, as well as the imposition of absolutist rule in most of Europe, must all be related to (indeed, should perhaps be derived from) the depression which marked the seventeenth century in the European metropolis and its impact on the process of capital accumulation on a world scale and on the transformation of the modes of production in various parts of the world. Although an analysis of this relation may be beyond the capacity of this book, the determinant influence of the "adverse" economic conditions of the seventeenth century on these political events and transformations may be stressed. This is not to deny that the international wars and national revolutionary movements themselves had far-reaching and lasting consequences for the course of capitalist development and capital accumulation. Absolutism—Louis XIV's "I am the State"—and mercantilist policy, as well as dynastic rivalry and aggressive wars, certainly were political instruments of particular class interests in the seventeenth century. There consequences included the elimination of Italy, Spain, Portugal, and Germany (as well as Turkey)—and the elimination within these countries of those classes whose interests were already associated with industrial development—from any future possible dominance and immediate benefit in the process of world capital accumulation. This elimination was followed or accompanied by the weakening of France and Holland vis-à-vis Britain. But these political instruments (or weapons in the international and intranational struggles) were wielded largely in response to cyclical economic circumstances, which made these instruments of absolutism, mercantilism, war, and revolution particularly timely and especially well-developed in Europe, precisely during the seventeenth century of depression which was "quiet" elsewhere in the world.

Without hazarding very far into the sociology and history—or even sociological history—of religion, art, and science, it may be observed that the seventeenth century of depression, and particularly its decades of most acute economic decline and crisis, were marked by many of the most important developments in European religious, artistic, intellectual, and scientific life. Religious persecution increased with (a) the Inquisition and the expulsion of the Moriscos (Muslims converted to Christianity in the sixteenth century) in Spain, (b) the persecution and emigration of the Huguenots in France, (c) the "religious" rivalry of the princes in the German wars, and (d) the large-scale persecution of the religious dissenters in England, which fed the stream of migrants to the New World. All of these were undoubtedly manifestations of the economically and politically troubled times. The persecutions, and the resistance to them, were instruments or weapons of the contending economic and political interest groups. In the arts and letters, the decline of Spain produced El Greco (1547–1614), Velazquez (1599–1660), and Murillo (1617–1682), as well as Lope de Vega (1562–1635), Calderón (1600–1681), and Cervantes (1547–1616). The latter's *Don Quixote* tilted the windmills that were inexorably driven by the ill winds of the Spanish decline while Cervantes was writing between 1605 and 1615 (Vilar 1964: 431–48). Troubled, but less so, France produced the tragedies of Racine (1639–1699) and the comedies of Moliére (1622–1673). Holland, whose golden century flourished at the beginning and again at the end of the seventeenth century, witnessed its golden age of painting in the intervening economically less auspicious period. Rembrandt lived from 1606 to 1669 and Hals from 1580 to 1666. In England, Milton retired from politics about 1655 and then devoted himself to his greatest work, *Paradise Lost*, which "is deeper and more tragic than the poem which Milton would have written twenty years earlier" (Hill 1967: 203). And Hobbes, Locke, and Petty were all politically moved by economic concerns of the mid-seventeenth century when they produced their respective contributions to philosophy and political economy.

Although innovation, in Schumpeter's sense of the term, naturally occurs during expansive upswings in the cyclical process of capital accumulation, scientific and technological invention would seem to be concentrated rather in periods of predominant economic decline and incipient revival (for evidence, see Chapter 5, section 7).* At least the "scientific revolution" produced by Kepler (1571–1630), Galileo (1564–1642), Bacon (1561–1626), Descartes (1596–1650), and in medicine by Harvey (1578–1657) occurred during the troubled times of the economic decline of the first half of the seventeenth-century depression. The second half of the seventeenth century was distinguished by Boyle (1627–1691), Leibnitz (1642–1727), and above all Newton (1646–1716), who published his *Principia* in 1679, that is, before the renewed economic upswing.

That this is not simply a temporal coincidence is suggested by Bacon's concern for the empirically grounded "mechanical arts," which yielded "substance or profit," as distinct from speculative scientific thought, which in his opinion did not; by Descartes' agreement with Bacon and his interest in constructing telescopes; by Boyle's essay entitled "That the Goods of Mankind May Be Much Increased by the Naturalist's Insight into Trades"; by Galileo's specific concern to use his research as a basis for constructing a more accurate clock for determining longitude in ocean voyages; by the creation of scientific societies after 1650; and by the employment of mathematicians and scientists by various governments in the seventeenth century to solve pressing problems of navigation and military technology. It may not be too much to hazard the suggestion that all

---

* Schumpeter argues that innovation is the cause of the upswing, but this is not necessarily so, since it may with the same or greater force be argued that innovation is rather the result of the upswing and its expanding profit possibilities.

these technological needs appeared—or indeed were—more pressing precisely when profitable opportunities were exhausted and military victories limited by existing technology during the long cyclical downturn, even if "the history of the interaction between motives, opportunities, skills and intellectual changes that brought about the Scientific Revolution had, in fact, yet to be written" (Crombie 1959, II: 124; Bernal 1969)

Chapter 3

The Political Economy
of Cyclical Expansion
and Rivalry, 1689–1763

*In fact, the veiled slavery of the wage workers in Europe
needed, for its pedestal, slavery pure and simple in the new
world.*

—Karl Marx, *Capital* (1867)

After the depression and structural transformation of the seventeenth century, the eighteenth century may be termed one of competitive expansion. On the European continent the century was typified by a seemingly unending series of wars, while overseas it was marked by the development of the slave-powered sugar plantation complex, principally in the West Indies, and the development of the slave and triangular trades between the West Indies, Europe, Africa, and North America. Both of these developments were integrated into the process of world capital accumulation and became major factors in this process. Later in the century India and, to a lesser extent, Indonesia would suffer transformations that would render their participation in this process qualitatively and quantitatively different. The precious metals to lubricate this expansion were supplied by the renewed increase of silver production in the old mining regions of Spanish America and for a time by the supply of gold from Minas Gerais in Portuguese Brazil. After the elimination of Dutch power, marked by their wars with the English at the turn of the century, and the relative weakening of Spain, the wars of the seventeenth century—and their worldwide theaters—increasingly expressed the commercial rivalry between France and Britain and played an important role in resolving this conflict in favor of the latter. The growth of Britain's production and even more so its expanding export of textiles in this political and economic climate prepared that country for "take-off," at the end of the seventeenth century, into what has since been called the Industrial Revolution. Far from being smooth or regular, this development was marked by incessant short economic fluctuations, which may be roughly grouped into the following major expansive and depressive cyclical phases: 1670–1688 depressive, 1689–1720 expansive, 1720–1746/7 depressive, 1747/8–1761 expansive, 1762–1789 depressive, 1790–1815 expansive. To understand the seventeenth- and eighteenth-century rivalries and expansion it will be useful to review these periods through the Seven Years War, leaving developments after the 1763 Peace of Paris for examination in connection with the Industrial Revolution.

The outcome of the commercial revolution of the eighteenth century was a victory for the British. Although the capital and technology that had opened the Caribbean to the production of sugar (after the Dutch expulsion from Brazil) had been primarily Dutch, the early expansion and implantation of sugar, at the end of the depression of the seventeenth century, was primarily British and secondarily French. For Britain, the eighteenth century had already begun in the seventeenth century; it was ushered in by the Glorious Revolution of 1688, which was followed by a generally expansive period lasting until 1720. This expansive period was accompanied, if not propelled or generated, by the revival of Spanish American silver production after the 1680s and by the discovery in 1697 of gold in Minas Gerais, Brazil, which was mined in significant quantities after 1708. The expansion was interrupted by some apparently depressive years associated with the Anglo-Dutch and French wars until 1697, and the War of the Spanish Succession between 1702 and 1713. These wars, however, were of lasting commercial benefit to Britain. The definitive elimination of Dutch power and commercial rivalry as a result of the Anglo-Dutch wars sealed the seventeenth century. Moreover, a need for political protection against Spain and France during the hostilities again forced Portugal into the hands of the British. In 1703 Portugal and Britain signed the Treaty of Methuen, which extended to British industry and commerce important privileges in the Portuguese and Brazilian trade for the period of its renewed expansion, initiated by the recent discovery of Brazilian gold. The Treaty of Utrecht in 1713, among its other provisions, transferred from France to Britain the *asiento* privilege of the sale of specified amounts of slaves to the Spanish possessions in America, and thereby symbolized and stimulated what would become the lifeline of eighteenth-century development: the slave trade.

These developments were reflected in significant transformations in English and international production and trade. The European trade was increasingly supplemented and even replaced by the colonial trade, a development that transformed the whole pattern of European trade. During the last four decades of the seventeenth century, British exports increased faster than manufactures, and re-exports faster than domestically produced exports. At the beginning of the eighteenth century, 85 percent of the domestically produced exports were manufactures, mostly wool cloth. But of the total exports, wool cloth accounted for only one half; one-third of all exports were really re-exports of colonial products, of which sugar, tobacco, and calicoes were two-thirds. These three colonial products, which also constituted two-thirds of all imports into Britain, reflected the expansion into the Caribbean and southern North America, and, in the case of calicoes, the revival of the Orient trade which was now based increasingly on textiles produced in India rather than on spices from Indonesia. This commercial expansion in the last four decades of the seventeenth century was marked by significant British investments in commerce rather than manufacturing, which resulted in a trebling of re-exports between 1660 and 1700 (D. B. Davis, in Minchinton 1969: 78–79).

Although at the end of this period, in the 1770s, re-exports would account for a still higher share (37 percent) of British exports, the intervening years would witness a relative shift of emphasis to domestic manufacturing and an expansion into new products. The increasing demand from the mining regions of Brazil and Spanish America, from the plantations of the Caribbean, and from the American South and Northeast supported this expansion of British manufacture, as did the import of certain British manufactures by Africa, the Mediterranean, and the Baltic areas.

Relying primarily on Gregory King's calculations for 1688, Deane and Cole offer the following estimates for Britain at the beginning of the eighteenth century: a *per capita* annual income of £9; government expenditures of 5.5 percent of net national product; and a rate of capital formation of less than 5 percent of net national product. Ten percent of the British national product resulted from receipts from abroad. With imports of £7.1 million and exports of £4.3 million, Britain had a trade deficit of £2.8 million, but received £3.5 million from foreign service payments, and thus enjoyed a net foreign investment of about £0.7 million, or 1.5 percent of national income. Europe still absorbed 82 percent of the domestic exports from Britain and supplied 62 percent of the imports to that country, while the New World accounted for 10 percent of exports and 20 percent of imports, and the Orient 3 percent of exports and 13 percent of imports (the last figure includes imports from the Orient that were re-exported by Britain) (Deane and Cole 1967: 2–3, 34, 87).

1. Cyclical Wars, 1689–1763

This expansion could not take place without considerable internal conflict in each of the participating countries and colonies, as well as commercial and political rivalry, including wars, among them. All of these tensions were intimately related to the cyclical ups and downs of the period. In France, Minister of Finance Colbert had represented the maritime and colonial economic interests against the agrarian and continental ones represented by the minister of war and generally favored by King Louis XIV and his successors. France was a continental power with a strong and prosperous landed class, which resisted unnecessary "adventures" overseas. Consequently France failed to generate any substantial overseas migration. Although its population was three times the size of Britain's, only 20,000 French peopled the vast interior of North America from the mouth of the St. Lawrence to that of the Mississippi in 1688, while the relatively small British colonies along the Atlantic seaboard already had 300,000 settlers. A century later (1763), the French territories had about 70,000 whites and the thirteen English colonies about 2.5 million. The landed interests in England, who, like their counterparts in France, supported a European or continental-oriented policy, were represented by the Tory party and symbolized by Hugh Walpole in the eighteenth century. The rising manufacturing interests, particularly of Lancashire, and the financial interests of London were more typically represented by the Whigs under the leadership of William Pitt (Hill 1969: 231; Dorn 1963: 147–48; Sideri 1970: 73–74): these interests would make their influence felt on British policy, particularly after the Glorious Revolution of 1688.

The eighteenth century of commercial and sugar revolutions has also been called the century of the second hundred years war, from 1689 to 1815. Nonetheless, Dorn, writing in 1940, argued in his *Competition for Empire* that

> among recent historians, especially in Great Britain and America, a tendency has arisen to belittle the importance of war as a contributing force in the building up of modern nations . . . [yet] for good or for evil, militarism became one of the constituent elements of European civilization at the very time when European influence was being extended over the rest of the world. It is a notorious fact that the history of colonial expansion is also the history of incessant warfare. (Dorn 1963: 12–13)

Moreover, although the wars appeared dynastic and continental—and no doubt were so in part—they were also fought substantially for reasons of commercial rivalry, which was to extend increasingly to all parts of the globe, focussing particularly on four centers of rivalry and theaters of war outside of Europe: North America, the West Indies, Africa, and India. These four centers already played a role in the War of the Austrian Succession between 1740 and 1748, and they became crucial theaters of combat in the Seven Years' War of 1756–1763.

The three Anglo-Dutch wars in the late seventeenth century were evidently fought for commercial ends and helped England to suppress Dutch shipping. England became an independent commercial power, established itself more firmly in the reviving oriental trade (at that time still based on spices rather than on textiles) and made a bid for the trade that would become the hallmark of the eighteenth century, the slave trade. The War of Spanish Succession (1701–1713) pitted England against its remaining principal political and economic opponent, France, in a rivalry that would shape the course of the entire eighteenth century, beginning with the inconclusive War of Austrian Succession, followed by the defeat of the French in the Seven Years War, and concluding with the total victory of the

British in the Napoleonic Wars. The tone of the period was already set by the Treaty of Utrecht following the first of these wars in 1713, by which England received the *asiento* right to supply the Spanish colonies with a certain number of slaves and the privilege of a *navio de permiso* to call on Spanish colonial ports, which up to that time had been legally closed. These privileges provided England with a series of further legal and illegal sources of access to the weakened Spanish empire. At the same time, the Treaty of Methuen (1703) with Portugal gave British trade access to the growing Brazilian market. These and other circumstances generated, during the years following, an often speculative expansion, symbolized by the South Sea Company in Britain and the Mississippi Company founded by John Law in France. Both led to a financial crash in 1720—the year of the "South Sea Bubble"—which initiated a generally depressive phase of the long trade cycles, lasting almost three decades. "One student after another has revealed the ebb and flow of economic life in these years. Almost all sectors—agriculture, trade (home and foreign), industry, population growth—show a weaker momentum from the twenties to the fifties, when the forward momentum was strongly resumed" (Wilson 1971: 276).

The decades following 1720 seem to have been marked by retarded expansion and recurrent crises and depressions. In his *Economic Fluctuations in England 1700–1800*, Ashton appraises many of these years as quite prosperous, but his own data and analyses are equivocal and admit a contrary interpretation (see especially Ashton 1959: 58–60, 92–95, 120–23, 143–47.) In any case, many students of the period, including Ashton himself (1959: 148 and elsewhere), agree that it was not until nearly the middle of the century that an expansive boom in both production and trade began. Relatively depressive years, especially in the sugar trade, have been noted by several students of the period.

> Between 1720 and 1739 the British sugar industry in the West Indies experienced a severe depression, occasioned chiefly by a falling off in exports to Europe. Recovery did not come until the secular increase in sugar consumption in Britain, together with favourable legislation, once more raised prices to remunerative levels. During this period of depression the political power of the West Indies plantation owners was brought into play to check the growing trade between New England and the French West Indies, and in 1733 the British Parliament passed

the Molasses Act, which imposed prohib tive duties on sugar, molasses, and rum imported into the British North American colonies from the foreign West Indies. The statute was passed against the strenuous opposition of New England and represented a major political victory for the West Indian interests. (Easterbrook and Aitken 1967: 105)

The victory was hollow, however, since the act was not, and at that time could not, be enforced.

But if legislation offered no immediate solution, there was the hope that stronger action might.

Depression in the English West Indies affected too many English interests to be tolerated; and in that time of truculent trade rivalry, if peaceful measures [the reference is to the Molasses Act] would not serve, war was welcomed as a possible solution of commercial problems. War offered the English an opportunity to cripple French sugar production, since they could not defeat it in open competition. Planters on both sides disliked the acquisition of fresh sugar producing territory; they feared that increased production would lower prices within their protected markets. Each side hoped not to acquire and exploit the enemy's colonies but to destroy and depopulate them. . . . Failing the destruction of the enemy's colonies, the next-best thing was to cut off their trade, starve them of provisions and slaves, and prevent them from selling their sugar. In this war naval activity was, in practice, almost confined to this second type of operation. By 1744 the energies of both combatants were taxed elsewhere, in Europe and North America. Forces were not available for major operations in the West Indies, and the fighting there was little more than a rehearsal for the much sterner struggle which was to break out in 1756. (Parry and Sherlock 1971: 113–14)

A contemporary pamphleteer left no doubt: "We should not only distress our enemy to the last degree, but by ruining their commerce, and destroying their colonies . . . we should in a great measure retrieve our own, and make them flourish again as formerly" (quoted in G. Williams 1966: 63). And another pamphleteer insisted in 1745: "By a well-managed descent upon their sugar islands we should at once ruin them, and promote the welfare of our own for many years. This might be done by only destroying their sugar works, and carrying off their slaves" (quoted in G. Williams 1966: 67–68).

This then was the Caribbean—and cyclical—background to the British wars against Spain and France that are better known as the War of Jenkins' Ear which began in 1739 or the war of the Austrian

Succession which began in 1740. According to Dorn: "In its essence the war was a commercial one, a struggle of rival merchants" (Dorn 1963: 164). Williams agrees: "The real significance of the war was that it was the first major conflict between European powers fought because of overseas disputes. . . . Colonies were regarded as integral parts of the national economy, and overseas commerce of sufficient importance to justify open war (G. Williams 1966: 63).

In Europe much of the war was fought for the control of Flanders, and in North America it was fought over the French fortress of Louisbourg on Cape Breton Island. In India the French and British East India companies fought between themselves as such, without yet bringing their respective governments into open conflict there. For the British, this war had a further indirect benefit: by weakening the French competition in the Caribbean, they temporarily expanded the market for Portuguese sugar grown in Brazil—and thereby the market for British textile exports to their captive customers (Fisher 1971: 39). But the war itself resulted in a stalemate. The Treaty of Aix-la-Chapelle of 1748 settled no outstanding issues—most conquests were mutually returned—and left the balance of power substantially as it had been settled by the Treaty of Utrecht in 1713 (G. Williams 1966: 70–72; Parry and Sherlock 1971: 116). Another war was virtually inevitable—and it came a decade later.

After 1750 the demand for sugar and its price, and indeed economic conditions generally, were increasingly favorable (Sheridan 1970: 75; Ashton 1959: 148). The years 1748–1756 were "the golden age of British sugar" (Parry and Sherlock 1971: 117). Yet, although the West Indies were still Britain's commercially most valuable colonies, British interests were already beginning to shift from them to North America, which increasingly provided the more important market for British manufacturing exports (Dorn 1963: 270–71). This shift was reflected in the Seven Years War which began in 1756 after eight years of "cold war." British Prime Minister William Pitt, who in connection with the previous war had declared that "when trade is a stake it is your last entrenchment: you must defend or perish" (quoted in G. Williams 1966: 78–79), now definitely centered his attention on the colonial war in North America with the intention of eliminating the French strategic threat to the exposed hinterland of the North American colonies. Meanwhile, the planter interests in the West Indies were already beginning to lose their dominant influence on British politics and policy, and they no longer offered, as they had done in the previous war, strenuous resistance to the annexation of competing foreign sugar producing colonies. Accordingly in the Seven Years War the British strategy was no longer simply to pillage the French colonies but to annex them. Parry and Sherlock (1971: 108) attribute this change in British strategy to the desire to use captured islands as bargaining counters at the peace settlement. They are supported by Williams, who adds that the British planters desired to eliminate French harassment of their shipping and to remove the French military threat to their own plantations. These were probably factors but they could also have been factors in the previous war. Dorn (1963: 147–48) emphasizes the internal division between the Pitt and Walpole interests, which no doubt was a factor in both wars and in both peace settlements. An additional and perhaps more decisive factor that explains the *difference* in British strategy between the two wars is, I suggest, the following. During the earlier period sugar markets were glutted, and this provided Britain with the opportunity of increasing its profits by eliminating rival *production*—hence a policy of destruction. In the 1750s the sugar market was much more buoyant, and it may have been economically more rational and politically more feasible to seek the elimination of *rival* production and to profit from it oneself—hence a policy of annexation.

In 1762, during the Seven Years War, the British captured Havana, the crown of the Spanish Antilles. They rapidly expanded the shipment of slaves to Cuba and initiated the process that would convert that island into the nineteenth century's principal sugar plantation. They likewise captured Spanish Manila in the Philippines, although too late in the war to make any difference. In Africa, Britain took the island of Gorée, the principal French slaving station, off the coast of Senegal, and effectively disrupted the French slave trade, which was vital to the economic survival of the French West Indian colonies. Finally, in a military action that would turn out to be determinant for the process of British and world capital accumulation during the remainder of the eighteenth century and all of the nineteenth century, the British succeeded, with the assault on Pondicherry, in eliminating French economic and political rivalry in

India; and, at the Battle of Plassey in 1757, they suppressed local military resistance, allied to the French, in Bengal. Thus the French challenge in India, which had begun modestly with Colbert's establishment of trading posts on the mainland in 1688 and which had become increasingly threatening under the leadership of Marquis Dupleix since 1732—and almost successful when, after 1744, he presented an economic threat to the British in Bengal—was eliminated for ever after. The economic opportunities derived from the progressive breakdown of Moghul power in Eastern India during the first half of the eighteenth century would be inherited, not by the (for a time) more aggressive French, but by the British, under the direction first of Robert Clive, the victor at Plassey, and then of the Marquis of Hastings.

The last years of the war, after 1761, were years of renewed economic crisis. Pitt, the representative of the industrial and commercial interests in Britain, was replaced as prime minister by the Earl of Bute, representing the landed and continental interests. At the bargaining table at the Peace of Paris in 1763, Bute ceded back to the French most of what they had lost on the battlefield, a surrender that was severely criticized by Pitt at the time and has generally been deemed unnecessary by historians, since the British preferred to keep Canada and hand back the sugar island of Guadeloupe, a decision consistent even with Pitt's strategy. But in the perspective of later history, the French lost North America and India, and would soon lose their major sugar colony in St. Domingue anyway. The British, in addition, gained some Caribbean islands and Florida from Spain in exchange for the return of Havana. (Spain also received from the French title to the Louisiana territory west of the Mississippi.) After 1763 British supremacy was all but assured, and the course of future world capital accumulation was mapped out at the Peace of Paris.

2. Money Supply from Brazil and Portugal to England

What was the relationship between monetary expansion and the commercial revolution of the eighteenth century? This is the issue raised by Vilar, recalling the monetary and price revolution of the sixteenth century and its intimate relation—often claimed to be causative—to the earlier expansion of European-centered mercantile capitalism. The eighteenth century witnessed, on the one hand, a long secular expansion in the supply of monetary gold and silver and a generally upward trend in prices and, on the other hand, an increase in production and a "revolution" in commerce with which the century had been baptized. The association is striking and certainly important. The average growth rate of the stock of gold was three times higher in the eighteenth century than it had been in the sixteenth century and that of silver twice as high. The absolute annual production of gold was over 20,000 kilos for six decades after 1720, whereas it had never exceeded 10,000 kilos in the earlier centuries. The average annual output of silver, which had reached 423,000 kilos in the first two decades of the seventeenth century and had then declined to an annual average of 337,000 kilos in the two decades prior to 1680, began to rise again thereafter, surpassed its earlier maximum in the decade after 1720 and doubled that amount by the end of the eighteenth century. Nonetheless, we may agree with Vilar that the causative influence of this monetary production, though not insignificant, was relatively less than it had been in the earlier century. On the one hand, since the eighteenth century began with a higher initial stock of money, the percentage changes were less significant and more stable. On the other hand, the relative and absolute increase in production and trade of other goods was much higher. British and French foreign trade trebled during the first seven decades of the century; and the structural transformation of production and productive relations, except in sixteenth-century Mexico and Peru, was generally much greater in the eighteen century than in the earlier one. Vilar suggests that the relationship between money and production or trade was reciprocal, rather than a one-way causal influence. The long depression lowered prices— that is, raised the price of monetary metals—and stimulated the discovery and mining of precious metals. They, in turn, facilitated trade in general, and particularly in the special cases of Spanish America, Brazil and Portugal, the Baltic and the Orient (Vilar 1969: 228–30, 265–68, 312–14). I will examine each of these special cases.

In Spanish America, the production and export of precious metals increased again during the eighteenth century. For most of the century this increase was gradual, but it accelerated rapidly during the last two decades of this century and during the first decade of the nineteenth century. Mexico, which by the end of the century produced about two-thirds of the silver in the Spanish empire, approximately doubled its average annual output during the first eight decades of the century, from 164,000 kilos annually in the first two decades to 366,000 kilos in the last two decades of this period (Vilar 1969: 348; Fisher 1971: 4). Potosí never recovered its earlier splendor, but elsewhere mines were brought into renewed or new production, especially the gold mines of Nueva Granada (Columbia). Humboldt (summarized and interpreted by Vilar 1969: 353–54) estimated the comparative costs and profits of silver production in a Mexican and a German mine: with 4.5 times more workers in the Mexican mine than in the German mine, capital moved 50 times more ore, mined 36 times more silver, and obtained 33 times more net profit, even though the wages paid out in the high price region of the Mexican mine were 6 times more than in the European mine. Yet mineowners in Spanish America were more often than not on the verge of bankruptcy and permanently in debt for working capital to merchants and other financiers. The mining regions, of course, had a permanent merchandize trade deficit with the rest of the colonial economy, the colonial economy with the Spanish metropolis, and Spain with other parts of Europe, particularly England and France. These trade deficits were paid for through the flow of silver in the opposite direction, of which England received from Spain and its colonies about £14 million, or the equivalent of about 3 percent of all English imports, between 1712 and 1770 (Fisher 1971: 4–5). In return, England sent its manufactures, principally woollen textiles, and re-exports of its Indian cotton textiles and North Atlantic or North American fish, as well as, of course, African slaves. Further British exports reached the southern regions of the Spanish empire through contraband from Brazil via the La Plata region to Chile and Upper Peru (Bolivia) from whence further silver flowed extra-legally in return.

The revival of mining in various parts of Spanish America generated an increase in *hacienda*-produced livestock and cereal production, as well as in *obraje* sweatshop-produced textiles, to supply the mining and urban demand. The German geographer, Alexander von Humboldt, who studied Spanish America at the turn of the eighteenth–nineteenth century, wrote in his *Political Essay on the Kingdom of New Spain:*

> Travelling along the ridges of the Andes, or the mountainous part of Mexico, we everywhere see the most striking examples of the beneficial influence of mines on agriculture. Were it nor for the establishments formed for the working of the mines, how many places would have remained deserted? How many districts uncultivated in the four intendancies of Guanajuato, Zacatecas, San Luis Potosi and Durango? . . . . Farms are established in the neighborhood of the mine. The high price of provision, from the competition of the purchasers, indemnifies the cultivator for the privations to which he is exposed from the hard life of the mountains. Thus, from the hope of gain alone . . . a mine which at first appeared insulated in the midst of wild and desert mountains, becomes in a short time connected with the lands which have long been under cultivation. (Humboldt 1811, II: 407–8, quoted in Frank 1972: 27–28)

"The beneficial influence of the mines" extended far beyond the mining regions or even their contiguous agricultural areas (see, for example, the account of the Bajio in Mexico in Wolf 1955). It was also responsible for the eighteenth-century development of *latifundio* agriculture in Chile to supply the mining regions of Upper Peru and its metropolis, Lima (Góngora 1960; Sepúlveda 1959; Frank 1969) Although the vast majority of the population was engaged in agricultural activities, and for many of them this meant subsistence farming, the axis on which these activities and in general the entire Spanish empire in the eighteenth century turned was mining. Even special regions, such as cocoa-producing Venezuela or indigo-producing Guatemala, exported most of their production to consumers in the mining economy of Mexico or to those dependent on it in Spain (Arcilla Farías 1950: 195). The often frustrated Spanish attempts to maintain a monopoly of the trade with their colonial empire gave way, during the final two decades of the century, to policies of trade liberalization, and these in combination with the economic climate of the early Industrial Revolution, generated a final silver and economic boom in the Spanish empire before its collapse (see Chapter 5, section 3).

The expansion of sugar production into the Caribbean in the middle of the eighteenth century and the fall of sugar prices after 1670 led to the decline of the old sugar-producing regions of the Brazilian Northeast after that date. These circumstances and the associated increase in the price of monetary gold stimulated the search for, and the subsequent mining of, gold in the region farther south and inland that came to be known as Minas Gerais (General Mines). Gold was discovered in 1693–1695. Serious production began in the first decade of the eighteenth century at an annual average of about 2,000 kilos. After 1720, production increased still further, to an annual average of over 8,000 kilos for the next two decades; and it reached its peak of nearly 15,000 kilos per year between 1740 and 1760. After that Brazilian gold production fell off sharply to about 10,000 kilos for the next two decades and declined to an annual average of only 5,000 kilos during the last two decades of the eighteenth century (Simonsen 1962: 298, after Soetbeer). The quantitative importance of Brazilian gold production between 1700 and 1770 becomes evident when it is compared with production at other times and places. It was equal to the entire amount of gold produced by the Spanish American colonies between 1492 and 1800, and it represented nearly one-half of the rest of the world's output of gold during the sixteenth, seventeenth, and eighteenth centuries (Simonsen 1962: 258). The qualitative importance of this Brazilian gold cycle lies in the role it played in the commercial revolution and in the early ascendancy of British industry in the eighteenth century.

In Brazil, the "golden" era shifted the focus of economic, political, and cultural life from the Northeast to the Center South, a shift that was symbolized by the move of the capital from Salvador de Bahia to Rio de Janeiro, which became the principal port for the exploitation of the interior. Indeed, the gold rush initiated the unification into a single country, or at least colony, of what had previously been hardly more than separate regions, each of which was tied, although in different ways, to the same metropolis in Portugal. The gold rush attracted capital and slave labor from the decaying Northeast. It stimulated livestock production in the dryland Sertão in the Northeast and even more so in the southern Bandeirante region of São Paulo, which supplied the mining region with mules for transport, hides for packaging, meat for consumption and other foodstuffs, and building materials for the mining population. But the resources already existing in Brazil were insufficient to fill the gold rush, and it attracted further capital, adventurers, and laborers from Europe, and slaves from Africa. Much of the mining and ancillary work was done by slaves, but by no means all. Though the productive and property relations of the Minas gold mining (and after 1728, also diamond mining) region were fundamentally equivalent to those of the Brazilian or Caribbean sugar plantations and the Spanish American silver mining economies, the very nature of gold mining introduced a significant difference. Gold placer mining (or washing), as distinct from deep shaft silver mining or sugarmilling, could profitably be undertaken with lesser investments of capital and significantly greater dispersion in the ownership of the mining installations and their product. In the extreme case, as in the famous California, Alaska, and Australia gold rushes of the nineteenth century, it required only a stake to keep body and soul together, a pan to wash gold, and randomly distributed luck. The resulting economic and social structure was relatively more egalitarian and led to different and greater development initiatives—including industrial production—in Minas Gerais after gold production faded out during the last decades of the eighteenth century. But these initiatives arose at a moment when Portugal and Britain had particular interests in frustrating them. They were stamped out by political and economic force, and Minas Gerais declined into a depressed area from the turn of the century onward (Simonsen 1962; Furtado 1965; Frank 1969).

Brazilian gold flowed to Portugal and from there to Britain to pay for their respective excess of imports over exports; and from Britain it flowed largely to the Orient. The seventeenth-century Anglo-Portuguese commercial treaties had fallen into substantial abeyance during the commercially recessive times prior to the Glorious Revolution of 1688, and Portuguese textile production had received a new—albeit short—lease on life. But the economic and political circumstances of the turn of the century led Portugal to sign the Treaty of Methuen in 1703 and to begin another period of even greater political and economic dependence on Britain, which lasted at least as long as the gold rush in Brazil. The Treaty of Methuen provided for the exchange of British textiles and Portuguese wine, an exchange which was sanctified a century later by Ricardo in his "law" of comparative advantage. British political and commercial rivalry with France and Tory-Whig agreement led Britain to transfer the import of wine from France to Portugal, thereby denying France this foreign exchange (most of the wine had been paid for with silver). This meant dearer wine in Britain, but it opened an assured and steady market for British textiles which were largely paid for in gold rather than wine. The arrangement was not without its critics in Portugal, so much so that the Portuguese envoy to Britain, Luis da Cunha, argued against it: "France would sacrifice its wine before its manufactures; England would prefer to buy dearer than to abandon her clothes. . . . What the British want is to improve their manufactures, and to ruin those situated in Portugal" (quoted in Sideri 1970: 75, 59). The British succeeded, as the Portuguese Prime Minister Pombal would sadly observe six decades later:

> The contribution of Brazil to the English "Commercial Revolution" has also been neglected by historians. This neglect stems not only from the English trade statistics which show no trade with Brazil and fail to reveal the importance of Luso-Brazilian trade for English trade with Portugal. . . . (Fisher 1969: 6)

Two important studies were subsequently published in 1970–1971 to partially remedy this neglect: Fisher's own *The Portugal Trade* and Sideri's *Trade and Power*, the former emphasizing the consequences for Britain and the latter emphasizing the consequences for Portugal.

The contribution to Britain and the commercial revolution generally was both direct and indirect, as well as circumstantial. *The British Merchant* observed: "Since our Treaty with Portugal, we have exported yearly to that country prodigious Quantities of our Woollen Manufactures vastly greater than we ever did before; vastly greater than we ever did to France" (quoted in Sideri 1970: 44). Indeed, between 1697–1700 and 1706–1710 British exports to Portugal—many of which went on from there to Brazil—increased 120 percent and imports from Portugal only 40 percent. Portugal became Britain's third largest customer for all exports and the fourth largest for manufactures (Sideri 1970: 44–45), accounting for about 10 percent of the former and 13 percent of the latter (Fisher 1971: 126). Later, during the relatively depressed 1730s and early 1740s, Portugal—with Brazil always behind it—came to take 12 percent of total British exports, including re-exports, 18 percent of Britain's exports of manufactures, and up to 23 percent of Britain's exports of principal woollen textiles (Fisher 1971: 126). Not only did Brazil and Portugal become a very important customer for British manufactures, therefore, whose growth they stimulated at a time when British manufactures were increasingly excluded from the European market; but they supported that growth precisely during the 1720–1745 recessive phase of the long commercial cycles of the eighteenth century, when even the Caribbean sugar business sank relatively into the doldrums.

But there was yet another golden contribution. Britain maintained a steadily growing merchandize export surplus with Portugal for the whole period, which grew from an annual average of about £200,000 at the beginning of the century to about £500,000 in the 1720s, £700,000–800,000 during the 1730s and 1740s, and then exceeded an annual average of £1 million in the late 1750s, before it declined again to little over £200,000 by the late 1760s and 1770s (Fisher 1971: 16). This British merchandize export surplus (or Portuguese merchandize trade deficit) was covered by Portugal with Brazilian gold, as were British earnings on "invisibles" in its shipping, merchandizing, credit, and other services to Portugal. For this period as a whole, these surpluses (or deficits) may have reached the sum of £25 million and accounted for 6 percent of all recorded imports into Britain (Fisher 1971: 128). This was the basis for the displacement of silver and Britain's establishment of the gold standard at that time. Not only did this gold serve to oil the wheels of British fortune in general during the eighteenth-century "preconditions for take-off" into the Industrial Revolution (to use Rostow's terminology), but it also financed much of the British revival of the Orient trade. Britain imported from the Far East lighter textiles for re-export to the warmer climates of Europe, Africa, and the Americas; but Britain had no ready means of payment other than Brazilian gold. Furthermore, this arrangement freed the scarcer silver for use to finance the Baltic trade, also characterized by deficit, which provided Britain with certain raw materials needed to support the development of her manufactures and their export. Fisher summarizes:

> Thus between 1700 and 1770 Anglo-Portuguese trade contributed in not unimportant ways to the development of the English economy, and

expecially so in the first forty years of the century when the rate of overall development was not particularly impressive. Without the growth of this trade, without the expansion of Brazilian gold output on which so much else turned, English commercial, financial and industrial advance would have been much slower. . . . Whilst the growth of foreign trade may not have directly precipitated the Industrial Revolution, its contribution was nevertheless notable. (Fisher 1971: 138–39)

3. Sugar and Slave Plantations in the Caribbean

Another, perhaps the major, contribution to the eighteenth-century commercial revolution came from the sugar revolution and the associated slave and triangular trade among manufacturing Europe, the Caribbean sugar plantations, and the source of slaves in Africa. As Sheridan observes, "the rise of the plantation colonies must be seen against the background of major economic and social recession and secular adjustment which has been termed 'the crisis of the seventeenth century.' The collapse of Spain and her imperial economy in America was only one aspect of the crisis" (Sheridan 1970: 60). This crisis also determined the "neglect" observed by Adam Smith, which the Caribbean suffered or enjoyed relative to Spain's mining colonies. In consequence, first the Dutch, after their expulsion from Brazil in the middle of the seventeenth century, and then predominantly the British expanded into the erstwhile Spanish Caribbean to develop slave plantation-grown sugar on island after island. After 1713 the British were increasingly challenged by the French, who were able to produce at lower cost using better organization and more fertile virgin lands.

British sugar production, initially using Dutch capital, began in the middle of the seventeenth century in Barbados, which was transformed from a yeoman farming to a slave plantation society between 1645 and 1667. After that the Barbadian boom petered out. The next major island to be converted to sugar planting by the British was Jamaica, first conquered in 1665. However, Jamaica did not come to rival Barbados in slave population and sugar production until the first decade of the eighteenth century. After that the number of sugar plantations in this larger island increased much more rapidly, and by the early 1770s they were producing ten times more than Barbados. By 1773–1774 Jamaica had over 200,000 slaves on 775 sugar plantations and a medium-sized sugar plantation would employ some 200 blacks working about 600 acres, of which perhaps 250 were in cane. The total profit to Britain from Jamaica for the year 1773 was estimated at over £1.5 million, of which about one-third came from production for export and two-thirds from profits on trade (Sheridan 1970: 41,101).

The French expanded into the Caribbean later, after Colbert had chartered the West Indian and African trading companies. Martinique was originally colonized in 1635, but by 1671 there were still only twelve sugar plantations on the island. During the next three decades, the population trebled to about 20,000, although the proportion of blacks and whites still remained roughly the same, 2:1. After that expansion was much more rapid, especially in the black population, which passed 70,000 in 1770 and exceeded the white population by 6:1. The major French plantation colony and eventually the largest producer of sugar in the Caribbean was St. Domingue (later Haiti) on the island of Hispaniola, which began to rival and then to exceed British Jamaica in the second and third quarters of the eighteenth century. By 1775 it had attained a black population of over 250,000, but the slave revolt of 1791 all but withdrew it from the world sugar market (Sheridan 1970: 48–55). The French also produced sugar on Guadeloupe and the British on Antigua, St. Christopher, and Grenada among others, over twenty islands in all. Their relative importance appears from the following average tonnages of legal imports into the metropolitan countries: in 1741–1745, out of a total of 150,000 tons, 65,000 were French, 41,000 British, and 34,000 Portuguese from Brazil; in 1766–1770, out of a total of 193,000 tons 78,000 were French, 74,000 British, and 20,000 Portuguese. The Spaniards produced only about 2 percent of the total, exceeded even by the Dutch and the Danish (Sheridan 1970: 22–23).

The "plantation system" came to dominate the Northeast of Brazil, most of the Caribbean, and subsequently the South of the United States, as well as other scattered regions in the New World. Lacking substantial mines, dense populations, to say nothing of high civilizations, these lowland tropical areas evidently did not permit the kind of exploitation that the Spaniards imposed in Mexico and Peru. But their geographical and climatic characteristics did permit their participation in, and their substantial contribution to the process of capital accumulation during the commercial revolution, provided their natural resources could be suitably combined with the labor, capital, and organization necessary to make them produce at a profit. It was these circumstances which initiated the mode of production that has determined the historical fate of most of these regions until this day.

Lewis Gray summarizes:

> The plantation system had its genesis in the economic organization of the early joint-stock company. . . . The plantation system was the natural successor of the colonizing company. With quasi public functions of colonial foundation accomplished and the functions of government taken over by public agencies (after the initial private colonizing investments had largely proved to be commercial failures), the remaining task was to finance immigration and settlement. The plantation system afforded a convenient method of uniting capital and labor in the business of production. It would have been impracticable for the European capitalist to advance to each laborer the necessary expenses of emigration and settlement, leaving him to work out his own success and to repay the debt at will. The planter was the effective agent through whom European capital might be so employed, and the plantation was the agency of colonial expansion which brought together and combined three separate factors in utilizing the natural resources of the New World: the labor of the industrial servant or the slave, the capital furnished by the European merchant, and the directive activity of the planters. In some instances, of course, the planters themselves furnished part or all of the capital. (Gray 1958, II: 312, 311)

Frequently,

> the establishment of private plantations followed as a third stage, favored by the fact that the new enterprises were not compelled to assume the expenses and responsibilities of initial colonization, had the advantage of experience with the new environment and the opportunity in some cases to acquire at small cost the lands, improvements, and equipment of the unsuccessful colonizing agencies. With the development of regular trade the latter was provided not only with market outlets for his products, but also a means of procuring on credit the requisite servants, slaves, and equipment. (Gray 1958, II: 341)

Elsewhere Gray specifies:

The most characteristic institution of the plantation colony was the plantation system, which may be formally defined as follows: *The plantation was a capitalistic type of agricultural organization in which a considerable number of unfree laborers were employed under unified direction and control in the production of a staple crop.* . . . The definition implies also that (1) the functions of laborer and employer were sharply distinct; (2) the system was based on commercial agriculture, except in periods of depression; (3) the system represented a capitalistic stage of agricultural development, since the value of slaves, land, and equipment necessitated the investment of money capital, often of large amount and frequently borrowed, and there was a strong tendency for the planter to assume the attitude of the business man in testing success by ratio of net money income to capital invested; and (4) there was a stong tendency toward specialization—the production of a single crop for market. It is significant that three of the characteristics developed in manufacturing by the Industrial Revolution—commercialism, capitalism, and specialization—were attained in Southern agriculture as early as the first half of the seventeenth century through the establishment of the plantation system. (Gray 1958, II: 302) (Emphasis in original)

Though referring specifically to the Caribbean, the economic, social, and political consequences of the implantation of the plantation system in the New World is summarized by Sidney Mintz.

Caribbean regional commonality is expressed in terms of nine major features as follows: (1) lowland, sub-tropical, insular ecology; (2) the swift extirpation of native populations; (3) the early definition of the islands as a sphere of European overseas agricultural capitalism, based primarily on the sugarcane. African slaves, and the plantation system; (4) the concomitant development of insular social structures in which internally differentiated local community organization was slight, the national class groupings usually took a bipolar form, sustained by overseas domination, sharply differentiated access to land, wealth, and political power, and the use of physical differences as status markers; (5) the continuous interplay of plantations and small-scale yeoman agriculture, with accompanying social-structural effects . . . the distinction between coastal plain and rugged highland foretold a sharp divergence of enterprise that has typically marked Caribbean (and other plantation regions') agriculture with plantations concentrated on the coasts and in island valleys, and small-scale enterprise and some hacienda forms occurring in mountainous sectors. (Mintz 1966: 915, 917)

As was observed and emphasized already by Smith and Marx, and of course by the planters and slaves themselves, the initial conditions

of plenitude of land (subject to some restriction only in the Caribbean by the small size of some of the islands, which on the other
hand constituted impediments to escape) and the scarcity of labor
meant that the plantation enterprise could operate with profitable
low cost labor only if the latter was subject to force in the form of
indenture or slavery. Ultimately, indenture became unmanageable
because of reduced supplies from Europe and because of increased
difficulties of enforcement in the colonies—and black slavery became
the dominant, though never the only, source and form of plantation
labor.

The moment of development and boom of the plantation economy
differed from island to island, in a sense repeating on a larger scale
the incorporation of the islands into the process of capital accumulation under Columbus and his Spanish successors, who had gone on
to greener pastures after eroding the economic virginity of the ones
incorporated first. In the seventeenth-nineteenth centuries, of
course, this process of successive maximum exploitation of the islands was complicated by the competition among rival metropolitan
powers.

The production regimes and relations varied among the islands as
a function of (1) this rhythm of successive though overlapping temporal exploitation, (2) the major boom and bust cycles of the sugar
business that to some extent they shared in common, and (3) the
variety of geographical or topological production possibilities. In
general the smaller islands specialized in the monoculture of sugar to
a greater degree than the larger ones or the mainland coastal regions,
which were relatively less dependent on imports of foodstuffs, etc.
Some of these imports were produced by and for the slaves themselves on inland or mountainous "provision grounds" of relatively
lower fertility, most notably in Jamaica. This economic circumstance, which was mutually beneficial to both planters and slaves,
also offered the latter a relatively greater opportunity to escape from,
or at least to resist, the total oppressiveness of the sugar "factory in
the field."

It is appropriate here to mention the argument that has recently
been resurrected by the publication of books like *Slave and Citizen* by
Frank Tannenbaum and *Slavery* by Stanley Elkins in the United
States and in *The Mansions and the Shanties* and other books on

Brazilian slavery by Gilberto Freyre. These writers argue, in a manner reminiscent of the crude Weberian argument about the Protestant ethic (which, incidentally, was not Weber's own), that supposed cultural and institutional differences between the slave owners or their respective societies are sufficient to account for supposed differences in slave societies, cultures, or personalities, and in the degrees or kinds of oppression the slaves suffered. This argument has been severely criticized by Eugene Genovese and Sidney Mintz among others. The former shows that, on the one hand, the supposed docility of "Sambo" was not confined to the South of the United States, as Elkins supposes, and that, on the other hand, this supposed docility did not prevent numerous slave uprisings that occurred, some unsuccessful and some successful as in Haiti (Genovese 1967). Mintz, in his review of Elkins, argues further that

the question, then, does not seem to hinge on the presence of a tradition in one case and its absence in another. . . . The rate of growth of the slave plantation, then, did not hinge on matters of race, civil liberties, protection of the rights of individuals slave and free, or the presence or absence of one or several religious codes. . . . The differentials in the growth of the slave plantations in different colonies are to be understood as resulting from different ecologies, different maturation of metropolitan markets and industries, and different political relationships between creole governing bodies and the metropolitan authorities. . . . Industrial slavery of this sort [as in the most commercial plantation colonies] effected a more complete dehumanization of the slaves than did other forms of slavery [and especially domestic slavery]. (Mintz 1961: 584)

Mintz thus supports Adam Smith's observation as well as my argument that the relatively benign regime in the Spanish colonies was due not to cultural or institutional differences but to economic differences. Because of the change in economic conditions, the severity and oppressiveness of the Spanish slave regime during the first half century after the conquest of the Caribbean (and other parts of its empire) and again during the nineteenth century after sugar became king in Cuba, was no less than it was in the worst Protestant North European colonies of the eighteenth century. Moreover the kind and degree of oppressiveness of slavery also varied over time within the latter, primarily as a function of economic requirements.
  Even Genovese—who, although he rejects the Tannenbaum-

Elkins thesis, is generally contemptuous in all of his writings of what he calls "excessively economic determinist misinterpretations" and specifically finds Mintz's thesis quoted above to be too extreme— recognizes that

> the *Code Noire* of 1685 set a high standard of humanity and attempted to guarantee the slaves certain minimal rights and protection. It was treated with contempt in the French West Indies, especially when the islands began to ride the sugar boom. . . . On the eve of the Haitian Revolution probably not one of the protective articles of the *Code Noire* was being enforced. (Genovese 1969: 300)

But this observation of Genovese, which is by no means original with him, leads us even further than Mintz seems prepared to go; for it implies that the treatment of slaves (like that of other kinds of agricultural workers and tenants since then) varies as a close function of the booms and busts of the agricultural business—not because he may or may not be excessively "economic determinist," but because the relations between the owners of capital and labor, to say nothing of the use of capital (including slaves), is in fact determined more economically and politically than institutionally or culturally, let alone psychologically, if these can be significantly distinguished.*

Harry Hoetink, in his comparative study on "Race Relations in Curaçao and Surinam," observes that the social relations in the two colonies were quite different, although subject to the same Dutch Protestantism, laws, and institutions.

> For Curaçao it is enough to note that the social roles of master and slaves produced an institutionalized and mutually complementary pattern of behavior for both master and slaves. . . . [because] Curaçao had no real plantations, no real latifundios producing for the world market. . . . The situation was totally different in Surinam. There were vast sugar, coffee, cotton, and lumber plantations. There were large concentrations of hundreds of slaves . . . [where] at no time did the number of whites exceed 7% of the number of slaves. . . . At the end of the eighteenth century in Surinam there were about 3,000 whites and about 5,000 slaves. In Curaçao the number of whites was

---

* For a discussion of this issue at the microlevel, see, for instance, Erich Fromm and Michael Maccoby, *Social Character in a Mexican Village* (1970: 230): "The social character is the result of the adaptation of human nature to the given socioeconomic conditions [in the next paragraph they say "class role"], and secondarily tends to stabilize and maintain these conditions."

more or less the same, but there were only one-tenth as many slaves. These statistics alone help to explain the more severe treatment of the slaves in Surinam. (Hoetink 1969: 181–82)

Elsa Goveia argues, on the other hand, that

> in spite of the religious differences between the Catholic French and the Protestant British in the West Indies, both their religious attitudes and their general behavior toward the slaves showed striking similarities during the course of the eighteenth century, and these similarities were in marked contrast with the attitudes and behavior accepted in Cuba until that colony began to develop a great plantation system. . . . All the evidence points to one conclusion. As they were actually administered during the eighteenth century, the French slave laws differed far less from their English counterparts than might be imagined. The enforcement of the *Code Noir* [which under other circumstances Colbert had sponsored to protect slaves more for commercial than human considerations] during this period [became increasingly lax]. . . . The law tended to become more and more a dead letter. (Goveia 1969:168, 134, 131)

This was, of course, during the 1763–1789 boom years of the French sugar colonies. David Brion Davis explains:

> Whenever slaves were worked under boom conditions, as in the West Indies in the mid-eighteenth century and the Brazilian coffee plantations in the nineteenth, the institution was one of grinding attrition. A more relaxed paternalism tended to appear when prices had fallen, when there was little incentive to maximize production. (D. B. Davis 1969: 67)

> It is perhaps significant that accounts of Latin American slavery often picture the relaxed life on sugar plantations after their decline in economic importance, and ignore conditions that prevailed during the Brazilian sugar boom of the seventeenth century, the mining boom of the early eighteenth century, and the coffee boom of the nineteenth century. (D.B. Davis 1969: 73)

In summary then, the principal determinants of the labor conditions on the slave plantations—and also in the mining and other colonial labor systems—were external economic and internal political imperatives. Additional, though related, circumstances that contributed to the definition of labor conditions and social relations in general were the size and concentration of the productive units and the replacement conditions of the labor force. Thus the slave regimes were most severe in areas, such as the smaller islands, that were highly specialized—especially in boom times—in large plantation agriculture; they were somewhat less severe, and yet more characterized by slave revolts, in areas such as Jamaica, where the hilly interior hinterland offered some possibilities of subsistence agriculture and military refuge; and they were relatively least severe in parts of the southern United States, where plantations, or rather farms, and concentrations of slaves were often smaller and more dispersed. Similarly, the treatment of slaves was most severe (a "useful" life of seven years or less) where and when the possibilities of the replacement of this "working" capital were greater and cheaper (absolutely or relative to boom time profits); and most "humane" where the useful lives of slaves had to be extended in accord with the needs of the master, and what is more, where and when the supply of slaves was dependent largely upon their own reproduction.

A related argument of old, which assumes greater and lesser political importance at different moments in history, is whether race prejudice is the cause or the effect of race discrimination and specifically of black slavery. One side seeks to justify—to themselves and to others—their own discrimination and exploitation of others, alleging that some races are inferior to others and that such sentiments do in fact exist; while the other side argues that these sentiments (i.e., prejudice) are really the historical and social result of the relations and system of discrimination and exploitation and, what is more, that any racial superiority/inferiority differences that may now be observable are themselves the sociohistorical result of such exploitation and oppression. The latter point out the symbolic importance of Shakespeare's *Othello,* a play that does not display nor reflect any race prejudice of whites toward blacks. Others have criticized Shakespeare for not having sufficiently reflected the race prejudice that was then supposedly already in existence. A detailed analysis of this question is not possible here, but it should be clear that the entire thesis of this book is consistent only with the thesis that race sentiment is fundamentally the consequence and not the cause of racial oppression and exploitation. The interested reader should see writers who have seriously examined and defended this thesis such as C. L. R. James, Eric Williams, and—though his defense is much more guarded—Eugene Genovese. In conclusion, C. R. Boxer's observation, referring to the oft-claimed "lack" of race prejudice among the Portugese, seems irrefutable: 'One race cannot systematically enslave members of another on a large scale for over three centuries without acquiring a conscious or unconscious feeling of racial superiority" (Boxer, quoted in Foner and Genovese 1969: 246).

4. The Slave Trade in Africa

"A large-scale slave trade would have been impossible if Africa had been truly primitive. . . . But Africa was not primitive" (Bohannon and Curtin 1971: 264). Slavery in the Americas and the Atlantic slave trade necessarily drew Africa into the process of capital accumulation and did so on a new basis. In the words of Samir Amin:

> During this period of incubation covering three centuries, the American periphery of the Western European mercantilist center played a decisive role in the accumulation of money-wealth by the merchant bourgeoisie of the Atlantic countries. Black Africa played a no less important role as the "periphery of the periphery." Reduced to the function of supplying slave labor for the plantations of America, Africa lost its independence. It began to be shaped according to external requirements, namely, those of mercantilism. (Amin 1976: 320)

Slavery and slave trading had a long history in Africa, but prior to the Atlantic slave trade they existed on different social bases and had other economic functions and consequences than they would have under the aegis of world mercantile capitalism (Hargreaves 1967). Davidson (1961) divides the development of the Atlantic slave trade into three prineipal largely successive stages: (1) piracy; (2) warlike alliance between slave-raiding Europeans and coastal chiefs who began by supplying slaves under duress and ended by producing them for profit; and (3) more or less peaceful partnership between the European slavers and the coastal suppliers who in turn traded or captured slaves in the raids of the inland wars.

The slave trade affected four major regions in Africa: the Congo, the Niger Delta, the Guinea Coast, and parts of East Africa—and it affected them differently, damaging the population base much more severely, for instance, in the more sparsely settled South, which was the main source for the Portuguese, than in the more densely settled Northwest of the Anglo-French slave trade (Oliver and Fage 1962: 121). Thus while the total flow of slaves increased from less than 2,000 a year before 1600 to an average of about 55,000 annually for the eighteenth century as a whole, and an average of 70,000 to 75,000 annually (over 100,000 in some individual years) during the peak decade of the 1780s, the African source of the slaves also shifted in a southwesterly direction. The supply from the Gold Coast suffered a relative decline, therefore, from about 25 percent in the 1720s to 8 percent in the 1790s, while the supply from the Bight of Biafra rose from only 2 percent in the earlier decade to 42 percent in the first decade of the nineteenth century; and the supply from Central Africa doubled between the 1770s and the 1780s. For the period 1711 to 1810 as a whole, Senegal, Gambia, and Sierra Leone together supplied about 5.5 percent, the Windward Coast about 7.7 percent, the Gold Coast 9.2 percent, the Bight of Benin 19.5 percent, the Bight of Biafra 16 percent, and Central and Southeast Africa 42 percent (Curtin, cited in Bohannon and Curtin 1971: 269–71). "In short, while the demand for slaves was relatively steady, it was met by rapid shifts from one source of supply to another, depending on African political conditions or the development of new trade routes from the interior" (Bohannon and Curtin 1971: 269). But more important than these regional differences for an appreciation of the operation and consequences of the slave trade for Africa was the difference between its operation on or near the coast and its far-reaching effects in the interior hinterland areas. Davidson writes in *The African Slave Trade:*

> It isolated the peoples of the interior from any contact with Europe except through the sale of captives. The chiefs of the coastal peoples throve and defended their power by purchasing European firearms; those in the rear, deprived of any direct link with Europeans, were reduced to impotence or involvement in the trade themselves. Increasingly, they chose or were driven to involvement. (Davidson 1961: 154)

Thus, some Africans, particularly rulers in the coastal belt, took an active and concious part in the slave trade as exporters of one commodity, slaves, in exchange for other commodities; just as elsewhere the local purveyors of the fruits of colonial and then neocolonial labor and the compradore bourgeoisie have always participated actively in the export-import trade and the political or military regime necessary to support it.

> It is wrong to consider the Guinea [and other African slave trade] experience as one that was simply ordered and imposed from the outside, with the African part in it a purely negative and involuntary one. This view of the connection mirrors a familiar notion of African incapacity, and it has no place in the historical record. Those Africans who were involved in the trade were seldom helpless victims of a commerce they did not understand; on the contrary, they understood it as well as their European partners. They responded to its challenge. They exploited its opportunities. Their great misfortune—and this would be Africa's tragedy—was that Europe only wanted slaves. (Davidson 1961: 201–2)

On the other hand,

> the wounds of the slave trade had become really inescapable. . . . At no point were they [Africans] presented with any choice except that of forgoing European trade altogether—to the a most certain profit of their rivals and their own peril—or else of surrendering to the incessant demands of Europe. . . . Dahomey's power to resist Oyo (itself in turn subjected to the same pressure) depended on delivering slaves to the coast; the drastic but inescapable alternative was to enslave others—in order to buy firearms—or risk enslavement oneself. This indeed was the inner dynamic of the slaving connection with Europe; and it pushed Dahomey, as it pushed other states, into wholesale participation in slaving. No single state could safely or even possibly withstand this combination of guns and captives. . . . Dahomey was caught in the slave trade's ruinous chain of cause and effect. . . . Huge quantities of firearms were poured into West Africa during the major period of the slave trade. . . . European dealers on the coast might regret this flood of weapons, for it strengthened the bargaining power of their African partners; but there was nothing they could do about it. Like the Africans, they too were caught in the chain of cause and effect. They had to have slaves, and to get slaves they had to pay with guns. Even if European traders wanted to refuse guns, they were far too distrustful of one another to operate any sort of common policy. (Davidson 1961: 240, 238, 241–42)

In some coastal areas the slave trade generated new settlements or new forms of settlement.

> The swamplands of the Niger Delta were thinly populated or void of people before the coming of the sailing ships. . . . Yet within a

hundred years there had emerged amid this maze of inland waterways
. . . a close-knit system of trading states; and within another hundred
years these states had built themselves into a well-nigh impregnable
position of commercial monopoly. They had become the indispensable
middlemen between Europe and the densely populated lands behind
the Delta. . . . The history of these little states . . . belongs to the Atlantic and to Africa. They were almost as much children of the Guinea
trade—the slave trade—as were the plantation colonies of the Caribbean and North America. And yet they remained strongly African
in accent and ideas. (Davidson 1961: 205–6)

Along the entire slave coast,

the slave trade became inseparable from the workings of chiefly rule.
Wherever the trade found strong chiefs and kings it prospered almost
from the first; wherever it failed to find them it caused them to come
into being. Whether in the accumulation of wealth by custom duties,
gifts, or trading profits; or in the political authority which slaving lent
to those who organized it; or in the military superiority which derived
from the buying of firearms, slaving built up the power of the chiefs
where it did not exist before, or else it transformed that power, where it
was already present, from a broadly representative character into an
autocratic one. (Davidson 1961: 225)

The firearms were the vital link between the coastal states and the
more densely populated interior.

Widespread use of firearms changed the course of history in the [Niger]
delta as surely as in other parts of Africa. It was their concentration of
firepower that enabled the delta chiefs to outface and overawe the
numerically far stronger peoples of the interior. And muskets were
almost certainly decisive in enabling the Aro trader-priests to maintain
their monopoly—and keep the oracle respected—in face of mounting
opposition from those who suffered from the system. The Aro priests
do not appear to have used the guns themselves. They hired others for
that purpose. They called up mercenaries from the professional
soldier-guilds of Iboland. . . . Thus the trade was organized by god
and gun on one side as surely as by ship and plantation on the
other. . . . Relations between the hinterland states were increasingly
poisoned by a fight for monopoly privilege in the supply of slaves.
Feudal wars widened into commercial wars. Commercial wars, duly
sanctioned by religion, degenerated into a free-for-all where any man
might seize another . . . if only his power sufficed. (Davidson 1961:
213, 226)

Thus in the states of the interior the Atlantic slave trade tended to
have consequences rather the opposite of those it had on the coast.

The interior had long maintained trade with the outside world, but across the Sahara (see Chapter 1, section 1). Where this trade still survived, it had to be suppressed by force—as the French did in what is today Senegal-Mali (Amin 1976). A more important consequence was the stagnation and political weakening of the previously existing imperial states.

> All the great states of the forest—Oyo, Benin, those of the Akan and Dahomey—became deeply involved in the slave trade; and each was influenced by its strains and pressures. More often than not, however, the consequences were in notable contrast with the political growth that occurred along the coast and most of all in the delta city-states. For whereas the peoples of the delta absorbed new tensions by evolving new forms of social organization, the states of the interior showed an increasing rigidity and resistance to political growth. Often enough, although with many local variations, their feudalisms turned inward on itself, their elected rulers became tyrants, and the fabric of their social life grew dangerously stiff and insensitive. Though trading vastly with the coast, they traded increasingly to their own ruin. They grew powerful in this commerce, but their power proved mortal. (Davidson 1961: 225)

Some states, like the Kongo-Angola and the Yoruba federation, were destroyed or disintegrated under the impact of the slave trade.

The apparent exception to this rule might seem to be the Ashanti state, for it grew up and expanded during the eighteenth century to become the most powerful African state of the middle ages of African history—and it did so in an inland region centered on its capital city, Kumasi. Its founders and empire builders are still remembered and revered today. But if the power and glory of Ashanti was exceptional, it was so in that it successfully challenged the coastal Fulani and Ga claims to the monopoly of the slave trade, and established itself as an intermediary between them and the North—rather than remaining marginal to, or being destroyed by, the slave trade. Then as now, ultimately it was the slave trade and the production of gold which was the economic basis of Ashanti power and of its state formation (Fynn 1971).

Another significant effect of the slave trade and slave wars was their contribution to the de-democratization, stratification, and authoritanization of African society. Not only was the power of the chiefs enhanced (or in some cases virtually created) and their legitimacy perverted—a process that had already occurred in the sixteenth century in the Indian caciques of Spanish America, and would reemerge at the turn of the twentieth century in colonial Africa—but as a counterpart

> the status of many common people became depressed and the division of society into different classes became more rigid. . . . Active involvement in the Atlantic slave trade invariably meant the increase of such servile categories in the societies where they existed, and their creation where they had not previously existed. Thus it was that by the end of the eighteenth century a sizeable proportion of the inhabitants of West Africa found themselves under some sort of servitude. . . . In the period of the Atlantic slave trade a punishment as drastic as sale into slavery was introduced for a larger and larger number of offences, descending right down to the most trivial. In effect the common people had lost the security of person which the customary laws had guaranteed them in the past. . . . Priests were usually involved on the side of the slave traders, along with powerful spiritual institutions such as secret societies. Religious authorities were adept at uncovering instances of witchcraft which meant that the accused were sold to the Europeans. There was obvious chicanery in these procedures, although the practice of witchcraft may have increased under the disturbed conditions of the slave-trade era. Another area of darkness is that of moral values. (Rodney 1967: 37–39)

Finally, we may ask what were the immediate consequences for Africa's own economic development as a result of her participation in the slave trade and its contribution (through the slave trade) to the world process of capital accumulation during the years 1650–1850? Rodney writes:

> The trade certainly did not stimulate any productive resources in Africa, as it did in Europe and the New World. On the contrary it distracted efforts away from agriculture and manufactures. The introduction of European goods in itself brought no economic benefits, since the goods were consumed without creating growth in the economy. . . . the economy stagnated and human resources were wasted. (Rodney 1967: 39)

Without any doubt, this stagnation and waste was greater than the African contribution, great as it was, to economic development elsewhere.*

---

* The social, economic, and political basis that the slave trade laid for Africa's participation—again, on a new basis—in the process of world capital accumulation in the nineteenth and twentieth centuries is examined in Chapter 6 of the author's forthcoming *Dependent Accumulation and Underdevelopment*.

Chapter 4

The Transition in India to the Transformation of Asia

Nearly all our major problems today have grown up during British rule and as a direct result of British policy; the princes; the minority problem; various vested interests, foreign and Indian; the lack of industry and the neglect of agriculture; the extreme backwardness in the social services; and, above all, the tragic poverty of the people. The attitude to education has been significant. . . . To all these methods must be added the deliberate policy, pursued throughout the period of British rule, of creating divisions among Indians, of encouraging one group at the cost of the other . . . . by organizing Quisling classes. . . . Imperialism must function in this way or else it ceases to be imperialism.
—Jawaharal Nehru. *The Discovery of India* (1960)

1. The Superficial European Impact on Asia

Before the British conquest of Bengal in the second half of the eighteenth century, the most far-reaching European impact in Asia was that of the Dutch East India Company in some islands of Indonesia—and even this was modest enough, although foreshadowing developments in the nineteenth century (van Leur 1955: 273, and *passim*). It was in several of the smaller islands of Indonesia that specialization in export agriculture was first demanded and enforced in South Asia. By making each of these islands specialize in the production of a particular spice, to the exclusion of others, the Dutch sought to strengthen their monopoly position. This meant that the Dutch began to exercise political control, at least in the form of "indirect rule" by local rulers. Moreover,

> with the extension of Dutch territorial control in Java, large quantities of products which had hitherto been paid for at market prices began to be received on more advantageous terms under contracts and treaties concluded with the Indonesian rulers. In addition to demanding specific amounts of rice, sugar, pepper, and coffee from the people of Java, the Dutch also required personal services in the manufacture of salt, cutting of timber in the forests, dredging of canals, construction of roads and bridges, and all kinds of public works. Moreover, the officials of the Company exploited this source of labor for their own private purposes. (Bastin and Benda 1968: 25)

Nonetheless, the Dutch exploitation of Indonesia was primarily limited to "skimming cash crops off the surface of an immobilized subsistence economy. . . . Its impact on the Indonesian ecological pattern as a whole was marginal and unsystematic" (Geertz 1963: 52).

Clifford Geertz's argument about the nature of the Dutch impact on Indonesia has been sustained most forcefully by J. C. van Leur, who argues:

> It seems to me that, until explained otherwise, these facts are in opposition to the concept of a languishing, retarded Indonesian world and an all-dominating Company. . . . To summarize, then, the course of Indonesian history, when checked in regard to a few episodes and economic concepts, does not appear to have coincided with that of the Dutch Company, no more than the history of any European political foothold in Asia in the eighteenth century directed the general course of Asian history. (van Leur 1955: 281, 284)

J. D. Legge comments that van Leur

> tended to overstate his case in order to counter the overstatements of the opposition. There would be general agreement today with his argument that the arrival of the Portuguese and Dutch did not constitute a dramatic break in the continuity of the history of Asian trade. There would be less general agreement with the implication that the arrival of the European represented almost no change at all. (Legge 1964: 61)

What then was the impact of European mercantile capitalism on Asia in general prior to the Industrial Revolution and the nineteenth century, and how did it differ from its impact on Latin America and Africa? I am in basic agreement with van Leur's review and evaluation:

A general view of the whole can only lead to the conclusion that any talk of a European Asia in the eighteenth century is out of the question, that a few European centers of power had been consolidated on a very limited scale, that in general—and here the emphasis should lie—the Oriental lands continued to form active factors in the course of events as valid entities, militarily, economically, and politically. . . . One should call to mind the picture of the overall political situation in eastern and southeastern Asia during the eighteenth century. . . . Persia, then, was in the eighteenth century a country still intact. In India the establishment of local, even regional, power by France and England did not disturb the power of the Mogul Empire more than fleetingly [though the latter declined of its own and was replaced by British power in Bengal during the last four decades of the century (see below secs. 4–8)]. Burma and Farther India harboured inviolate states. The excellent organisation of the mandarin bureaucracy in Annam and Tonkin was to disappear only with the colonial wars of the French under the Second Empire [of Napoleon III after the mid-nineteenth century]. Under the Manchu emperors, eighteenth-century China reached a pinnacle of political power and cultural achievement. Emperor K'ang Hsi (1662–1723) once more extended the military influence of the empire as far as into West Turkestan and placed Tibet under Chinese suzerainty. Emperor Ch'ien Lung (1736–1796) made the distant western borders secure, drove Nepal out of Tibet back over the Himalayas, and gained recognition of Chinese suzerainty from Burma (1769) and Annam (1789). "Never, not even under the T'angs were such vast regions in Mongalia and Turkestan so completely annexed to the empire. . . . Never in all history had China's power and supremacy seemed to be so securely safeguarded" [quoting J. J. L. Duyvendak, *Wegen en Gestalten der Chineesche Geschiederis*]. In Japan the shogunate remained unshaken. The new development of more influence shifting to a "bourgeois" class of rich merchants, speculators, and money-holders did not affect the existing order of things; the reverses through volcanic eruptions, floods, droughts, and crop failures were of a completely static nature. Also deserving consideration is the social and economic significance of the great masses of population: from sixty or eighty to a hundred million people in China, twenty-six million in Japan, a hundred million in India—as opposed to the number of people in France, the most heavily populated European country, nineteen million at the end of the seventeenth century and twenty-three million at the end of the eighteenth (England counted only six-million inhabitants; with Scotland, seven). Such a comparison has a far-reaching validity in a world whose means of subsistence were practically equal technically in Asia and in Europe. Then, on the other hand, one should look at the position of European outposts in Asia. Russia had pushed across Siberia to the Sea of Akhotsk, but it remained completely peripheral in relation to China (as is shown by the treaties of 1688 and 1724) as well as to Japan. Nor had it yet begun its central Asian conquests. In the older strongholds in southeast Asia, did a change take place, did the balance shift and the Western element come to dominate? In the seventh-century political picture the Asian element had dominated completely when compared to that of the tiny outposts the Europeans had established. Was a balance struck later, and did the scales tip the other way in the eighteenth century? Certainly not for China, Japan, Indo-China, India, and Persia. Not even for India. The beginning of British territorial control dated from Plassey, 1757. (van Leur 1955: 274, 270, 271–72)

Two equal civilizations were developing separately from each other, the Asian in every way superior quantitatively. The equality remained as long as the magic poison of modern capitalism had not yet enchanted Europe and northeastern America to produce steam, mechanics, and grooved cannon. (van Leur 1955: 284–85)

2. Asiatic, Feudal, and Capitalist
Modes of Production

Bhowani Sen begins his chapter on "Heritage of the Past" in his *Evolution of Agrarian Relations in India* by stating, "Historians differ as to the nature of the ancient land system in India. It is beyond the scope of this book to go into the details of this controversy" (Sen 1962: 37). The same may be said with regard to other parts of Asia (see for example Jean Chesneaux 1969) and the scope of the present discussion. Much of the discussion has turned on the "Asiatic mode of production." Bartra (1969: 21) recalls that "the concept of the Asiatic mode of production or oriental despotism has a long history in Western thought," which he traces back to Plato and Aristotle, passing through Machiavelli, Hobbes, and Montesquieu, and in the nineteenth century Hegel and John Stuart Mill, before it was reformulated by Marx and Engels. In the twentieth century, this discussion died down during the Stalinist years, only to be revived as a pseudoscientific ideological weapon of anticommunism in the cold war years of the 1950s by Karl Wittfogel's publication of *Oriental Despotism.* * Thus the concept of the Asiatic mode of production degenerated into little more than a political weapon. Recently however, and especially since the translation and publication in various languages of Marx's *Grundrisse*, more serious research and debate has again revived among Marxist circles as well who have sought to vindicate the Asiatic mode of production as a scientific concept and to apply it in research from a historical materialist perspective (see, for example, Hobsbawm 1964b; Godelier 1969a; CERM 1971).

Bartra summarizes and defines:

> The Asiatic mode of production is a system in which a very strong—political and economic—state power appears which is based on the generalized exploitation of the village communities in the territory dominated by the state, an exploitation which works through the extraction of the surplus of the village production through tribute in kind or in labor (rarely in money). . . . The Asiatic mode of production should be considered as a class social formation. Or we may establish that we are dealing with a transitional mode of production. . . . In the Asiatic mode of production there is not only a low general level of the productive forces, but also an internal disequilibrium in their development. . . . There is a greater utilization of the productive force *human labor* than the productive force *means of production*. We find there a superexploitation of the labor force which compensates the underutilization of technological possibilities. . . . This is the disequilibrium which conditions the stagnation that is characteristic of the Asiatic mode of production; but this is an economic *historical* phenomenon, which has a structural factor, not a *natural* one, at its base. The socio-political instrument which permits the maintenance of this disequilibrium is represented by the state apparatus. Under these conditions, the society can only reach a high level of civilization through the strict, despotic, organizing and centralizing control of the state; for when this control disappears, there is lost the possibility of massive superexploitation of the labor force, which is spread through and perfectly integrated in the village communities which constitute the *relatively unchangeable* base of the system. In that case, up to a point frequent in the Asiatic world, of the decline of the power of the state, the traditional communities again turn in upon themselves to their

---

* For a non-Marxist critique, see Robert McC. Adams (1960) and Angel Palerm (1955).

isolated and self-sufficient life, without having acquired technical innovations that could permit their development. (Bartra 1969: 15–17)

It was this sort of concept, sometimes lending more emphasis to the supposed immutability and stagnation and sometimes less emphasis to village life and the state system as a whole, which characterized much of Western observation of Asia from Plato to Marx. Since then the Asiatic mode has been "found" also in parts of Africa, pre-Columbian America, and the classic Mediterranean civilizations. These discoveries have lent increasing emphasis to the internal dynamic and transitional features of the mode of production, so that some authors now recommend the elimination of the regional reference to "Asia" (where in fact it is far from universal), and its replacement by "village-despotic" or some other term (Chesneaux 1969).

Several considerations, among them the Stalinist insistence on the supposed primitive-slave-feudal-capitalist historical sequence, and the political and Eurocentric misuse of the Marxist concept of the mode of production to suggest the "superiority" of European pre-capitalist social formations, led to the replacement of the earlier Marxist interpretation in terms of the concept Asiatic mode of production, especially in regard to India, by other theses. Soviet writers and Indian students associated with the Communist Party of India (led by S. A. Dange) particularly have sustained the thesis of a feudal India:

> In the sixteenth to eighteenth centuries, feudalism in India developed quite rapidly. . . . When the Europeans appeared in India, the feudal mode of production was dominant there. (Levkovsky 1966: 2)

> Some form of feudalism, somewhat different from the European, had developed during the rule of the Gupta dynasty. . . . We have already noticed that the general features of feudalism explained above began to develop in ancient India more than 2,000 years ago. We have also indicated that the special feature of Indian feudalism was the *tributary form;* that is, unlike European serfdom, forced labour was not a general feature, the lord or overlord received only tributes. . . . Under Muslim rule, land system in India was divested of much of its primitiveness, characteristic of the Asiatic system, and developed into a type of feudalism, which resembles, in some respects, the western classical form. (Sen 1962: 41, 47, 51)

[In the seventeenth century] the mercantile bourgeoisie were still decisively subservient to the feudal power of Indian society. . . . In short, the decaying feudal forces of society neither provided the basis for the cultural renaissance which India witnessed in this period nor could they maintain their hold over India for long. . . . The Indian mercantile bourgeoisie . . . as a class could neither rise above the feudal forces of the country nor could they by that time have a decisively upper hand over the European merchants, and specially over the English Company. (Mukherjee 1955: 111, 123)

A further question is that of the fate of "feudalism" in India. A. I. Chicherov writes in the Introduction to his *India: Economic Development in the Sixteenth to Eighteenth Centuries:*

There are two basic trends in Soviet Indology with regard to the subject of the present study. The first is represented by scholars who believe in the emergence, in one form or another, of capitalist elements in India's feudal economy from the 17th to the early 19th centuries. This thesis was first advanced in Soviet historiography in the early 1950's by I. M. Reusner and taken up by A. M. Dyakov, V. I. Pavlov, E. N. Komarov, A. I. Levkovsky and others, who gave the first documentary proof of the existence of embryonic capitalist relations on the subcontinent. . . . The other trend is represented by scholars who either deny the emergence of capitalist elements or consider that these were so few that they can be ignored. This trend is particularly vividly expressed in the works of K. A. Antonova. Recently K. A. Antonova's views have undergone a certain evolution and are now closer to those held by the above-mentioned group of researchers. (Chicherov 1971: 11–12)

Chicherov's own views are also close to this group:

Source material at our disposal enables us to speak of the emergence and development in some areas in India in the 17th–18th centuries of capitalist relations, which transformed merchant's capital into industrial capital through the organization of capitalist domestic industry. (Chicherov 1971: 181)

The deepening of the social division of labour (the separation of handicrafts from farming, of towns from the countryside, development of commodity-money relations) in the feudal economy presumably led to the emergence of rudiments of new, *capitalist* relations, which involved the hiring of wage labour for the production of surplus value. The emergence of these relations was connected with the growing demand on the home market and, especially, on the foreign market. The considerable volume of trade carried on by Europeans was *only one of the factors* that made for the development of these phenomena, *which on the whole were linked directly with Indian and other Asian capital rather than with European captial.* (Chicherov 1971: 234) (Emphasis in the original)

Nonetheless,

a feudal structure of society, in varying degrees of development, seems to have prevailed in the various states of the Indian subcontinent in the 16th–18th centuries. Their economies were based mainly on feudal landownership. . . . The feudal mode of production had not yet exhausted their development potential. . . . We thus come to the conclusion that at the end of the 18th and the beginning of the 19th centuries India was apparently approaching the beginning of the manufacturing stage in the development of capitalism within the framework of her generally feudal economy. . . . A large, if not the main, part of the nascent bourgeois elements was most probably destroyed in the fire of feudal wars, anti-feudal movements and particularly, the colonial subjugation and plunder. (Chicherov 1971: 230, 236, 237)

Some Indian students extend the argument still further, both backward and hypothetically forward. "Eminent authorities on the question, like Baden-Powell and Radha Kumud Mukherjee, maintain that private property and peasant proprietorship existed in India even in the Vedic period" (Sen 1962: 37). And V. B. Singh argues that:

the direction of this change might have led Indian economy to capitalism had the natural evolution not been thwarted by British rule. . . . But the British intervention did not allow this natural process to grow: by creating landlordism, British rule reversed the development of capitalist relations of production in agriculture and introduced a semi-feudal economy. . . . My contention is that left to herself India (as other underdeveloped countries) would have in due course followed the path of industrialisation with all its implications, and that the present state of underdevelopment has been imposed on her by imperialism. . . . Capitalism in India could have grown even if there had been no Plassey and no Clive. (Singh 1970: 2, 15, 8, 31)

This is the thesis, current for a long time among many communist parties, that mercantilism, capitalism, and imperialism reinvigorated and maintained feudalism in the colonial world, if they did not introduce it outright, and that it was and is through this feudalism that imperialism has imposed and is continuing to impose underdevelopment in these countries.

Serious Indian analysts of their own history are increasingly re-jecting all of these facile models of the Indian past and calling for much more detailed studies. For instance, K. S. Shelvankar re-calls:

> what Indian agrarian development created was thus a multiplicity of simultaneous and co-ordinate claims on the land. They were broadly of three kinds: the customary claims of the peasants in the village; the delegated or derivative claims of the intermediary; and the superior claims of the sovereign. Private property in land, as ordinarily under-stood, can only arise when this triple claim has been systematised and unified in some form or other. . . . None of the major conflict in Indian history had for its object the exercise of rights over the village. They were conflicts between overlords of various grades for the right or power to get payment from the peasant, not to seize his land. . . . . The Indian conflict was one between lords who were concerned not at all with methods of cultivation, but only to draw income from the peasantry. . . . The issue was always between different claimants of the sword. (Shelvankar 1969: 150–52)

D. D. Kosambi also attempts to formulate a new interpretation, stating that "Indian feudalism differs so much from its European counterpart, at least, as regards the superficial manifestations, that the very existence of feudalism in India has sometimes been denied" (Kosambi 1969: 148), and "the question of who owns the land? could not be answered because ownership had totally different meanings under Indian feudalism and the European bourgeois or proto-bourgeois mode" (Kosambi 1969: 149). Shelvankar adds, "For these reasons—the invincible toughness of the village and the political importance of the bourgeoisie—the evolution of Indian economy was inhibited and the spontaneous emergence of a capitalist order was rendered impossible" (Shelvankar 1969: 154).

Irfan Habib, for his part, goes so far as to argue that Marx and Engels qualified or even abandoned their earlier theory of the Asiatic mode of production in the *Origin of the Family, Private Property, and the State*, and is suspicious of recent attempts to revive the concept. He ridicules those, like Dange, who sought to find feudalism in India as part of the supposedly universal Stalinist developmental schema, and still more those who see seventeenth-century India as containing "potentialities of capitalistic development," which he terms an opportunistic appraisal. What Marxist historians should first and foremost concentrate on is surely a study of class struggles. . . . If we are able to base ourselves firmly on revolutionary Marxism, and steadily carry on painstaking research work there is no reason why some day we should not break through the curtain of darkness imposed by reaction, and illumine the real history of the toiling people of India. (Habib 1969b: 67; see also Habib 1969a)

Part of this curtain is lifted by Habib and Kosambi themselves and by others who collaborated in B. N. Ganguli, ed., *Readings in Indian Economic History*.

3. India in Asia

It was during the years of general economic depression from 1762 to 1789 preceding the Industrial Revolution, that India's relations with the rest of the world were rapidly and qualitatively changed; and simultaneously India's internal political, economic, and social structure assumed a new world historical importance through its now crucial participation in the process of capital accumulation.

Though the British were not the first Europeans to win a foothold in India, they succeeded where their Western rivals all failed. Their victory was due to slow and patient penetration, which bore fruit [after 1757] only after more than a century and a half of continuous contact with India. Moreover, they learned from the errors of earlier Western arrivals, benefitting from the techniques evolved after long experience by the Portuguese, Dutch and French. The British epoch of Indian history may be seen as the final fruition of some two and a half centuries of European experimentation and penetration in South Asia. Its roots go back to late-fifteenth-century Lisbon. (Wolpert 1965: 64)

But successive qualitative changes in this history took place throughout the eighteenth century.

Two major themes dominated the history of India in the first half of the eighteenth century: Mughal disintegration, and Anglo-French rivalry along the fringes of a collapsing empire. To Indian aspirants for the Mughal dominions the former seemed by far the more important. The outcome of the Anglo-French conflict, however, was destined to decide who the true successors to Mughal imperial might would be. While Marathas, Afghans, Rajputs, Mughals, and Sikhs wore each other out in indecisive warfare, the European rivals were left relatively free to determine between themselves [and relying on rival Indian political and armed forces as allies] whether Britain or France would inherit an Indian empire. (Wolpert 1965: 72)

In relation to both internal Indian and world historical developments during the eighteenth century, five major periods may be distinguished: (1) until the death in 1707 of Aurangzeb, the last of the great Moghul rulers in India (see Chapter 2 on the seventeenth century); (2) from 1707–1714 to 1739–1742 or 1744, beginning with the War of the Spanish Succession in Europe and the beginning or acceleration of Moghul disintegration in favor, particularly, of Maratha expansion in India, to the important Moghul defeat and checking of the Maratha advance by Persians in the North in 1739, the appointment of Dupleix to French command in the South, and the Anglo-French confrontation in Madras during the War of the Austrian Succession; (3) the intensified Anglo-French rivalry in the Carnatic and the displacement of competition northward to Bengal, leading to Clive's historic victory over the Bengalis at the Battle of Plassey in 1757 and the virtual elimination of French power in India through the seige, capture, and destruction of their fort at Pondicherry during the Seven Years War in 1761; (4) the period from 1757–1765 to 1793, notorious for the "rape of Bengal" and the extension of British power northward and westward under the leadership of Clive and Hastings, which notably coincided with the long economic downswing before the Industrial Revolution in Britain— including the marked decline of Brazilian gold production and largely preceding the late eighteenth-century recovery of Mexican silver production; and finally (5) the decades from 1793 to 1816–1817, marked by the introduction of the "permanent" *zamindari* land settlement during the administration of Governor-General Cornwallis and the destruction of Maratha power during the administrations of the Marquis of Wellesley and Lord Hastings, which coincided with the period of the Napoleonic wars and the beginnings of the Industrial Revolution in England. (Romesh Dutt divides the last two periods at 1784, apparently because of the passing of Pitt's India Act in that year and the departure of Hastings the year after, although the reforms instituted by his successor, Cornwallis, did not begin to go into effect until 1791/1793.)

Here we will briefly review the first three periods (up to 1757), and examine more fully the fourth period (1757/1765 to 1793). (The general question of European capitalist penetration in South Asia and the theoretical problem of the modes of production, their transformation, and the transition from feudalism to capitalism in India was already discussed in sections 1 and 2 of this chapter.)

The Europeans—Portuguese, Dutch, French, English, and others—had traded on the outskirts of the Moghul empire for over two centuries without becoming a crucial factor in the qualitative transformation of the existing mode of production or of Indian social transformation. Had it not been for the rapid internal disintegration of Moghul power after 1700, the European-dominated world capitalist development—despite its "needs" for "external" sources of primitive capitalist accumulation and for external markets during the century from 1750 to 1850—might not have made significantly greater inroads in India than it managed to make in China; and the development of capitalism would have been very different from what in fact it has been.

Many regions of India had established interregional and international long distance trade since the fourteenth century and before (see Chapter 1, section 1 and Chapter 2, section 3). Bengal, Golconda, and Gujarat maintained a "favorable" balance of trade and imported precious metals. Bengal, beyond exporting grain and other products to other parts of India, maintained trade relations with many parts of the Far East, Southeast Asia, Africa, and the Middle East, exporting cotton and silk textiles and agricultural produce. The Coromandel Coast also traded with these regions, exporting the same kind of goods as well as iron and steel products. Increasingly, since the sixteenth century, European traders, at first the Portuguese and Dutch and then the French and English, had taken over part of this inter-Asian trade and other external Indian trade. Nonetheless, "a considerable part of India's foreign trade continued to remain in the hands of Indian and other Asian merchants practically throughout the 18th century" (Chicherov 1971: 128–29).

At the beginning of the eighteenth century, £817,000 out of a total of £1,852,000 of Bengali foreign trade was in European hands, much of it inter-Asian trade (Chicherov 1971: 130).

Exports to Europe . . . were exceeded by far by the volume of India's trade with Asian and African countries. . . . Exports of goods to Europe during this period did not play a decisive role in the development of production in Bengal. . . . Even in Dacca, one of the biggest foreign trade centers, the export of cloth to Europe did not play the decisive role in the mid-18th century, since it accounted for only 30% of the total trade. (Chicherov 1971: 129–30)

4. The Rape of Bengal to 1793

The original British East India Company obtained its charter on December 31, 1600. After a century of touch-and-go rivalry with other merchant groups and especially with the stronger Dutch, the company was reorganized and assured a monopoly in 1702. Meanwhile, Colbert had directed French attention to India with the founding of the French East India Company in 1664 and the founding of a trading post at Chandernagore in Bengal in 1688. Nonetheless, French interest and activity in India remained insignificant until the founding of the Perpetual Company of the Indies in 1720 and especially the appointment of Joseph Dupleix as governor at Chandernagore in 1732. Although in 1732 they had no ships at all in daily use, by 1742 the French company and its employees had fifteen or twenty ships in daily use (Sinha 1961, I: 35–36). Between 1728 and 1740 the company's exports from India increased tenfold (G. Williams 1966: 107). In 1740 Dupleix moved to Pondicherry in Madras, and under his leadership the French accentuated their design to become the major European power in India. The strategy changed from the traditional one of trading from isolated coastal positions to achieving territorial control, at least along the eastern Carnatic coast of India and northward, taking advantage of alliances with some local rulers and with pretenders against others. Dupleix was limited by inadequate financial support from France, because at that time India had far from priority claim on imperial attention. This attention was directed, rather, toward the Americas, which became the center of Anglo-French imperialist contention in the two wars of 1740–1748 and 1756–1763.

Unlike the "private" English East India Company, the French company was directly controlled by the state, and hence more vulnerable to other state priorities and political changes. Moreover the French company was much poorer than the English one. For both reasons, Dupleix, after an imposing victory in the first Carnatic War, was obliged to cede before the British in the second one, and indeed was removed from command. The English East India Company, backed by the British fleet, thus gained a "decisive victory . . . over its French rival [and] the treaty of 1754 between the two companies . . . dealt a mortal blow to the French Power in India" (Mukherjee 1955: 78). What remained of the French position in India was dealt the coup de grace by the British capture of Pondicherry in 1761 during the Seven Years War, again relying on superior naval power. Nonetheless, James Mill would later write in his *History of British India:*

> the Europeans in India, who hitherto had crouched at the feet of the meanest of the petty governors of a district, were astonished at the progress of the French, who now seemed to preside over the whole region of the Deccan. A letter to Dupleix, from a friend in the camp of Salabat Jung, affirmed that in a little time the Mogul on his throne would tremble at the name of Dupleix; and however presumptuous this prophecy might appear, little was wanting to secure its fulfillment.
> (Quoted in Mukherjee 1955: 75)

British policy in India began to change at mid-century, perhaps encouraged at first by French pretensions under the leadership of Dupleix, and then impelled by its own logic with the defeat by Robert Clive of Bengali resistance at the Battle of Plassey in 1757. After Clive returned from England in 1765, he organized and directed British policy in India. Increasingly, military conquest and political power became the handmaiden and indeed the basis of commercial policy. Successive regions and peoples were brought under military, political, and economic control. During the rest of the eighteenth century and before the Industrial Revolution, India was transformed from the net importer of European capital (through the bullion settlement of its export surplus) that it had been for centuries, into a net exporter of capital to Europe. This completely reversed the essential basis of English trade with India, a reversal that continued during the nineteenth and twentieth centuries, by transforming India from the manufacturing exporter that it had been for centuries, into a market for the developing industries of European capitalism. After Europe had been obliged for two centuries to pay for Indian exports with bullion extracted from the Americas and the earnings on service account from inter-Asian trade,

> the situation underwent a qualitative change after the Company captured Bengal, and eventually the whole of India. Henceforth, "methods of power could be increasingly used to weigh the balance of exchange and secure the maximum goods for the minimum payment.". . . The Company was now "able to throw the sword into the scales to secure a bargain which abandoned all pretence of equality of exchange." The policy of the Company was established to extract from the Indian producers as much as possible, and to give them in return virtually nothing or so meagre a remuneration that they ultimately became unable to maintain even the reproductive rate of the economy. This decision of the Company, pursued with unwavering resolution, was first put into practice in Bengal after 1757, and in the course of time it spread all over India with the subjugation of her territory, directly or indirectly, by the Company. (Mukherjee 1955: 171, quoting Dutt)

The British government became alarmed at the recklessness of the company's exploitative activities and took measures, especially after 1793, to safeguard at least that part of the reproductive capacity of the Indian economy which was essential to world capitalist development. Thus the official Shore inquiry of 1789 reports that, compared with the earlier trade pattern, "from the year 1765 the reverse has taken place. The Company's trade produces no equivalent returns. Specie is rarely imported by foreign companies, nor brought into Bengal from other parts of Hindustan in any considerable quantities" (quoted in Dutt 1970, 1: 58). On the contrary, according to Sinha, "import of bullion almost entirely ceased not long after the battle of Plassey and export of bullion for aiding [the conquest of] other Presidencies and for helping China trade began almost systematically" (Sinha 1961, I: 14).

Again, the Select Committee's Ninth Report in 1783 observed:

> when an account is taken of the intercourse, for it is not commerce, which is carried on between Bengal and England, the pernicious effects of the system of investments from revenue will appear in the strongest point of view. In that view, the whole exported produce of the country,

so far as the Company is concerned, is not exchanged in the course of barter, but it is taken away without any return or payment whatever. (Quoted in Dutt 1970, I: 46)

One of Clive's lieutenants, Scrafton, had already reported in 1763 that the company and its servants "have been enabled to carry the whole trade of India (China excepted) for three years together, without sending out one ounce of bullion" (quoted in Mukherjee 1955: 194). Nor did the British pay for Indian goods with their own merchandize during this period, as is evident from the import and export figures quoted below.

It must again be emphasized that this new (or, for the history of world capital accumulation, renewed) reliance on the sword to tilt the balance of "exchange" in Europe's favor—permitting the whole trade of India to be carried on without an ounce of bullion—was inaugurated precisely at the moment when the Brazilian source of British gold alarmingly dried up after 1760, and before the economic depression and other factors encouraged the renewed increase in the supply of silver from Mexico (beginning about 1775 but accelerating only during the 1780s and particularly between 1790 and 1810). Moreover, while the French Caribbean and France still enjoyed their greatest prosperity in the 1760s, the English Caribbean and the English economy already suffered hard times, which were only to be exacerbated by the nonimportation policy and the subsequent American War of Independence in the 1770s. In this context, both the novel Indian balance of trade and the associated "drain" of capital from India to England (to be examined below) assumed a very special importance.

In 1765 the de jure but hardly de facto emperor in Delhi granted the "dewani" or political administration of Bengal to the East India Company. This initiated the total political, economic, and social transformation of the countryside, first in Bengal which had been the granary of adjacent parts of India, and then increasingly in other regions. The instruments and process of this transformation were recorded by innumerable contemporary commissions of inquiry and in the statements of the very British governors themselves who were sent out to "remedy" the misdeeds of their predecessors. Clive's successor as governor of Bengal from 1761 to 1770, Harry Verelst, writing of his own administration, recalled in 1772:

In the provinces of Brudwan and Midnapur, of which the property and jurisdiction were ceded to the Company by Mir Kasim in the year 1760, . . . a plan was adopted in 1762 productive of certain ruin to the province. The lands were let by public auction for the short term of three years. Men without fortune or character became bidders at the sale; and while some of the former farmers, unwilling to relinquish their habitations, exceeded perhaps the real value in their offers [of revenue to keep their own lands], those who had nothing to lose advanced yet further, wishing at all events to obtain an immediate possession. The numberless harpies were let loose to plunder, whom the spoil of a miserable people enabled to complete their first year's payment. (Quoted in Dutt 1970, I: 29)

Philip Francis, a member of the council of the governor-general, writing in 1776, added:

The greater part of the Zemindars [hereditary landlords] were ruined and dispossessed of the management of their lands, and there were few people of rank and family left, or of those who had formerly held high employments, such as there were, looked for large profits, which the country could not afford them and pay the rents also. People of lower rank were therefore of necessity employed at Amils or collectors [of rent] on the part of the Government. These people executed a contract for a stipulated sum for the district to which they were appointed, and in effect they may be considered as farmers of revenue. They then proceeded from the Sudder, or seat of government, to the districts, to settle with the Zemindars or tenants for the revenue they had engaged to pay. (Quoted in Dutt 1970, I: 40)

Dutt continues:

In 1777 the five years' settlement made in 1772 came to an end. The auction system was somewhat modified, and preference was now given to hereditary Zemindars [instead of new British-created ones]. But the harshness of the system was greatly exaggerated when it was declared that the estates would be let, not for five years, but annually. Lands were thus let annually to Zemindars in 1778, 1779, and 1780. The country groaned under this economic tyranny; the revenues failed once more. . . . All the great Zemindars of Bengal, all the ancient landed families, suffered under this system of annual settlement, frequent enhancements, and harsh methods of realisation, such as they had never known before. Descendants of old houses found their estates pass into the hands of money lenders and speculators from Calcutta. (Dutt 1970, I: 41)

The peasants and artisans who produced the commodities that, through this expedient, were converted into further primitive accumulation, no longer in India, but now in Britain, suffered still more. The same Select Committee's Ninth Report in 1783 stated: "Notwithstanding the [resulting] famine in 1770, which wasted Bengal in a manner dreadful beyond all example, the Investment [purchase of Indian goods by British merchants], by a variety of successive expedients, many of them of the most dangerous nature and tendency, was forcibly kept up . . ." (quoted in Dutt 1970, I: 46).

In 1773 the British Parliament passed a Regulating Act and designated Hastings to remedy the settlements of his predecessors. Thus Hastings, who had become governor of Bengel in 1773, became governor-general responsible to the British parliament in 1774. Yet even he, referring to his predecessor's administration, had written in 1772:

> Notwithstanding the loss of at least a third of the inhabitants of the province, and the consequent decrease of the cultivation [due to the famine of 1770–1772], the net collections of the year 1771 exceeded even those of 1768. . . . It was naturally to be expected that the diminution of the revenue should have kept an equal pace with the other consequences of so great a calamity. That it did not was owing to its being violently kept up to its former standard. (Hastings, quoted in Dutt 1970, I: 35–36)

The results of Warren Hastings' administration have been observed above, and he himself had to be removed (and later impeached by parliament) as the Indian economy's reproductive capacity was increasingly damaged and Britain became increasingly alarmed. Parliament passed Pitt's India Bill in 1784 and placed the company under the control of the Crown. In 1785 Hastings was replaced by Cornwallis, who was charged with the mission of finding ways and means to put the house in order. By 1790, Cornwallis was able to report:

> Twenty years have been employed in collecting information. . . . Like our predecessors, we set out with seeking for new information, and we have not been three years in collecting it. Voluminous reports have been transmitted. . . . The consequences of the heavy drain of wealth from the above causes, with the addition of that which has been occasioned by the remittance of the private fortunes, have been for many years past, and are now, severely felt, by the diminution of the current specie, and by the langour which has thereby been thrown

upon the cultivation and the general commerce of the country. . . . A very material alteration in the principles of our system of management has therefore become indispensably necessary, in order to restore this country to a state of prosperity, and to enable it to continue to be a solid support to the British interests and power in this part of the world. . . . We are, therefore, called upon to endeavour, to remedy evils by which the public interests are essentially injured, and by granting perpetual leases of the lands at a fixed assessment we shall render our subjects the happiest people in India. (Lord Cornwallis' Minute, dated February 5, 1790, quoted in Dutt 1970, I: 62)

In Bengal, Bihar, and Orissa the decennial *zamindari* land settlements had by 1789–1790 provisionally replaced the no longer acceptable former short-term settlements. As a result of the recommendations of Cornwallis and others, these decennial land settlements were converted by Cornwallis' proclamation of March 22, 1793, into the ever since famous, or rather infamous, "Permanent Settlement" land grants and revenue rates to *zamindaris* in these and later some other regions of India. It should be observed, however, that "British interests" after 1793 were no longer precisely those that they had been during the drive for primitive accumulation that had characterized the previous three depressive decades; instead they came to reflect the economic expansion that began in 1790, the Industrial Revolution and its bourgeoisie, and the immediate wartime needs and dangers of the Napoleonic Wars, when Napolean sought to recover India from the British.

5. The Transformation of Agriculture, 1757–1793

It may be useful to review this rapid succession of land and labor systems again from another perspective. Like the Spaniards before them in sixteenth-century Mexico and Peru, the Dutch in eighteenth- and nineteenth-century Indonesia, the European colonial powers in Africa in the nineteenth and twentieth centuries, and even the Latin Americans themselves who were bent on "liberal" reforms in the nineteenth century, the British in India, and especially in Bengal, initiated a succession of institutional disasters, each consciously designed to remedy the faults of the last, and each—driven down the well-known path to hell, paved with good intentions, and impelled by the economic imperative of surplus extraction—more disastrous than its predecessor.

For the first sixteen months after July 1757, following the military victory at Plassey, the East India Company, with Frankland in charge, collected the land revenue itself. But this system proved impossible to administer effectively, and anyway as a former acting governor of the company in Calcutta, J. Z. Holwell remarked, "keeping the lands in our hands will never lead us to knowledge of their real value." Therefore, he suggested, the lands should be put up to public auction; and in 1759 they were. As a result, the old *zamindaris* and many of their subordinate farmers were displaced by the essentially speculative tax farmers. Holwell himself became one of them. The increased payments by the peasants and the widespread abuses by the new *zamindaris* led to immediate complaints. Accordingly, the 1760 treaty under which the East India Company acquired Burdwan, Midnapore, and Chittagong from Mir Quasim included a provision to the effect that the company "shall continue the [existing] *zamindaris* and renters in their places." But the high payments demanded by Mir Quasim and, for instance, Verelst as chief in Chittagong, ruined many *zamindaris*, old and new, who went into arrears in their payments and had to relinquish the farms. Other "men of substance and character," as Verelst called them, were loath to take their place, so, when Verelst was appointed resident in Burdwan in 1765, he abolished the public sale of lands and offered assurances to the new revenue farmers that they would not be similarly displaced. Then "a torrent of corruption in land-revenue administration swept away all existing barriers." The system became "embarrassed and confused"; Verelst as governor decided to put an end to the "state of power without control, of knowledge without participation, and of influence without any effective counteraction" (Sinha 1968, II: 21–45).

The results were, as Verelst himself remarked in 1772, "productive of certain ruin to the province" and led to the famine of 1770. More than a third of the population died and a third of the land was returned to jungle. Social life was disorganized and lawlessness became widespread. Warren Hastings, reared in India, was appointed governor to remedy the situation. He would later write:

"My everlasting theme of the Famine (as the gentlemen are pleased to call it) I must continue to insist on as an event the effect of which must still be felt for many years" (quoted in Sinha 1968, II: 65), and on which Hastings himself was pleased to blame the failure of his own remedy: "I lengthened the period of the leases which before was annual to five years. This was considered by many as a bold innovation" (quoted in Sinha 1968, II: 71).

This "bold innovation" turned out to be still more disastrous, inasmuch as it extended the overassessments from one to five years, precisely at the time that the famine—"an event the effect of which must still be felt for many years"—reduced the ability to produce and to pay. The collector soon commented: "It is amazing how fast they run into arrears." Accordingly in 1776, the Amini Commission was set up and charged to inquire into land values, farm accounts, and especially into ways of protecting the *ryots* or peasants. After the commission's report and the issue of a plan by Philip Francis, Hastings himself had second thoughts, with the result that all the previously let farms were recalled on April 13, 1777. Henceforth, the *zamindari* system was restored; and many of the old *zamindaris* were reinstated. According to Hastings, he sought "to remove every interference and embarassment from the present system of control to afford every relief and ease both to the *ryots* and the *zamindars*. . . conformable to the constitution of the country. . . for the settlement of a fixed revenue during the lives of the actual incumbents." Although it was claimed (again) that the "new" system "led to a more correct estimate of the value of the lands," Hastings himself was obliged, on February 8, 1780, to admit that the revenue demanded was "exceeding the abilities of the *zamindars* in many parts." But far from being let for life, the farms were again let annually, though with certain options for renewal, both in theory and in practice, but not enough to induce any long-term investments on the land.

In any event, as we observed above, the debacle continued and grew worse. Hastings was removed and impeached. In 1784 Pitt's India Act was passed to transfer control increasingly to the Crown, and the East India Company was enjoined "to enquire into the alleged grievances of the landholders and if founded in truth to afford them redress and to establish permanent rules for the settlement and collection of the revenue and for administration of justice founded in the ancient laws and local useages of the country" (Sinha 1968, II: 147). In 1786 Cornwallis arrived to take charge and to implement this "new" policy. After the extensive inquiries of 1786 to 1789, the annual settlements were commuted to decennial settlements in 1789 and 1790; and after the opposition to increasing permanency had been overcome or overridden the settlements were made "permanent" in 1793. Cornwallis wrote:

> Twenty years have been employed in collecting information. . . . Like our precedessors, we set out with seeking for new information [about] . . . the diminution of the current specie, and . . . the languor which has . . . been thrown upon the cultivation and the general commerce of the country. . . . A very material alteration in the principles of our system of management has therefore become indispensably necessary, in order to restore this country to a state of prosperity, and to enable it to continue to be a support of the British interests and power in this part of the world. (Cornwallis, quoted in Dutt 1970, I: 62)

Cornwallis' Permanent Settlement became the pattern and model of British administration in large parts of India during the nineteenth century, and it did indeed support British interests and power in that part of the world; but far from restoring India to prosperity, this settlement—even more so than those of Cornwallis' predecessors—plunged India into yet deeper misery and made it permanent.

6. Trade and Manufactures

The political administration of the sword also changed the balance of exchange in inland trade. The purchases of the East India Company for ultimate shipment abroad were called "investments." These were made in principle by the company itself, in practice more frequently by its "servants" on their own private account, and were effected initially through paid Indian agents, or *gomastas*, under the supervision of the company's servants. The enrichment of the company's servants, to the detriment and near bankruptcy of the company itself, led to the increasing displacement of the Indian agents by the company, and to the (largely unsuccessful) attempt to control the activities of the company's servants. The "payment" for these "investments" was the forced "sale" of other commodities.

Some consequences for Indians in general and Indian merchants in particular were recorded by contemporary Indian and British officials. The Bengali puppet ruler, Mir Quasim, complained of the new *gomastas* as early as 1762.

> From the factory of Calcutta to Cossim Bazar, Patna, and Dacca, all the English chiefs, with their Gomastahs, officers, and agents, in every district of the government, act as Collectors. Renters, Zemindars, and Tealookdars [estate holders], and setting up the Company's colours, allow no power to my officers. In every pargana, every village and every factory they buy and sell salt, betelnut, ghee, rice, straw, bamboos, fish, gunnies, ginger, sugar, tobacco, opium and many other things. They forcibly take away the goods and commodities of the ryots [small farmers] and merchants for a fourth part of their value. . . . they oblige the ryots to give five rupees for goods which are worth but one rupee. And every man with a Company's Dustuck in his hand regards himself as not less than the Company . . . . they expose my government to scorn and are the greatest detriment to me. (Quoted in Mukherjee 1955: 174, 177 and Sinha 1961, I: 79)

Also in 1762, one Sergeant Brego reported:

> A gentleman sends a Gomastah here to buy and sell; he immediately looks upon himself as sufficient to force every inhabitant hither to buy his goods or sell him theirs; and on refusal (in the case of non-capacity) a flogging or confinement immediately ensures. This is not sufficient even when willing, but a second force is made use of, which is to engross the different branches of trade to themselves, and not to suffer any person buy or sell the articles they trade in; and if the country people do it, then a repetition of their authority is put in practice; and again, what things they do purchase, they think the least they can do is to take them for a considerable deal less than another merchant, and oftentimes refuse paying that; and my interfering occasions an immediate complaint. These, and many other oppressions more than can be related, which are daily used by the Bengal Gomastahs, is the reason that this place is growing destitute of inhabitants; every day numbers leave the town to seek a residence more safe, and the very markets, which before afforded plenty, do hardly now produce anything of use. (Quoted in Mukherjee 1955: 75)

The English merchant, William Bolts, himself confirmed in 1772:

> Inconceivable oppressions and hardships have been practised towards the poor manufacturers and workmen of the Country, who are, in fact, monopolized by the Company as so many slaves. . . . Various and innumerable are the methods of oppressing the poor weavers, which are duly practised by the Company's agents and *gomastas* in the country;

such as fines, imprisonments, floggings, forcing bonds from them, etc., by which the number of weavers in the country has been greatly decreased. . . . In this situation of things, as the trade of the Company increased, and with the inland trade of individuals also in a much greater proportion, those evils, which at first were scarcely felt, became at last universal throughout the Bengal provinces; and it may with truth be now said, that the whole inland trade of the country, as at present conducted, and that of the Company's investment for Europe in a peculiar degree, has been one continued scene of oppression; the baneful effects of which are severely felt by every weaver and manufacturer in the country, every article produced being made a monopoly; in which the English, with their *banyans* [Indian agents] and black *gomastas*, arbitrarily decide what quantities of good each manufacturer shall deliver, and the *prices* he shall receive for them. (Quoted in Mukherjee 1955: 172) (Emphasis in the original)

The cotton growers, spinners, weavers, silk growers and winders, etc. were also affected by other economic changes and circumstances. The Proceedings of the Bengal Board of Trade for January 3, 1776, noted: "The Dacca fabric for these six or seven years past has been upon the decline as to quality, great part whereof may be attributed to the ravages of the famine in 1770 carrying away great numbers of the best spinners and ryots who cultivated the cotton plant. The loss is not yet recovered nor will it for many years to come" (quoted in Sinha 1961, I: 160). Accordingly the price of cotton thread and goods rose considerably. The war in America further increased the demand for Indian cotton, and during the years 1785–1789 European demand for the products of Indian spinners and weavers was again high, despite depressed economic conditions. It could perhaps be argued that since much of the European demand was for goods that would be re-exported, the depressed economic conditions were themselves in part responsible for the sustained high demand. In certain respects, these circumstances temporarily favored the Indian producers, since they were able to command higher prices. But the company paid the weavers 20–30 percent below market price (Sinha 1961, I: 225), and the weavers tried to sell to other foreign merchants. In 1786, the Board of Trade noted that "nothing can be done with the weavers without that they are paid a price more equal to their labour than they receive at present" (quoted in Sinha 1961, I: 163). But beyond paying them the market price, let alone their real value, there still remained another possibility. That

same year the company/government issued a consolidated list of
twenty-one regulations, including Regulation XI, stating: "Upon
any weaver failing to deliver cloth according to the stated period
agreed upon, the Company's Agent shall be at liberty to place peons
upon them and keep them under restraint," and Regulation XII,
stating:

> If any weaver in the Company's service shall be convicted of selling
> cloth either by himself, any of his family, journeyman or by any agent,
> to any other merchants or dealers whatever, whilst he is deficient in his
> deliveries according to the stated periods of his agreement with the
> Company, such offenders shall be punished in a regular process on
> conviction in the judicial court. (Quoted in Sinha 1961, I: 164)

The impartiality of the judicial court may be left to the imagination!

7. Private "Investments" in India and China

The policy of Clive, Hastings, and their subordinate "servants" of
the East India Company was "Money! Money! and no time be lost"
(*Memoirs of Sir Philip Francis*, quoted in Sinha 1961, I: 221). Clive,
who had left England a poor man, amassed a private fortune, though
he would later tell parliament. "at this moment I stand astonished at
my own moderation." Whatever that may have been, Clive himself
reported that "fortunes of £100,000 have been obtained in two years"
by others. As for himself, he testified:

> I never sought to conceal it, but declared publicly in my letters to the
> Secret Committee of the India Directors that the Nabob's generosity
> had made my fortune easy. . . What pretence could the Company
> have to expect, that I after having risked my life so often in their
> service, should deny myself the only opportunity ever offered of ac-
> quiring a fortune. (Quoted in Mukherjee 1955: 191–92)

Wolpert recalls,

> Clive set the tone for his subordinates, giving them a target at which to
> aim. The young apprentice or writer who joined the Company for the
> passage east received a salary so small it would hardly pay for the
> clothes he wore, yet each man knew that if he played the game wisely

once in Bengal, using his influence and opportunities for the purpose of private trade rather than Company service, he could earn a fortune. . . . For the young men of England after 1760 the universal cry of ambition was "Go East." (Wolpert 1965: 76–77)

We may ask with Sinha: "How did the servants of the English Company send their wealth to Europe in the sixties and seventies of the eighteenth century" (Sinha 1961, I: 234)? After examining the commercial correspondence of these merchants, he summarizes: "thus Canton, Bencoolen, Calcutta, Bombay, Jedda, Mocha, Aleppo, Basra, Cairo, and even Madeira—every British trade outpost—helped Barwell and many others in sending their wealth amassed in Bengla to England. The French, the Dutch and the Danes were also helpful" (Sinha 1961, I: 235–36). All undertook the tasks of taking the goods on consignment and negotiating the bills of exchange of the company's "servants" who could not employ the company's official channels to remit their private fortunes home (Sinha 1961, I: 233–36).

Particularly important as an intermediary—a role that portended its destiny in the nineteenth century—was China and its port of Canton.

The practice of sending silver from Bengal to China commenced as early as 1757 [the date of the Battle of Plassey]. . . . So long as clandestine opium trade with China could not be fully organized bullion poured into China from Bengal in the sixties at the rate of about twenty-four *lakhs* [one *lakh* = 100,000 rupees] a year, in the early seventies about twenty *lakhs* a year. In the 1790s it became perhaps unnecessary to send bullion for the purchase of tea in China. (Sinha 1961, I: 233)

China resembled India in one respect: it did not wish nor require European manufactures in payment for the goods, principally tea, that the European sought to acquire there. In 1793 the Chinese emperor, Ch'ien Lung, would write to King George III in England, through the English ambassador who had been sent there to "open" China: "As your Ambassador can see for himself, we possess all things. I set no value on objects strange or ingenious, and have no use for your country's manufactures. . . . there was therefore no need to import the manufactures of outside barbarians in exchange for our own produce" (quoted in Schurmann and Schell 1967, I: 108–9). However, there was one very important difference between

China and India after 1757: the Chinese emperor remained in political authority and, far from permitting European inland trade, let
alone political administraticn, restricted foreign traders to regulated
exchange at Canton. The emperor's boast was not strictly correct,
since there was in China a demand for Indian raw cotton, as well as
for a variety of luxuries from Southeast Asia. But the supply that the
British and other Europeans could offer of these was far less than
their demand for Chinese tea, which consequently they were obliged
to pay for in silver.

After 1760 the exigencies of remitting private fortunes from Bengal and later from other regions of India back to Britain required
the swift development of an intermediary entrepot and the supply of
merchandize that could suitably serve as the physical vehicle of
remittance. Accordingly, the private traders who engaged in this
important mission first appeared in Canton in the 1760s (Fairbank
1969: 60). John Fairbank explains (albeit with a perspective as seen
from China):

> The most powerful economic factor at Canton was the need for cargoes
> to sell to China. Something more than British woollens was required in
> the tropical climate of Canton to balance the mounting exports of tea
> and silk. The Company's tea shipments out of Canton rose from
> 2,626,000 lbs. (worth £831,000) in 1761 to 23,300,000 lbs. (worth
> £3,665,000) in 1800. Here the so-called "country" trade (the trade
> between India and China) entered the scene as the necessary link in the
> triangular commerce between India, China, and England. This country
> trade was conducted by private individuals who were licensed by the
> East India Company in India and remained under its control in the Far
> East. It represented the final entrance of the British flag into the
> native-carrying trade in South East Asia. . . . Until 1823 raw cotton
> from India was the largest staple import. . . To avoid dependence on
> the British Company's rate for bills of exchange on London, the British
> private traders bought bills of exchange from American merchants.
> With these they could remit funds from Canton to London more
> advantageously than could be done from Bombay. These operations
> helped funnel the profits of India through Canton to England. . . .
> Ships avoided British restrictions when necessary by sailing under
> Danish or Portuguese colors. . . . As the next step in the disruption of
> the old Canton system, the ingenuity and energy of these newcomers
> on the Chinese scene became focussed upon importing opium. This
> grew into a tide which could not be checked The origin of the drug
> traffic lay first of all in the Chinese demand for opium . . . [but] the
> most obvious economic reasons for its importation has been noted

above, namely, the constant pressure to balance the Canton tea trade. Indian raw cotton had at first served this purpose equally well, but . . . the production of opium in India had become a great vested interest [first of the private traders who required a means to remit their Indian earnings, and then] on which the government had come to rely for revenue. . . . There were two general types of opium, grown in eastern and western areas of northern India, respectively. The chief type grown in Bengal was called Patna . . . [the other] opium was called Malwa [and was shipped through Bombay] . . . . Silver inevitably moved out [of China] as opium moved in. (Fairbank 1969: 59–64, 75)

Although the tide of opium trading would not sweep over China, causing and benefiting from the Opium Wars, until the mid nineteenth century, the requirements of British merchants in India and China thus already initiated the flow of opium in the period under review. The shipment of Indian opium to Canton increased from 800 chests in 1770 to 3,000 in 1775, and 7,800 in 1795 (Devèze 1970: 123–24). The number of British flagships (often Indian-built) plying the trade to China, mostly from or via India, was 33 in the period 1764–1773, 94 in 1774–1783, and 217 in 1784–1793 (Devèze 1970: 161–62). Other European shipping also participated in this growing trade. Both their own trade and the competition from others then encouraged the British to seek intermediate bases on the route from India to Southeast Asia. The British desire for such bases in Southeast Asia became one of the factors that caused the Anglo-Dutch conflict in Indonesia and the capture of Dutch Batavia by the British Sir Thomas Stamford Raffles during the period of the Napoleonic Wars.

8. The Drain from Bengal

It remains to inquire how much these methods of primitive accumulation, so reminiscent of those the Spaniards had already employed two centuries earlier after their conquest of America, cost India and contributed to the accumulation of capital elsewhere. Opinions are widely different, of course. Moreover, as in all cases of oppression and exploitation, one may make a distinction between the costs—economic, social, political, cultural, and psychic—to those who suffer, and the (no doubt) much smaller contribution to those who benefit. Furthermore, in restricting our assessment of the process of capital accumulation to the period up to 1793, it is necessary to recall that part of the so-called drain from India was, as we have observed, effected indirectly via China and other places. Perhaps more important still, we confront the almost impossible task of estimating the delay in the drain from Bengal, since a substantial part of the capital raised there by the British was first employed in financing their subsequent conquests elsewhere in India, and then successively served to promote other colonizing enterprises. As Nehru recalled, "India had to bear the cost of her own conquest," as have so many other parts of the colonial world as well. Moreover, many, if not all, of them had to bear the costs of each others' conquests by their common colonizers, as we shall see in an analysis of the "informal" "imperialism of free trade" in the nineteenth century (Frank 1978; 1976).

As for the intercourse between Britain and India—recall that the Select Committee Report for 1783 said it could not rightly be called commerce—the tonnage of the East India Company's shipping to India increased as follows: 1765–1771: 6,185 tons, 1772–1777: 8,385 tons, 1778–1784: 10,489 tons, 1785–1791: 8,058 tons, and 1792–1798: 15,246 tons (Devèze 1970: 163). But the "balance" of imports and exports—at the prices established by the British!—was in 1772–1778 an annual average of British exports of £512,000 and British imports of £3.1 million through *the East India Company*, of which about half came directly from India and half (in part indirectly from India) from China. In the period 1792–1798, these totals rose to £1.5 million exports and £5.9 million imports annually; and of the latter £3.1 million came from India and £2.8 million from China. Already in the former period, French trade had fallen to no more than one-fifth of the British company's total (Devèze 1970: 134–38). Before Britain's "traditional" practice of buying textiles from India for re-export and resale elsewhere was replaced by the policy of selling textiles to India (a policy associated with the "take-off" into the Industrial Revolution after 1790), the balance of trade between England and India was consistently and indeed increasingly in India's favor. In other words, India exported far more than she received, as is indicated in the accompanying table.

Table 4.1
Anglo-Indian Trade, 1766–1805
(in thousands of pounds sterling)

	Indian imports from Britain	Indian exports to Britain
1766–1771	399	1,562
1772–1777	392	2,149
1778–1784	363	1,826
1785–1791	493	1,765
1792–1798	670	3,109
1799–1805	1,586	2,770

SOURCE: Devèze 1970: 163.

The methods of calculation of the drain from India during this period and the estimates of the size of the drain vary widely. For the first years after Plassey, Ramkrishna Mukherjee estimates:

> even taking the £5,940,498 (thus obtained in all in the eight years after the Company captured power) as the total sum looted from the Subah of Bengla, for no account is available in figures of the direct plunder of the people—the peasants, artisans and traders—it represented more than four times the revenue collection of the Nawab in the year 1765–6, when £1,470,000 were so collected. Such was the magnitude of this colossal plunder. (Mukherjee 1955: 193)

For the years 1766, 1767, and 1768, the governor of Bengal, Harry Verelst, computed £6,311,250 exports as against only £624,375 imports (Dutt 1970: 31). For the period 1765–1766 to 1770–1771, the gross collection in Bengal was over £20 million, of which about £7 million were spent in tribute to Indian rulers and commission, etc. to agents (some of which, however, ultimately was also exported), and £9 million were devoted to various civil and military expenditures, which, however, were in the nature of an investment that would permit the generation of future earnings. The remaining £4 million were immediately remitted abroad (Mukherjee 1955: 196). The already quoted Select Committee's Ninth Report of 1783, after referring to the famine of 1770 goes on:

The goods from Bengal, purchased from the territorial revenues, from the sale of European goods, and from the produce of the monopolies . . . were never less than a million sterling [annually], and commonly nearer £1,200,000. This million is the lowest value of the goods sent to Europe, for which no satisfaction is made. About £100,000 a year is also remitted from Bengal on the Company's account to China, and the whole of the produce of that money flows into the direct trade from China to Europe. Besides this, Bengal sends a regular supply in time of peace to those Presidencies [elsewhere in India] which are [still] unequal to their own establishment. (Quoted in Dutt 1970, I: 46)

Those presidencies, "unequal to their own establishment," were the more recently conquered regions, where revenues from Bengal served to pay for British domination until these regions could pay their own way. For this early period as a whole (from 1757 to 1780), the Indian historians Majumdar, Raychaudhuri, and Datta in their *Advanced History of India* estimate a total drain of £38 million (cited in Devèze 1970: 160).

For the period around 1780, Sinha (1961, I: 231) estimates an annual drain of approximately £16 million from Bengal. James Grant, writing in his *Analysis of the Finances of Bengal* in 1786, estimated a rate of annual drain on account of the British East India Company's investment alone of £10 million, and, including that for the China trade of about £2 million and that of other European companies and mercantile adventurers of £6 million, a total drain of £18 million a year (cited in Sinha 1961, I: 232, 236). Holden Furber, after studying English, French, Dutch, and Danish language invoices and bills for the period 1783–1792, and constructing his calculation on a different base than Grant, estimated an annual average drain from India as a whole also of £18 million (cited in Sinha 1961, I: 236).

For the entire period from 1757 to 1815. William Digby writes in his *"Prosperous" British India, a Revelation from Official Records*, first published in 1901:

What was the extent of the wealth thus wrung from the East Indies? No one has been able to reckon adequately, as no one has been in a position to make a correct "tally" of the treasure exported from India. Estimates have been made which vary from £500,000,000 to nearly £1,000,000,000. Probably between Plassey and Waterloo the last-mentioned sum was transferred from Indian hoards to English banks. (Digby 1969: 33)

In this regard Angus Maddison writes:

> There is a tendency among Marxist and anti-British historians to exaggerate the size of the Indian plunder. . . . In fact a good deal of the Indian revenue was used to finance local wars and did not reach the U. K. The latest scholarly estimates suggest that the transfer to the U. K. was about one-tenth of the amounts estimated by Digby. (Maddison 1971, 63 n.)

Maddison does not explain why plunder used to finance local wars (i.e., the conquest of the remainder of India and later of Burma, etc.) should be omitted from reckoning, unless he assumes that the rewards of empire, formal and informal, should also be omitted from all reckoning. However that may be, the Soviet scholar, A. I. Levkovsky, cites evidence submitted to the board of directors of the East India Company in 1813, and reaches the conclusion that "According to obviously minimised statistics, the British colonialists derived from India in 55 years (1757–1812) a direct income exceeding £100,000,000" (Levkovsky 1966: 10). And Digby remarks, "the connection between the beginning of the drain of Indian wealth to England and the swift uprising of British industries was not casual: it was causal" (Digby 1969: 31). He goes on to quote the oft-repeated opinion of Brooks Adams that "possibly, since the world began, no investment has ever yielded the profit reaped from the Indian plunder . . . . the effect appears to have been instantaneous, for . . . the 'industrial revolution' " (Digby 1969: 31–33). And, of course, for the inventions and innovations that initiated the Industrial Revolution. These, however, are questions that are examined in their respective contexts in the process of world capital accumulation as a whole in Chapters 5 and 6.

Chapter 5

Depression and Revolution, 1762–1789

Analyzing business cycles means neither more nor less than analyzing the economic process of the capitalist era. Most of us discover this truth which at once reveals the nature of the task and also its formidable dimensions. Cycles are not, like tonsils, separable things that might be treated by themselves, but are, like the beat of the heart, of the essence of the organism that displays them. I have called this book "Business Cycles" in order to indicate succinctly what the reader is to expect, but the subtitle really renders what I have tried to do.

— Joseph A. Schumpeter,
Business Cycles: A Theoretical, Historical, and Statistical Analysis of the Capitalist Process (1939)

1. Depression and Accumulation

The three decades from 1762 to 1789 decidedly were marked by recurrent and predominant economic depression—and they in turn mark what is probably the decisive turning point in the modern history of humanity. J. D. Bernal writes in his *Science in History*:

The seventy years from 1760 to 1830, and particularly the thirty from 1770 to 1800, are a decisive turning point in world history. They mark the first practical realization of the new powers of machinery in the framework of a new capitalist productive industry. . . . The critical transition came as a culmination of changes in technology and economics which reached, as has been shown, a breakthrough in Britain, on the

167

technical side, around the year 1760, and in France, on the economic and political side, thirty years later. The changes were not easily effected; it was no accident that the period was one of unprecedented revolutions and wars. (Bernal 1969, II: 535)

I might add that it was also no accident that the period was one of widespread economic depression. These closing decades are remembered for a series of world-historical events, each of which receives different emphasis according to the relative importance assigned it by the perspective and interest of each writer. These events include the highpoint of the eighteenth-century Enlightenment, which replaced faith by rationality in Europe; the cluster of mechanical inventions associated with the Industrial Revolution in England; the French Revolution against the remnants of feudalism, which offered the world bourgeois "liberty, equality and fraternity"; the American War and Declaration of Independence which has been heralded as a "model" for anticolonial revolutions; the beginnings of the attack on restrictions of the slave trade; the simultaneous conquest and plunder of India; the introduction of foreign-grown opium in China; the European exploration of the Pacific; the Russian penetration south and eastward; the economic and political awakening of the Spanish empire and of the Ottoman Empire as well—in short, the birth of industrial capitalism as we know it. I shall examine some of these events below, but I must warn with Bernal that

> Although there is ample material and even adequate analysis of the political, the economic, the technical, and the scientific transformations of the eighteenth century, these studies have remained largely separate and the combined analysis of them has yet to be written. It would be impossible to embark on it here. (Bernal 1969, II: 520)

The decades of the sixties, seventies, and eighties of the eighteenth century were predominantly depressive in Europe, the Caribbean, and North America, although for France and her possessions this destiny was delayed for nearly a decade. In his *Economic Fluctuations in England, 1700–1800,* T. S. Ashton labels fifteen out of the twenty-eight years between 1762 and 1789 as years of depression, and comments that "the inclusion of a year among the peaks does not necessarily mean that things were good, but only that they were better than they had been or were to be. Crises might appear at any point of the fluctuation, but generally they came just after a peak: they were precursors of depression" (Ashton 1959: 173). As years of depression he lists 1762, 1765–1769, 1773–1774, 1778–1781, 1784, 1788–1789. Ashton then examines these in greater detail:

In 1761 the London cabinet-makers were indicted for having combined to raise wages and shorten their hours of work, and there were similar reports of this "growing evil" among the shoe-makers, tailors, and peruke-makers. Even the Irish harvesters . . . were at odds with farmers about wages. . . . [This] precipitated the general crisis in August. The result can be seen not only in the statistics of finance—the upward movement of exchange rates, the fall in the prices of securities, and the drop in the Bank's ratio—but also in the fall of the price of wool, and a general decline in production. In 1761 the output of printed goods was 6.88 million yards: in 1762 it fell to 5.62 million yards. Similar, if less steep, decreases occurred in the manufacture of paper and glass—and presumably in the volume of building. In 1762 English exports declined by £1.4 million, and there was a marked fall of employment at sea. . . . The depression was at its lowest point in the last months of 1762 and the first months of 1763. Preliminaries of peace were signed at Fontainbleau on 3 November 1762, and the definitive treaty was concluded at Paris on 10 February 1763. As after the War of Spanish Succession, the first year of peace was, at best, one of moderate prosperity. . . . The year 1764 saw general prosperity. . . . The following year saw the beginning of a depression that dragged on for the rest of the decade . . . the trade of the northern ports was paralysed. . . . The iron industry was short of orders. . . . At the same time there was a depression in overseas trade, and especially in America. . . . The chief support for employment in these years came from building and public works. A reduced demand for capital by the export industries may have been one reason for the low rates of interest that were a condition for expansion here; and the release of able-bodied men from the army may have provided a large part of the labour force. . . . From 1769 to 1774 the story is different. . . . Overseas trade recovered in 1770, rose outstandingly in the following year, and, it would seem, remained at a high level for at least the first half of 1772. . . . The production of broad-cloth (four-fifths of which was sold abroad) increased from 2.7 million yards in 1769 to 3.6 million in 1772. Other series also tell of great activity in this year. . . . Sooner or later the drain of specie—external and internal—must have enforced a restriction of credit and brought the boom to an end. But, in fact, a whole series of untoward events conspired to this end. . . . [In] late 1772 [in] Holland, credit collapsed; and the panic spread rapidly to England. The shortage of currency was such that many concerns, in Lancashire and Yorkshire in particular, were obliged to pay wages in notes they themselves created. Manufacturers of repute, like Matthew Boulton, John Roebuck, and Henry Thrale, were in difficulties. According to Boulton, the trade in Birmingham was "so dead." . . . The decline in wages was 12½% for the relatively well-paid wool-comber, 16½% for weavers, 20-27% for the spinners near Halifax, and 30–40% for those at a distance. . . . The slump led to widespread emigration from Scotland and Ireland, and according to the *Leeds Mercury* of 17 May 1774, the same thing was happening here: "scarce a week passes without some setting off from this part of Yorkshire for the Plantations". . . . In the slump of 1773 producers concerned with the home market had suffered less than those dependent on overseas demand. . . . By the middle of 1774 . . . a new upward movement had begun . . . and in 1775 there was recovery here also. . . . In the early months of 1775 Britain drifted once more into war. . . . The recession set in in the later months of 1777; but it is reasonable to believe that the boom, like its predecessor of 1771–2, had carried with it the seed of decay, and that economic forces were mainly responsible for the slump. . . . A further increase of bankruptcies and depression in trade, manufacture, and building alike persisted for nearly three years. . . . Employment in shipping, which had been at a peak in 1778, dropped suddenly. And though an increase of shipments to the East Indies brought some relief in 1780, and increased greatly the number of merchant seamen, the accession of Holland to the list of Britain's enemies brought the figure down again the following year. . . . In June 1779 riots broke out . . . disorders . . . attributed to unemployment. . . . In the following year anti-machinery riots. . . . The depression continued throughout the year 1781. . . . The upward movement [of 1782] continued in 1783, but several factors prevented the development of an authentic post-war boom. . . . The crisis of the autumn of 1783 seems to have been due partly to an external drain and partly to losses sustained by merchants who had overestimated the strength of overseas demand for British goods. . . . the two downward fluctuations of the eighties—those of 1781–84 and 1786–9—were short and of limited amplitude. In both cases the crisis was relatively mild, and the increase of bankruptcies relatively small. In several series the following recessions appear as a retardation of the secular trend rather than a declivity. . . . There is evidence that in 1789 the depression was lifting . . . and between 1789 and 1792 the production of printed goods increased by half. . . . There are many indications that prosperity had created conditions of boom in 1792. (Ashton 1959: 150–66)

The evidence seems overwhelming that between 1762 and 1789, the entire British-dominated (and also French-dominated) "international" economy was going through a long crisis of accumulation (and not simply a series of fortuitously, or even agriculturally, caused commercial fluctuations). It will not be possible here (and, as Bernal suggests, it is probably nowhere yet possible) to analyze the fundamental causes and all of the consequences of this crisis. But in the pages that follow, I will examine some of the world developments that coincided chronologically with this crisis and, where possible, suggest some possible causative relations.

The production of Brazilian gold began to fall off significantly after 1760; consequently, because of Brazil's relative importance, so too did world gold production. According to the classic calculations of Adolph Soetbeer, accepted by Simonsen (1962) and others, the Brazilian production of gold, which had risen from about 1,000 kgs. annually at the beginning of the century to an average of nearly 15,000 kgs. at its highpoint between 1740 and 1760, declined sharply, because of the progressive exhaustion of the gold fields, to an annual average of about 10,000 kgs. between 1760 and 1780, 5,000 kgs. from then until the end of the century, and after that it fell below 2,000 (Simonsen 1962: 198). According to Furtado (1965: 85), Brazilian exports of gold dropped from £2.5 million in 1760 to less than £1 million in 1780. As a result, total world gold production fell from a maximum annual average of 781,000 ounces in 1741–1760 (not reattained until more than a century later), to 665,000 ounces in 1761–1780, to 572,000 ounces in 1780–1810 and still less after that (Vilar 1969: 421). And this was while the potential demand of quantitatively increasing world trade was for increasing means of payment!

The world output of silver, after the drastic decline of Spanish American production in the seventeenth century, had remained virtually stagnant until 1740. After that world output began to increase, but in Spanish America, particularly in Mexico, which came to supply two thirds of the total, silver production did not begin to increase until the end of the 1760s. According to Humboldt, the production of silver in Spanish America rose from less than 1.4 million marks in the 1760s to 1.75 million annually between 1770–1775, then to about 2.1 million annually until 1790, increasing again to 2.7 million annually during the last decade of the eighteenth century (Vilar 1969: 420). World silver production rose from an annual average of 14 million ounces in 1721–1740 to 28 million ounces between 1781 and 1810 (Vilar, 1969: 421).

This increase of silver production—with a decade and a half lag on the decline in gold output—cannot be attributed to chance or to the discovery of new mines. Two contemporary authorities, the viceroy of New Spain, Revillagigedo, in 1794, and the German geographer, Humboldt, in 1803, gave the following explanations.

> In the last few years, the output of the mines has increased considerably. . . . This increase has not been due to great bonanzas or greater purity of the metals; it is due primarily to the increased numbers of people working in the mines. . . . Many former merchants, accustomed to high profits and low risk in overseas trade, turned to agriculture and mining when they realized that the new commercial system would allow them lower profits and entail higher risk. (Revillagigedo, quoted in Frank 1972: 28–29)

> The enormous expansion of the produce of the mines observable in latter years is to be attributed to a great number of causes all acting at the same time, and among which the first place must be assigned to the growth in population on the tableland of Mexico, the progress of knowledge and national industry, the freedom of trade conceded to America in 1778, the facility of procuring at a cheaper rate the iron and steel necessary for the mines, the fall in the price of mercury, the discovery of the mines of Catorce and Velenciana, and the establishment of the *tribunal de mineria*. (Humboldt, quoted in Brading 1971: 156–157)

Indeed, by 1775 the Almaden mine had doubled its capacity for the output of mercury which was required for smelting silver (Brading 1971: 141). But this too had been possible only as a result of new investment in mining.

Why should this investment in silver mining and related activities take place at the end of the eighteenth century, even though there was a time lag that left a hole in the world supply of new metallic money between 1760 and 1776? Brading says that "any explanation of the great Mexican boom must be tentative," and goes on:

> It seems best to concentrate upon the boom of the 1770's which followed the recession of the 1760's. Here we can perceive several factors at work which combined to create a significant lowering of production costs sufficient to increase profits quite considerably. In mining itself, owners gained greater control over their workers, and in some cases were able to reduce their *partidos* and wages. Then the more extensive

use of gunpowder was encouraged by a cut in price and a more efficient supply. . . . tax exemptions. . . . cheaper and more abundant supply of mercury. . . . At the same time the local price of silver bar rose appreciably. . . . Trading profits in general and premiums on silver in particular fell during the 1780's. Here, then, is a possible causal sequence. The great boom of the 1770's sprang both from general cost reductions affecting all industry and from a remarkable series of current bonanzas in particular mines. Then, in the 1780's this boom was sustained and pushed still further by the entrance of mercantile capital into the industry and matched by greater willingness to plough back mining profits. . . . quite possibly it was the entrance of investment capital which made the difference. Proofs, however, are lacking. (Brading 1971: 157–58)

But may we not speculate, despite the lack of "proof," that the entrance of investment capital in *silver* mining, emphasized by both of the contemporary authorities above, may have been generated initially by the *low* prices of *all* other commodities, including (but not limited to) the material and labor inputs required for mine development and production, which was associated in turn with the general depression and the reduced gold supply? May we not suppose that, as I have argued in Chapter 2, section 3, the later sixteenth-century inflation of all prices reduced the price of silver money and encouraged the withdrawal of capital from silver mining? May we not also suppose that the late eighteenth-century depression increased the price of silver relative to all other prices (except gold whose known sources were being exhausted) and thereby encouraged renewed massive investment in silver mines and increases in silver output—but *not* until at least half the long cyclical downswing had run its course? Further presumptive evidence may be sought in the near substitute for gold and silver money, that is, paper money and bills of credit.

In 1776, Adam Smith wrote in the chapter on "Money" in *An Inquiry into the Nature and Causes of the Wealth of Nations*:

When, therefore, by the substitution of paper, the gold and silver necessary for circulation is reduced to, perhaps, a fifth part of the former quantity, if the value of only the greater part of the other four-fifths be added to the funds which are destined for the maintenance of industry, it must make a very considerable addition to the quantity of that industry, and consequently, to the value of the annual produce of land and labour. An operation of this kind has, within these five-and-twenty or thirty years, been performed in Scotland, by the erection of new banking companies in almost every considerable town, and even in some country villages. The effects of it have been precisely those above described. The business of the country is almost entirely carried on by means of the paper of those different banking companies, with which purchases and payments of all kinds are commonly made. Silver very seldom appears except in the change of a twenty shillings bank note, and gold still seldomer. . . . that the trade and industry of Scotland, however, have increased very considerably during this period, and that the banks have contributed a good deal to this increase, cannot be doubted. (Smith 1937: 280–81)

Smith continued:

By issuing too great a quantity of paper, of which excess was continually returning, in order to be exchanged for gold or silver, the bank of England was for many years together obliged to coin gold to the extent of between eight hundred thousand pounds and a million a year. . . . For this great coinage the bank was . . . frequently obliged to purchase gold bullion at the high price of four pounds an ounce, which . . . losing in this manner between two and a half and three percent. Upon the coinage of so very large a sum. . . . Scottish banks, in consequence of excesses of the same kind, were all obliged to employ constantly agents in London to collect money for them. . . . The bank of England, notwithstanding their great annual coinage, found to their astonishment, that there was every year the same scarcity of coin as there had been the year before . . . the state of the coin, instead of growing better and better, became every year worse and worse. . . . The over-trading of some bold projectors in both parts of the United Kingdom, was the original cause of this excessive circulation of paper money. . . . It is now more than five-and-twenty years since the paper money issued by the different banking companies of Scotland was fully equal, or rather more than fully equal, to what the circulation of the country could easily absorb and employ. Those companies, therefore, had so long ago given all the assistance to the traders and other undertakers of Scotland which it is possible for banks and bankers, consistently with their own interest, to give. They had even done somewhat more. They had over-traded a little, and had brought upon themselves that loss, at least that diminution of profit, which in this particular business never fails to attend the smallest degree of over-trading. . . . Upon their [the banks] refusing to extend their credits, some of these traders had recourse to an expedient which, for a time, served their purpose, though at a much greater expence, yet as effectually as the utmost extension of bank credits could have done. This expedient was no other than the well-known shift of drawing or re-drawing; the shift to which the unfortunate traders have sometimes recourse when they are upon the brink of bankruptcy. The practice of raising money in this manner had been long known in England, and during the course of the late war [1756–1763], when the profits of trade afforded a great temptation to over-trading, is said to have been carried on to a very great extent. . . . The practice of drawing and re-drawing is so well known to all men of business, that it may perhaps be thought unnecessary to give any account of it. (Smith 1937: 286–93)

Nonetheless, Smith explains at length to ' people who are not men of business":

> . . . all European nations, have given such extraordinary privileges to bills of exchange, that money is more readily advanced upon them, than upon any other species of obligation. . . . each endorser becomes in turn liable to the owner of the bill for those contents, and, if he fails to pay, he becomes too from that moment bankrupt. . . . Many vast and extensive projects, however, were undertaken, and for several years carried on without any other fund to support them besides what was raised at this enormous expence. The projectors, no doubt, had in their golden dreams the most distinct vision of this great profit. Upon their awakening, however, either at the end of their projects, or when they were no longer able to carry them on, they very seldom, I believe, had the good fortune to find t. (Smith 1937: 293–95)

That is, the whole house of cards came crashing down beginning with the crisis of 1762, which initiated a depression nearly a decade long, followed by only partial recovery, and nearly a decade more of hard times.

It is noteworthy that Smith recalls that the increasing recourse to paper money had begun twenty-five to thirty years before he wrote, that is, around the mid-eighteenth century upturn of business conditions *prior* to the Seven Years War of 1756–1763. Nevertheless, Smith attributes part of the optimism to profit opportunities offered by the war itself. Moreover, he emphasizes that when the banks would no longer extend further credit, businesses had additional recourse to private bills of exchange, which "for a time" continued to serve their purpose, albeit at a higher cost, until the whole system became overextended and had to retrench. (I shall discuss below the ways that it found to emerge from the crisis.) Seeking some further empirical evidence to link the process Smith describes to the development of the long depressive phase (with which, writing as he was in the early seventies, Smith was no doubt also concerned), we might check the ratio of bullion and coin to notes in circulation plus drawing accounts of the Bank of England. Although this ratio cannot reflect the entire credit structure, it offers some indication of the relative amount of paper financial instruments in use; that is, the lower the ratio of metal money to paper money and drawing accounts, the greater the paper structure. Ashton (1959: 189) provides this ratio for each year (with two exceptions) from 1720 to 1800. For the entire period 1720–1760, the average ratio is 39 percent; and for the last decade thereof, from 1751–1760, it is 42 percent. Yet for the recession years 1761–1769, the ratio of metal to paper falls to an average of 22 percent, rising again to 36 percent for the less depressive years 1770–1776 (though falling to 15 percent in the depressive year of 1773) and falling again to 24 percent for the years 1777–1785. Thus, for the whole period from 1761 to 1785, the average was only 27 percent. After that, from 1786 to 1795, the ratio rose to an average of 49 percent. Is this a "Keynesian" policy in operation, one which was insufficient, by itself, to stem the tide of depression?*

> Sweet smiling village, loveliest of the lawn
> Thy sports are fled, and all thy charms withdrawn;
> Amidst thy bowers the tyrant's hand is seen
> And desolation saddens all thy green.
> Only one master grasps the whole domain
>
> Far, far away, thy children leave the land
> Where then, ah! where shall poverty reside
>
> The rich man's joys increase, the poor's decay
>
> Where wealth accumulates, and men decay;
> Princes and lords may flourish, or may fade;
> A breath can make them, as a breath had made,
> But a bold peasantry, their country's pride,
> When once destroyed, can never be supplied.

Oliver Goldsmith wrote his classic poem "The Deserted Village" in 1770; I suggest it was not happenchance that he did so at that precise historical juncture.

Marx was no doubt right—and especially so if reference is to a time of temporary recession of the international market (as Hobsbawm [1971: 109] argues)—when he wrote

---

* For a similar discussion without these data, see Vilar (1969: 343–45), who says that in 1783 the Bank of England "for the first time" reacted to a gold loss and impending crisis by cutting its line of credit.

in fact, the events that transformed the small peasants into wage-labourers, and their means of subsistence and of labour into material elements of capital, created at the same time, a home market for the latter. . . . Thus, hand in hand with the expropriation of the self-supporting peasants, with their separation from the means of production, goes the destruction of rural industry, the process of separation between manufacture and agriculture. And only the destruction of rural domestic industry can give the internal market of a country that extension and consistence which the capitalist mode of production requires. (Marx 1954, I: 747–48)

But Marx had apparently been misled when he believed that "about 1750, the yeomanry had disappeared [in England]" (1954, I: 723). The Hammonds, citing Slater, note that both the number of acts of enclosure and the acreage of common fields enclosed increased about ten-fold during 1761–1801 from what it had been during the previous period, 1700–1760 (Hammond and Hammond 1927: 17). Deane and Cole, also citing Slater, record 56 acts of enclosure and 74,518 acres enclosed between 1727 and 1760 and 339 acts and 478,259 acres between 1761 and 1792 (Deane and Cole 1967: 272). Still citing the same Slater, Mantoux (1964: 141–42) records the following progression of Enclosure Acts:

1720–1730	33 acts
1730–1740	35 acts
1740–1750	38 acts
1750–1760	156 acts
1760–1770	424 acts
1770–1780	642 acts
1780–1790	287 acts
1790–1800	506 acts
1800–1810	906 acts

Whatever the discrepancy and the reasons for it, one thing is evident: relative to earlier times, the enclosure movement became an avalanche precisely during the depressive decade of the 1760s—just preceding Goldsmith's poem—and continued in the still relatively depressed decade of the 1770s. It then abated temporarily.

Mantoux comments further:

Between the sixteenth- and seventeenth-century enclosures and those of the eighteenth century, there was an essential difference. The former had been opposed by the King's administration, the latter on the contrary met with the assistance and encouragement from Parliament. . . . The great landowners were the first to undertake a methodical exploitation of their estates according to the precepts of the new agricultural science. They were men who bore most impatiently the obligations laid on them by the open-field system. And they, in almost every case, initiated the petition to Parliament for a Bill of Enclosure.

But the desertion of Goldsmith's villages did not occur quietly.

> After 1760 such protests became more frequent and forceful. The suppressed anger of the villagers would break out suddenly. In some parishes, the announcement of the enclosure caused riots. . . . Thus the enclosures and the engrossing of farms ultimately resulted in placing at the disposal of industry resources in labour and energy which made it possible for the factory system to develop. Industry was becoming, as it were, a new land in the very midst of the country, another America attracting immigrants by the thousands—with this difference: that instead of being a discovery it was a creation. . . . Many of the small yeomen and farmers, reduced to the condition of wage-earners, shared the fate of the labourers, who came to the towns in search of work. They possessed nothing, and could offer nothing but their labour. These were to form the working population, the anonymous multitude in the factories—the army of the industrial revolution. . . . There is, therefore, an intimate connection between the movement by which English agriculture was transformed and the rise of the factory system. (Mantoux 1964: 165–84)

Phyllis Deane likewise draws a direct connection between the acts of enclosure and the labor supply (Deane 1965: 158–59). Paul Bairoch, in describing the technical and other advances in Belgium (that is, Flanders and certain parts of Walloon) that occurred between 1760 and 1791, and those that occurred a decade earlier in France, is content merely to stress the technical/economic increase in the supply of agricultural products.

> In France, the first phase of the modifications that overcame agriculture was around 1750–1760. . . . It has been possible to estimate that the annual rate of increase of agricultural output was 1.4% between 1751–1760 and 1771–1780, while during the first half of this eighteenth century the increase in agricultural output did not pass 0.3%. (Bairoch 1969: 81–82)

But the importance of all of these transformations in agriculture goes far beyond the increase in agricultural products.

What were the political economic consequences of this late eighteenth-century accumulation crisis beyond the immediate attempts to ward it off by a wall of paper? (These attempts in fact only aggravated the final crash in the long run, as Smith observed at the time, and as subsequent crises to this day have continued to demonstrate.) One natural reaction of capital, as observed by Ashton and the contemporary witnesses he quotes, was to cut wages up to 40 percent. This, presumably, was intended to increase the rate of exploitation of the worker at home, irrespective of the "disturbances" generated, which, again presumably, were adequately dealt with—from capital's standpoint. Ashton writes:

> at times when activity in both [building and construction and manufacturing] was high, as in 1764, 1772, and 1792, there were complaints of a shortage of labour [and presumably relatively high wages and lowered profits], and it is possible that the ending of the booms was due to this influence quite as much as to growing pressure on supplies of capital and money. (Ashton 1959: 174)

Ashton does not clarify why one influence should be an alternative to the other rather than its predecessor—and indeed its cause.

A second reaction or consequence, as we have observed, was to increase the supply of silver by, among other things (as Brading recalls) increasing the rate of exploitation, or superexploitation, of the Mexican miners and vastly increasing the misery of the masses of the population in Mexico until they (unsuccessfully) rose up in revolt in 1810. A third reaction, as we shall see, was to try to exact more external indirect customs duties and to impose new internal direct taxes on the American colonists, as well as to seek greater revenues from the fur trade by closing the western frontier to settlement. This set of measures combined to incite the American colonists to go to war for their independence. A fourth reaction was the formation in London of a Society of West Indian Planters to lobby and pressure for the maintenance of their depression-threatened incomes (and to shift part of the burden on to the North American colonists). Other reactions included the decision to go to war against France and the exploration of a new frontier in the Pacific. But by far the most important reactions and consequences for world history were, on the one hand, the plunder of Bengal (that was subsequently extended to other parts of India) in a drive for primitive accumulation not witnessed since the Spanish conquered America and established slave plantations in the Caribbean; and, on the other hand, the domestic turn to enlightened rationalism, scientific research, mechanical invention, and, after the profit rate began to look up, innovation—in short, the Industrial Revolution.

Having examined the plunder of Bengal and India in the previous chapter, we can go on to the other political economic consequences of the late eighteenth-century accumulation crisis.

2. *The Caribbean after 1763*

Although at the Peace of Paris in 1763 the Caribbean sugar islands were a major bone of contention (should Guadeloupe be sacrificed for Canada?), ironically that year may be said to mark the beginning of the end of the economic and political reign of Caribbean sugar. Affected by the general economic crisis of the following decades, sugar prices declined, and there were periodic financial panics. The British sugar islands failed to maintain profitability through greater exploitation and output, apparently because their fertility was too exhausted, although perhaps also because sufficient British investment was not forthcoming. In any case, the cost of production in the British islands was significantly higher than in the French ones, and the British did not or could not bring it down. We may speculate to what extent the contemporary British turn eastward (go East, young man!) to India and the plunder of Bengal may have been related, as an attraction for potential investment and still more as a source of primitive accumulation, to the progressive exhaustion of the traditional West Indian "paradise." "Declining prosperity produced bitter wails of complaint and demands for legislative help" (Parry and Sherlock 1971: 142) from the West India interests, who achieved a temporary success with the Sugar Act of 1764. This Act sought to shift part of the burden of the recession on to the North American colonies, who in turn rebelled. But, by and large, along with the decline in their profits and in their relative importance to Britain, the sugar planters lost more and more political influence. Their increased visible activity through the Society of West Indian Merchants and the Society of West Indian Planters and other parliamentary lobbies reflected, rather than an increase in influence, their struggle to prolong and their vain effort to protect their waning economic and political privileges. British interest was shifting, first to North America and India, and after the loss of the former, still more to the latter. In Jamaica, the largest of the British sugar islands, between 1775 and 1791, 23 percent of the 775 plantations were sold for debt, 12 percent passed into the hands of receivers, and 7 percent were abandoned (E. Williams 1966: 123). Even so, although the North Americans had encouraged the British Caribbean to join them after the decline of sugar prices in 1773, the planters preferred to protect their declining fortunes from the threat of France by relying on the British navy (Parry and Sherlock 1971: 134–35).

In the French sugar islands, on the contrary, the trend was just the opposite to that in the British islands—up to a point. The French islands reached their "golden age" only after 1763 and were able to increase their output and presumably cut, or at least maintain, their costs of production up to 1790. "French sugar cost one-fifth less than British, the average yield in St. Domingue and Jamaica was five to one" (E. Williams 1966: 122). Production in St. Domingue nearly doubled between 1783 and 1789, and the importation of slaves increased still more (James 1963: 55). It has generally been asserted as an explanation of the French success that "the fertility of the French soil was decisive" (E. Williams 1966: 122). No doubt the more recently developed and less exhausted French islands were more fertile than the older English ones, but was this "decisive," or did it merely physically permit a greater degree of labor exploitation than in the English islands? And did this rate of exploitation not increase while the importation of slaves—and presumably the more rapid exhaustion of their "useful life"—increased much more rapidly even than yield and production? According to C. L. R. James, "[T]he slaves were being used for the opening up of new lands. There was no time to allow for the period of acclimatisation known as seasoning, and they died like flies" (James 1963: 56). The "humanitarian" protective clauses of the Code Noir were forgotten. Further, was French capital merely *enabled* to increase its rate of primitive capital accumulation from its Caribbean colonies? Or was it actually *obliged* to do so in order to stem the tide of the domestic economic and political crisis, which had been aggravated by the British exclusion of France in 1763 from the happy hunting grounds of both India and North America? Whatever the answers, all of the French efforts soon turned out to be in vain. Indeed, they aggravated the final outcome. In France itself the revolution came in 1789, and in St. Domingue (now Haiti) it came in 1791 under the leadership first of Toussaint L'Overture and then Jean Jacques Dessalines—"torn by inner and outer contradictions which in four years [from 1789] would split that [social] structure into so many pieces that they could never be put together again" (James 1963: 57). Although Toussaint's forces eventually failed to make the total revolution they sought, Napoleon's efforts to recover the colony failed as well. After twelve years of foreign and civil war, Haiti's export of sugar dropped from 163 million pounds to 53 million (Parry and Sherlock 1971: 170). This provided Cuba, which had been "opened up" by the British capture of Havana in 1762, with the opportunity of succeeding to the throne of sugar in the nineteenth and twentieth centuries, though by then, on a world scale, this represented no more than a minor principality.

3.   *Spain, Portugal, and Their Empires*

In the Spanish and Portuguese submetropolises and their empires, the period after 1763 was marked by profound and far-reaching contradictions. These were the Bourbon reforms under Charles III (1759–1789); and under the Portuguese Prime Minister Pombal (1750–1777) and his successors they have been characterized as a policy of "dependence resisted" (Sideri 1970). While the English- and secondarily French-dominated world economy suffered a long cyclical economic downswing, Spain and its empire prospered as never before in the eighteenth century. Indeed, such prosperity had not been experienced since the seventeenth century "decline of Spain," nor has it been experienced again since 1800.

Except for a brief five year period (1771–1775) [which coincided substantially with the temporary relative English recovery], the rule of Charles III (1759–1789) develops under the wing of an extremely favorable upswing. Prices and wages—more the former than the latter—are in distinct upsurge, and this coincides with a demographic, agricultural, commercial and industrial expansion of the country, where an almost uninterrupted increasing quantity of American precious metals arrive. Here in sum is the golden age of the eighteenth century. (Vicens Vives 1962, IV: 227–28)

Domestically, after 1760 Spain experienced a significant shift in economic activity, power, and interest from the inland regions to the coast, and especially to Cataluña or its capital, Barcelona. By the end of the century the wage rate in the latter was almost double that of Madrid. This economic and industrial growth was accompanied by the rise of new bourgeois forces and their increasingly successful political demands for the cessation of the monopoly privileges of the previously favored regions (Vicens Vives 1969: 25–33). Additionally, Spain, which had been almost as economically and politically dependent on France as Portugal had been on Britain, was temporarily favored by the disturbances associated with the revolution in France, disturbances that were perhaps already caused by the economic depression preceding it.

After 1763 the Spanish Crown embarked on a whole series of far-reaching reforms of the economic and administrative regulations governing its empire in America and the Philippines. These reforms have generally been attributed to the gradual or sudden "enlightenment" of Spanish despotism, under the influence of Bernardo Ward, Pedro Rodríguez Campomanes, Caspar de Jovellanos and others in Spain itself, as well as the influence of the Encyclopedists and Physiocrats in France. They have also been attributed to the momentary shock suffered when the British captured Havana (the staging center of the Spanish merchant fleet in America) and Manila, and threatened to capture Veracruz (the principal port of New Spain) in 1762, and to the increasing disquiet caused by the growing contraband incursion of Britain and France into the Spanish empire, of which in a sense the capture of these ports was symbolic (Stein and Stein 1970: 95–97). All of these factors were no doubt important; but they should also be interpreted in the context of the cyclical crisis of English, and to a lesser degree French, industry and trade and the simultaneous economic spurt of Spain itself—as well as the opportunity (examined above) for the increase of silver production in New Spain and elsewhere, and, indeed, of gold production in Nueva Granada (today Colombia) and in other Spanish possessions to partially fill the gap left by the decline of the Brazilian mines. In 1765 the monopoly of a single Spanish port (earlier Seville and later Cadiz) in the trade with America was abolished, and several Spanish and Catalan ports were authorized to trade with several ports in the Spanish Caribbean. In 1768 the same concession was extended to (then Spanish) Louisiana, in 1770 to Yucatan and Campeche in Mexico, and in 1776 to two ports in Nueva Granada. In 1767 the Jesuits were expelled from the Spanish dominions and their vast properties were subsequently put up for sale. In 1774 direct reciprocal trade among the Spanish colonies, previously prohibited except in special cases, was legalized. In 1776 a longstanding dispute over the riches of the Peruvian (now Bolivian) highland mining regions between the old submetropolis on the Pacific, Lima, and the newly developing one on the Atlantic, Buenos Aires, was resolved in favor of the latter, which became the capital of the new viceroyalty of La Plata, with the privilege to tax and trade with the mining regions. In February 1778 the ports of Argentina, Chile, and Peru were permitted "freedom of commerce" with Spain, and in October of the same year a host of other ports in Spain and its American empire were granted the same privileges in a new omnibus decree. In 1789 the same freedom was finally granted to the port of Veracruz in Mexico. It appears then that the Spanish Crown progressively relaxed its traditional trade restrictions—and often reduced taxes at the same time—in accord with the real or felt threat to its economic and political power in the area, beginning in the Caribbean after its losses during the Seven Years War. These relaxations were then extended to Louisiana and Nueva Granada, and most importantly to the La Plata region, where British and Portuguese contraband via Brazil and Colonia de Sacramento (in present-day Uruguay) was making increasing economic inroads and political friends; and last of all to Mexico, the brightest and safest jewel of the imperial crown. Mexico was, in fact, all of a (sub)metropolis itself, dominating much of the remainder of the Spanish empire in America, after the similar challenge of Lima had declined along with the declining output of the Potosí mines (Arcila Farías 1950: 13–15). The increasing liberation of trade in the remainder of the empire, moreover, was not very favorably received in Mexico, at least by its bigger merchants since the resulting "competition" undermined their monopoly power (Arcila Farías 1950: 13–15). It was also of course strenuously, if vainly, resisted by both the economic and political power in Lima (Kossok, 1959; Céspedes del Castillo 1947).

The economic recession in the English and French economies, the simultaneous economic revival of the submetropolises in Spain and Portugal (which, however, reflected the growth of the newer coastal regions at the relative expense of the older inland ones), and the threat to, and loss of, mercantile and political power of previously privileged sectors in the sub-submetropolises of Mexico and especially Lima had further varied consequences in the remainder of the Spanish dominions. Trade between Spain and America increased enormously, as did the growing import surplus of the latter, which was paid for by ever growing production and export of silver and gold. Yet by no means all of the additional Spanish American imports came from Spain originally. Although Spanish manufacture and manufacturing export increased—and the whole "liberalization" of trade with its colonies was intended to strengthen its export of manufactures and its import of raw materials and bullion—Spain did not and could not satisfy the import requirements of its colonies. Other colonial manufacturing imports from Spain were of foreign origin, and probably still more of the colonial imports were direct English and French contraband (or in the southern cone of the continent, indirect contraband via Portugal and Brazil). Such contraband trade in the Spanish colonies received a perhaps especially strong foreign impulse during this period, as a result of the stagnation of other export markets (especially those of Britain) and the newly increased "availability" of British re-exported Indian textiles. Moreover, while the contraband (like other) trade was partially hindered by the wars of the period, it was also facilitated by Spanish permission to some of its colonies for trade with "neutral" flag vessels. One thing is certain and recorded in documentary evidence from all of the Spanish colonies: their internal (including literally inland) markets were flooded with foreign manufactures from Spain, Europe, India, and also North America; and the local manufacturing establishments were massively put out of business (documented in Frank 1969: 51–55; 1972: 24–25). On the other hand, the production of raw materials, mining, and associated agriculture flourished in many areas; and merchant capital, where it was threatened by foreign competition and could do so, moved over into these recently more profitable activities.

From the innumerable contemporary testimonies to the consequences of these cyclical trends and associated reformist policies, I have chosen to reproduce only one, by Count Revillagigedo, viceroy of New Spain, in his *Instrucción Reservada* to his successor in 1794. (Recall that the trade reforms had arrived last and least in Mexico; although, on the other hand, the Crown had sent the most outstanding of its visitadores or inspectors, Jośe Galvéz, to Mexico to clean up and oil the administration of the viceroyalty. Later, as newly appointed intendente, Galvéz was commissioned not only to administer New Spain, but also to extend this administration and the Spanish dominions northward to meet the English, French, and now also Russian threat in California.) Revillagigedo wrote:

Far from a decline, in the years of free trade there was a considerable increase in the volume of goods and merchandize introduced as well as the amount of wealth and produce extracted. In these regions, there has been great progress in recent years: the export of products has nearly tripled in comparison with earlier years and consists principally of hides, dyes, cotton, Campeche wood [*palo de tinto*], and myrtle, and above all, the precious cochineal [dye]. Tanned products, soap, cotton, and flour were sent from these domains to Havana and the islands, where they were needed in agriculture. . . . the harvests of grains of all kinds have increased greatly in these domains. . . . In the last few years, the output of the mines has increased considerably. [For the reasons he gives, see the beginning of this chapter.] . . . In these domains it is very difficult to prohibit the manufacture of those things which are made here. . . . The only way to destroy such local manufactures would be to send the same or similar products from Europe, to be sold at lower prices. This is what has happened to the great factory and guild which existed for all sorts of silk textiles, now barely remembered; and much the same fate has befallen the factories manufacturing printed cloth. . . . The decline of the [Acapulco] trade was quite natural in view of the changes which haven taken place, the growth of European factories, and the generally inferior quality of Oriental cloth. Since the year 1789 [the year in which the liberalization of commerce was extended to Mexico, although elsewhere it had been introduced twelve years before that, with proportionately greater effects] there has been a steady increase in the textiles and goods that have been imported. (Revillagigedo 1966: 191–205, quoted in Frank 1972: 28–29, 24)

These economic developments in the Spanish colonies could not but have their social and political counterparts and repercussions. Those which ultimately led to the independence of the Spanish colonies between 1810 and 1820 may be left for later examination in relation to that period. In the meantime internal class contradictions sharpened in many regions of the empire and were reflected in the increase of vagrancy, criminality, and social banditry, and its sporadic outbursts, especially during agricultural crises or epidemics (Florescano 1969: 155–69), which further magnified the felt effects of the growing rate of superexploitation. Some of these became important social/political protest movements or rebellions that are still remembered, such as the riots in Mexico in 1786, the *comunero* revolt in Nueva Granada in 1780, and most of all the uprisings of the Inca descendants under Tupac Amaru in Peru from 1779 to 1783. The historian, Enrique Florescano, gives the following account of the situation in Mexico.

> From 1779 to 1803 the value of the tithes [10 percent received by the Church], which reflects the upsurge of agriculture, almost tripled. . . . For the first time the value of agricultural production (which was calculated on the basis of the value of the tithes) exceeded the value of mining activities, in spite of the fact that the height of mining prosperity was from 1779 to 1803. . . . When Humboldt visited New Spain in 1803, he was able to confirm that the increase of wealth in the last thirty years of the eighteenth century had aggravated the economic inequalities in colonial society. . . . In a word, the rise in prices had made the great landlords richer; the division between the prelates and the parish priests was deepened and the situation of the poor became more intolerable. . . . The growth of the *haciendas* [also associated with the mining boom] caused the displacement of a great number of rural laborers and the impact of cyclical crises increased. The number of unemployed rose and social tension in the cities grew. The inequalities caused by the increase in wealth were so dramatic that, in commenting on the situation which prevailed from 1803 to 1807, Humboldt, Fray Antonio de San Miguel, Abad y Queipo, and the liberal group writing in the *Diario de Mexico* predicted the outbreak of social conflict. In September 1810, after thirty years of continuous rise in prices, after the [food] crises of 1785–1786 and 1801–1802, and precisely when another inflationary wave reached its peak, Hidalgo initiated the [peasant] revolution [against Spain but immediately also against the ruling classes] which was to make New Spain an independent country ten years later.* (Florescano 1969: 193–95, quoted in Frank 1972: 29)

---

* At that time, however, New Spain was under the leadership of the very oligarchic groups which had fought against and defeated both Hidalgo and his successor Morelos and their poor peasant army

Sergio Bagú reaches similar conclusions:

> It is not by chance that the Marquis of Pombal, Prime Minister of Portugal, is contemporary of Charles III [of Spain]. His government was born out of similar necessities, confronted the same enemies and heard a national clamor which expressed itself in parallel terms. Of course, there are differences. (Bagú 1949: 153)

One might add that these statesmen responded to similar though not identical opportunities. Portugal was dependent on Britain (see Chapter 3, section 4), and its ability to finance its import surplus of British goods was diminishing with the progressive exhaustion after 1760 of its major source, the Brazilian gold fields, and with the increasing Brazilian inability to compete with French Caribbean sugar. The Portuguese reaction, begun under the leadership of Prime Minister Pombal, but still continued by his successor after 1777, was to face the simultaneous crisis in British trade and Brazilian gold by instituting a forced "import substituting" development policy at home and by promoting, through the formation of monopoly companies to exploit the North, and particularly Maranhao, the development of alternative sources of raw material income from her Brazilian colony. In Portugal, manufactures, especially textile production, were significantly expanded with state aid, as was the merchant marine, which then took advantage of the belligerency of the major powers—and the need for vehicles for private circuitous remittances of the "servants" of the British East India Company (see Chapter 4, section 7)—to extend Portuguese shipping and invisible earnings. Total Portuguese trade increased sixfold between 1774 and 1800, Portugal's imports from Britain declined, and its balance of trade turned favorable for various years during the period (Sideri 1970: 99–111). In Maranhao, Portugal took advantage of wartime interruptions in the supply of Caribbean cotton and North American rice to increase earnings from slave labor in its new colony. But it was all too little and too late. From the beginning of the nineteenth century onward, Portugal would relapse—even losing, as a side effect of the Napoleonic Wars, its Brazilian colony (which would also languish until the development of coffee in the South)—and Portugal would again become the model, selected by Ricardo in 1817, to illustrate the "comparative advantage" of the exchange of British manufactures for the world's raw materials.

4. Exploration and Expansion in the Pacific

Like other generally depressive phases, the one between 1762 and 1789 witnessed a European explorative and expansive movement into new areas, this time into the Pacific. The outbreak of hostilities among the English, French, and Spanish in 1739 (the War of the Austrian Succession and Jenkin's Ear) and the Anglo-French rivalry in Asia and especially India regenerated interest in a new route to the Orient. The search would soon be renewed for the long-sought northwest passage as well as for a northeast and southwest passage. In connection with the search for the southwest passage, interest revived in the discovery of the *Terra Australis Incognita*, long since "known" to occupy much (more than Australia) of the South Pacific region. Two British expeditions to find the northwest passage through Hudson's Bay failed in the 1740s.

It was not until after the Seven Years War that the Pacific enterprise began in earnest. In 1762 the British captured from the Spaniards not only Manila in the Pacific, but also Havana in the Atlantic, though both were later returned as part of the peace settlements. In 1763–1764 both France and Britain dispatched naval expeditions to the Malvina/Falkland islands off the coast of Argentina. Lord Egmont, Britain's first lord of the admiralty, referred to these islands on the eastern approaches to the Straits of Magellan as "the key to the whole Pacific Ocean"; and for good measure he added optimistically that "this island must command the ports and trade of Chile, Peru, Panama, Acapulco and, in one word, all the Spanish territory in that sea. It will render all our expeditions in those parts most lucrative to ourselves, most fatal to Spain" (quoted in G. Williams 1966: 161, 191).

Similar though lesser ambitions or illusions were entertained about the island of Juan Fernandez, reputedly that of Robinson

Crusoe (whose adventures reflect the spirit of the times; see Hymer 1971), off the coast of Spain. As it turned out, the importance of these islands was vastly exaggerated; nonetheless, Britain has to this date refused Argentina's demand for the "return" of the Malvinas/Falkland islands.

The expeditionary thrust into the Pacific came with the voyages of John Byron in 1764–1765, Philip Carteret in 1766–1768, Louis Antoine de Bougainville in 1767–1768, and most notably with the three voyages of Captain Cook in 1768–1771, 1772–1775, and 1776, the last of which was also designed to challenge the Russian thrust as well as Spanish suzerainty in North America. On this voyage, Cook turned northeastward after leaving Tahiti, "discovered" the Sandwich or Hawaiian Islands and reached California and the Puget Sound region (the present State of Washington in the United States and British Columbia in Canada). The mysterious continental *Terra Australis Incognita* remained unknown, of course; but the voyages served to open the door to the future European colonization of the Polynesian and Melanesian South Pacific islands as well as New Zealand and Australia, where the first shipment of British convicts was landed at Botany Bay on January 20, 1788.

5. The American Revolution
for Independence

One of the important world-historical consequences of the generally depressive economic conditions between 1762 and 1789 was the independence of the thirteen colonies of Britain in North America and the formation of the United States. Another was the French Revolution.

Most historians would now agree that Britain's North American subjects generally fared well under a policy of so-called salutary neglect and had little cause for complaint. A. H. Schlesinger (1918), among others, argued at the beginning of the present century that the colonial regulations of commerce did not seriously restrict the colonial fortunes of North America and in many ways promoted them through the colonies' participation in monopoly privileges. British mercantilist attempts to prohibit or even to restrict other manufacturing in the northern colonies were largely unsuccessful. The British program to produce naval stores in the northern colonies for colonial export to Britain did not attain its objectives and rather supported American development. And the regulations controlling the shipment or transshipment of certain enumerated products of the colonial trade between the New World and the European metropolis, through they adversely affected the agricultural export regions of the Caribbean and the South, did not hinder and in some ways—even if unintentionally—aided northern development and manufacturing. This was the case until 1764 of the molasses trade (despite the unenforced Molasses Act of 1733), which played an important role in generating northern distilleries of rum. The molasses trade in turn developed into an important item or link in the whole pattern of northern overseas trade and local capital accumulation, as we shall see below. There is now substantial agreement (for example, Harper 1964: 41) with Beard (1941) and Schlesinger (1918: 19–20) that laws against manufacturing did not adversely affect the northern colonies and that trade regulations did not seriously affect their interests before 1763. Another American historian, writing at the same time as Schlesinger, argued:

> We have lost sight of the fact that the amount of taxation imposed by England was insignificant in amount, and could not possibly be now considered as a serious burden. . . . Here again we lose sight of the fact that these commercial restrictions were in existence for a century without serious opposition, were vastly more liberal than those enjoyed by any other colonies in the world and had not prevented the colonies from making such progress in wealth and population as to attract the attention of all Europe. (Callender 1965: 122)

Only after the Peace of Paris in 1763, having incurred large debts in the preceding Seven Years War but having eliminated the French threat from North America (as well as from India), did the British impose new onerous revenue-generating regulations on their American colonies, which these writers and others argue interfered with the normal good business of the North American traders. This interference propelled the dominant merchants in the North to form an alliance with indebted southern planters and to issue the Declaration of Independence in 1776. But before we can fully appreciate the significance of the American Revolution for independence, it is important to understand the peculiarities of the early development of Britain's colonies in northeastern America, and in particular their insertion, participation, and function in the expanding system of mercantile capitalism and the process of world capital accumulation.

Adam Smith offered some explanations to account for the socioeconomic and political differences between the North and the South and other colonies. The settlement pattern and distribution of landownership in the North, as well as the relatively high wage level associated with the nonwage opportunities that these offered (as Marx also observed) cannot be simply explained by the physical availability of land, since it was initially greater in the South and elsewhere. On the contrary, it was the relative *poverty* of the land and climate, as well as, of course, the nonexistence of mines, in the Northeast which explains why access to it was less foreclosed than it was in the South and elsewhere. It was the possibility of extracting a profit from the land in the South—essentially through production for export—much more than in New England or even the grain regions of the Middle Atlantic states which was determinant in differentiating these regions. But this profit was possible in the South, as in the Caribbean, only if free access to land was limited by its monopolization in the best areas and by further restrictions on the mobility of labor through servitude or slavery, which were not profitable in the North.

These different profit possibilities also explain, as Smith observed, the reasons for the British "neglect" of the North relative to the "attention" devoted by the British (and French) to the South and to the sugar islands in the Caribbean and by the Spanish to their mining, though not their Caribbean and other possessions. If this attention did not make the colonies "thrive" better, as Smith remarked, it was of course because the political and economic controls and institutions that characterized such "attention" were designed precisely to exploit and develop the profit possibilities more efficiently—while the "neglect" of the northern colonies left them more nearly to fend for themselves. "British capital had little interest" in New England, observes Stuart Bruchey (1966: 40); and Curtis Nettels (1956: 10) argues that "the policies that affected the Middle Colonies and New England differed materially in character and effect from the policies that were applied to the South." The same may perhaps be said for some other "neglected" regions of the New World which, like New England, did not then have the mode of production and the exploitative colonial systems of the mining and plantation regions and which were not therefore already condemned to underdevelopment during mercantile capitalist times. But these other regions did not also share the peculiarly privileged participation of New England in mercantile capitalist development.

That which most particularly and unhappily distinguishes most of these Northern British Colonies, from all others, either British or any other nation, is, that the soil and climate of them, is incapable of producing almost anything which will serve to send directly home to the Mother Country. Yet notwithstanding this fatal disadvantage, their situation and circumstances are such, as to be obliged to take off, and consume greater quantities of British Manufactures, than any other Colonies; their long cold winters call for much clothing, but their deep and lasting snows, make it impossible to keep sheep, and thereby procure wool to supply that demand. Again, the same long winters, prevent the labour of slaves being of any advantage in the Colonies; this, together with almost endless countries lying back, yet to be settled and with inhabitants, makes hands so scarce, and labour so dear, that no kind of manufactures can be set up and supported in these Colonies: and thus it appears on one hand, that the inhabitants are obliged by necessity to take great quantities of goods from the Mother Country; so on the other, it is no less evident that nature hath denied them the means of returning anything directly thither to pay for those goods.

When these singular circumstances are fully known, and duly considered, it will easily be found what the cause is, that a much greater number of ships and smaller vessels are employed by the people of these Colonies, than of any others in the world: unable to make remittances in a direct way they are obliged to do it by a circuity of commerce, unpractised by and unnecessary in any other Colony. The commodities shipped off by them are generally of such a nature, that they must be consumed in the country where first sold, and will not bear to be reshipped from thence to any other; from hence it happens that no one market will take off any great quantity; this obliges these people to look out for markets in every part of the world within their reach, where they can sell their good for any tolerable price, and procure such things in return, as may serve immediately, or by severale commercial exchanges, to make a remittance home. ("An Essay on the Trade of The Northern Colonies of Great Britain in Northe America: 1764" in Callender 1965: 51–52)

In the first seven decades of the eighteenth century Anglo-American trade had increased five- or sixfold, from an annual average of *balanced* imports and exports of about £266,000 in the first decade to a still balanced annual average of £730,000 in each direction in the decade prior to 1745 (exports of £646,00 from England and imports of £617,000 during the fourth decade). After that, although the total Anglo-American trade continued to increase, it became increasingly imbalanced, until American imports from Britain reached an annual average of £3,280,000 in the years 1770–1774, while American exports to Britain amounted to only £1,334,000 (U.S. Bureau of the Census 1960: 757). This bilateral trade deficit of all the American colonies put together signifies much greater real imbalances among the individual colonies.

The northeastern colonies came to occupy a position in the expanding world mercantile capitalist system and in the process of capital accumulation which permitted them to share in the latter as a submetropolis of Western Europe with respect to the exploitation of the South, the West Indies, and indeed Africa, and indirectly the mining regions and the Orient. This privileged position, not shared by others in the New World, must be considered as a crucial factor in the economic development of the northeast during colonial times and in its successful political policy of independence and further development thereafter. This privileged position and role impinged on northern transport, mercantile and financial participation in southern and western export (and import) trade, the northeast's advantageous participation in the West India trade, the slave trade, and indeed world trade; northeastern manufacturing development largely for export; and the associated capital accumulation and concentration in northern cities.

While the southern plantation export colonies of Georgia and Carolina maintained a roughly balanced trade and often even an export surplus, Virginia and Maryland already had a modest import surplus with England. The northern New England and Middle Atlantic colonies imported much more from England than they exported to that country: about five times as much in the case of

New England and up to ten times as much in the case of Pennsylvania.

> The only articles produced in the colony [Rhode Island], suitable for remittance to Europe consist of some flax seed and oil, and some few ships built for sale; the whole amounting to about £5000 per annum . . . all of which bears but a very inconsiderable proportion of the debt contracted for British goods. It can therefore be nothing but commerce which enables us to pay it. As there is no commodity in the colony suitable for the European market, but the few afore-mentioned; and as the other goods raised for exportation, will answer no market but in the West Indies, it necessarily follows that the trade thither must be the foundation of all our commerce; and it is undoubtedly true, that solely from the prosecution of this trade with other branches that are pursued in consequence of it, arises the ability to pay for such quantities of British goods. (Remonstrance to the Board of Trade, passed by the Rhode Island Legislature, January 24, 1764, in Stavrianos 1966a: 118)

Not just Rhode Island, but all the North American colonies, particularly in developing New England, were heavily dependent on the trade with the West Indies and the market that was generated by the West Indies' mode of production.

> In 1770 the continental colonies sent to the West Indies nearly one-third of their exports of dried fish and almost all their pickled fish; seven-eights of their oats, seven-tenths of their corn, almost all their peas and beans, half their flour, all their butter and cheese, over one-quarter of their rice, almost all their onions; five-sixths of their pine, oak and cedar boards, over half their staves, nearly all their hoops; all their horses, sheep, hogs, and poultry; almost all their soap and candles. As Professor Pitman has told us, "It was the wealth accumulated from the West Indian trade which more than anything else underlay the prosperity and and civilization of New England and the Middle Colonies." (E. Williams 1966: 108)

Moreover, New England capital accumulation was substantially based on its own corner of the larger triangular trade.

> By the middle of the eighteenth century the New England slave trade was three-cornered, like the Liverpool trade, but it was simpler and even more symmetrical. Essentially it was based on three commodities: rum, slaves and molasses. At its home port the vessel would take on a cargo consisting chiefly or entirely of rum. . . . In Africa the rum would be exchanged for as many slaves as it would buy, often at the rate of two hundred gallons per slave. The black cargo would be sold to the West Indies, and part of the proceeds invested in molasses, usually

purchased in the French or Spanish Islands, where it was cheaper. On the final leg of the voyage, the vessel would carry the molasses back to New England, to be distilled into more rum, to buy more slaves. (Mannix and Cowley 1962: 159–60)

Benjamin Franklin, testifying to a committee of the British House of Commons in 1766, explained further how his Pennsylvania could import £500,000 worth of goods from Britain each year while exporting only £40,000 in return as he answered the question, "How then do you pay the balance?"

> The balance is paid by our produce carried to the West Indies, and sold in our own islands, or to the French, Spaniards, Danes and Dutch; by the same carried to other colonies in North-America, as to New England, Nova Scotia, Newfoundland, Carolina and Georgia, by the same carried to different parts of Europe, as Spain, Portugal and Italy. In all which places we receive either money, bills of exchange, or commodities that suit for remittance to Britain; which together with all the profits on the industry of our merchants and mariners, arising in those circuitous voyages, and the freights made by their ships, center finally in Britain, to discharge the balance, and pay for British manufactures continually used in the province, or sold to foreigners by our traders. (Quoted in Faulkner 1960: 80–81)

John Adams, one of the fathers of North American independence and freedom, noted the divine wisdom and benevolence of this whole mercantile capitalist system and development: "The commerce of the West Indian Islands is part of the American system of commerce. They can neither do without us, nor we without them. The Creator has placed us upon the globe in such a situation that we have occasion for each other" (quoted in E. Williams 1966: 121). Thus the surplus of goods imported from Britain was covered, (as the above quotations from contemporary documents and contemporary spokesmen record) by North American earnings from merchandize exports and services to other areas, principally the West Indies, Southern Europe and Africa. The pattern of trade of the northern and southern American colonies prior to their independence is summarized in the accompanying table.

The commerce between Britain and its North American colonies and its importance for the former was described and summarized by the merchants of London and Bristol, when they petitioned parliament in 1775 to remedy the causes and consequences of the Ameri-

Table 5.1
Colonial American Exports and Imports, 1769
(in thousands of pounds sterling)

To/From	North*		South		Total**	
	Exports	Imports	Exports	Imports	Exports	Imports
Britain	284	504	1,247	1,100	1,531	1,605
West Indies	556	594	192	195	748	790
South Europe	336	55	217	22	553	77
Africa	20	1	1	151	20	152
Total**	1,195	1,155	1,657	1,469	2,852	2,623

SOURCE: E. R. Johnson et al., *History of Domestic and Foreign Commerce of the United States*, cited in Faulkner 1960: 82.
 * North includes all colonies north of Maryland.
 ** Differences between totals and breakdown are due to rounding.

can embargo against British goods. This embargo had reduced American imports of British goods from over £2.5 million in 1774 to less than £200,000 in 1775. The petition stated:

That the petitioners are all essentially interested in the trade to North America, either as exporters and importers, or as vendors of British and foreign goods for exportation to that country; and that the petitioners have exported, or sold for exportation, to the British colonies in North America, very large quantities of the manufacture of Great Britain and Ireland, and in particular the staple articles of woollen, iron, and linen, and also those of cotton, silk, leather, pewter, tin copper, and brass, with almost every British manufacture; also large quantities of foreign linens and other articles imported into these kingdoms, from Flanders, Holland, Germany, the East Countries, Portugal, Spain, and Italy, which are generally received from those countries in return for British manufactures; and that the petitioners have likewise exported, or sold for exportation, great quantities of the various species of goods imported into this kingdom from the East-Indies, part of which receive additional manufacture in Great Britain; and that the petitioners receive returns from North America to this kingdom directly, viz. pig and bar iron, timber, staves, naval stores, tobacco, rice, indigo, bees wax, pot and pearl ashes, drugs and dying woods, with some bullion, and also wheat flour, Indian corn and salted provisions, when, on account of scarcity in Great Britain, those articles are permitted to be imported; and that the petitioners receive circuitously from Ireland (for flax seed, &c. exported from North America) by bills of exchange on the merchants of this city trading to Ireland, for the proceeds of linens, &c.

imported into these kingdoms from the West Indies; in return provisions, lumber and cattle, exported from North America, for the use and support of the West India islands, by bills of exchange on the West India merchants, for the proceeds of sugar, molasses, rum, cotton, coffee, or other produce, imported from those islands into these kingdoms; from Italy, Spain, Portugal, France, Flanders, Germany, Holland, and the East Countries, by bills of exchange or bullion in return for wheat flour, rice, Indian corn, fish, and lumber, exported from the British colonies in North America, for use of those countries. (Quoted in Callender 1965: 155–56)

For their part, the West India planters, similarly alarmed, petitioned parliament the same year that:

if the Acts and the parts of Acts of the British Parliament therein mentioned, are not repealed, they [the Americans] would not directly or indirectly, export any merchandise or commodity whatsoever to the West Indies; and representing to the House that the British property in the West India islands amounts to upwards of £30 million sterling; and that a further property of many millions is employed in the commerce created by said islands, a commerce comprehending Africa, the East Indies and Europe; and that the whole profits and produce of those capitals ultimately center in Great Britain, and add to the national wealth, while the navigation necessary to all its branches, establishes its strength which wealth can neither purchase nor balance . . . and therefore praying the House, to take into their most serious consideration the great political system of the colonies heretofore so very beneficial to the mother country and her dependencies, and adopt such measures as to them shall seem meet, to prevent the evils with which the petitioners are threatened, and to preserve the intercourse between the West India islands and the northern colonies, to the general harmony and lasting benefit of the whole British empire. (Quoted in Callender 1965: 157–59)

The schoolbooks teach us that the Americans rose up against "taxation without representation" and certain commercial restrictions. But, as has often been observed, "the more rigid enforcement after 1763 no doubt increased their injurious effects, but even then it is impossible to make them out a grievous burden" (Callender 1965: 122).

We may ask with Guy Callender: "Why, then, did they, along with insignificant taxes, stir up such fierce opposition? Why were the Americans willing to endure the horrors of a long and costly war for what seems now so small a cause" (1965: 122)? In answer, Callender suggests:

A partial explanation may be found in the economic and social conditions existing at the time. In the first place, there was economic depression in nearly all the colonies during the ten years which preceded the war. This chiefly affected the commercial classes in New England and the middle colonies, and was no doubt connected more or less with the more rigid enforcement of the commercial restrictions. Commerce, it must be remembered, was the chief source of private fortune in these colonies, and almost every prominent man was connected with it. Economic depression in Virginia had nothing to do with commerce, but affected the planter class, and was ever more serious than in New England. It was natural enough that a people already suffering economic depression should feel strong opposition to any increase of taxation, however slight, and be irritated by any changes in commercial regulations likely to affect them. It was not alone an excessive devotion to abstract principles of constitutional and political rights which caused so much agitation and excitement in Massachussetts and Virginia. It was the fact that those abstract principles were invoked to remedy an economic depression which was seriously felt. (1965: 122–23)

Other historians agree:

The most cursory examination of the factors in the controversy leading to the Revolution, as suggested in this chapter, leads one to discard quickly the old theory that the Revolution occurred because an English despot was seeking to regain his lost powers, as well as the other explanation that it was fought in protest to taxation without representation. Deep-seated causes of long standing were behind it. . . . Undoubtedly one potent cause in bringing about the separation was the period of depression or "hard times" which preceded the Revolution. . . . The hard times in England were reflected in America; decreased buying power in England combined with the enforcement of the mercantile system was disastrous. (Faulkner 1960: 125, 123)

Chester Wright remarks that:

the abnormal conditions that mark this period as a whole exercised such great influence on the immediate course of events and varied so from time to time it is necessary to divide the period into sections corresponding to the changes in general conditions and so make the account more nearly a chronological narrative than for other periods; only thus can the rapid changes and extensive interaction of the various developments be explained. Along with this narrative of wartime reactions and their aftermath, often closely influenced by them, will be found developments tending to bring enduring changes in the structure of industrial society. (Wright 1941: 189)

We may then briefly follow Wright and other historians in reviewing the highpoints of this chronological narrative. Aptheker recalls:

> the exacerbations were aggravated or alleviated by fluctuations in business conditions. In the 1750's, prior to the Seven Years' War, there was a recession in the colonies; with the war, until 1763, an upturn. Recession followed, to the point of rather severe depression from 1764 through 1769, an upturn starting in 1770 lasted for about two years; then from 1772 to the outbreak of actual hostilities in 1775 the colonial economy was in the grip of recession. Of course, depression then, as now, meant unemployment, falling prices for farmers and merchants, special hardship for debtors, increased bankrupcies—all of which reflected itself politically in increased restlessness and sharpened dissatisfaction with the status of subordination to the interests of the British rulers. (Aptheker 1960: 34–35)

The Seven Years War and the 1763 settlement at the Peace of Paris aggravated economic problems for the British, which were already concerned with those generated by the economic recession that had begun two years earlier in 1761. Indeed, it has been claimed that the British chose to make an early peace and, through the new Bute government, agreed unnecessarily to French demands because the economic recession rendered the continuation of the war excessively burdensome. Thus the economic recession served to raise the political fortunes of the "little Englanders" represented by Bute as against the more "imperial" interests represented by the Pitt administration which had started the war. One consequence of the war and the peace settlement was the elimination of the French threat in the trans-Appalachian–Mississippi region. This tilted the political balance in the longstanding conflict between the English settlers and the fur traders, whose interests were virtually mutually exclusive, in favor of the latter. A royal proclamation in 1763 forbade land grants and settlement beyond a "proclamation line" running through the crest of the Allegheny-Appalachian mountain ridge. This prohibition adversely affected the interests of "little people," intent on moving westward in the North and especially in the South, and infuriated the land speculators allied to the urban commercial fortunes. The economic interest tied to the fur trade, and concentrated more particularly in regions that later remained loyal to the British and formed the nucleus of present-day Canada, were, on the contrary, favored by the measure.

The recession conditions, the vast war debt, and the elimination of the French threat in North America encouraged the British to increase the taxes on the Americans, who, it was claimed, were beneficiaries of the war; to extend the administration of the colonies; and to intensify the pacification campaign against the Indians, which required military and other expenditures. The result was the Sugar Act of 1764, the Quartering [of troops] Act of 1765, and the now notorious Stamp Act of 1765, which first levied direct taxes on the colonists. Opposition to the Stamp Act achieved its repeal in 1766, though in the Declaratory Act of the same year, the Crown reaffirmed its right in principle to levy such charges. In the next year, 1767, new customs duties were levied through the Townshend Acts. Probably far more important, though less readily visible in its effects, was the 1764 prohibition against the issue of bills of credit or paper money in all of the colonies. This resulted in a deflationary shortage of money and severe hardship to debtors—always more populous and poorer than the creditors—who had incurred their debts during inflated wartime conditions.

> So far as the colonists actually experienced economic losses, it is probable that the general depression and the scarcity of money were by far the most important causes responsible for them, and that the Sugar Act and the Stamp Act were minor factors. Yet it was these acts, particularly the Stamp Act, the burden of which on the masses could not have been great since the estimated receipts were only between 15 and 20 cents *per capita*, that aroused the greatest outcry. . . . These facts made the Stamp Act the strategic point of attack against which these [more well-to-do] groups could most easily rally the masses whose suffering and discontent were chiefly caused, though only half understood, by other conditions. The ignorance of the masses about the real causes in the complex operation of economic forces under which they suffer in a period of depression and about the proper remedies thereof has been used throughout history in manifold and devious ways to further the purposes of some special groups. (Wright 1941: 194)

Beginning in 1770, coincident with (and, it may be argued, in consequence of) the renewed short cyclical economic upturn, there was a change of policy both in England and North America. The new ministry of Lord North in England responded to the American nonimportation policy by repealing all of the Townshend Act duties, except that on tea, which, being a non-English product, was maintained as a matter of principle. For their part, the more conservative northern merchants in New York, Philadelphia, and elsewhere— apparently frightened by the prospect that the popular wrath that they had unleashed would swell beyond their control and turn increasingly against property, law and order, and themselves— opted for conciliation and repealed the nonimportation agreements, also except for tea and other dutiable articles. The following two years of relative economic prosperity were also years of renewed political calm and significantly reduced political support for the more radical leadership.

The year 1773 brought on the economic and political events which were to lead to the Lexington and Concord "shot heard around the world" on April 19, 1775, and to the Declaration of Independence on July 4, 1776. Recession set in again. Meanwhile, halfway around the world, the British East India Company's ravaging administration of its newly conquered Indian territories had brought on, simultaneously, the severe famine of 1770–1772 and the virtual bankruptcy of the company. The collective fortunes of this company were sacrificed under Clive to the private ones of its "servants," i.e., the administrators and especially Clive himself (see Chapter 4, section 7). In India, Clive was replaced in 1772 by Warren Hastings, representing parliament; and in Britain the parliament was persuaded to safeguard the national interest and that of the company's stockholders by finding a suitably profitable market for the stock of otherwise unsaleable tea on hand. The result was the Tea Act of 1773, which sought to dump the tea under what amounted to monopoly privileges for the company on the market of the Americans. The Americans reacted by dumping it in Boston Harbor during the Boston Tea Party, locking it up in warehouses, or sending it back to England. The British reaction was to seek the American payment of damages to the company through the Intolerable and Quebec Acts of 1774, both of which signified an escalation from economic demands to political repression. Although formal independence had been and still was far from the intention of most American colonists, the subsequent events precipitated its declaration in 1776 and its achievement after the war.

"Was the revolution a majority movement?" asks Aptheker, and what were the class interests, conflicts, and alliances involved? Opinions still differ. But perhaps there may be common agreement on a summary such as the following:

> We may now raise the questions: What groups or economic interests were injured by these various acts of England? Who led in the opposition aroused? What were the results? Doubtless all groups except the relatively self-sufficing frontier settlements suffered more or less from the economic depression, though it was chiefly felt in the larger trading centers; and the tobacco planters were particularly hard hit during the decade. Next in importance, judging by the number affected, and closely bound up in its influence with the depression, was the prohibition of paper money which especially affected the debtor classes of the middle and Southern colonies. The prohibition of western land grants directly affected only a small, though rather influential group interested in land speculation. The Stamp Act chiefly concerned lawyers, publishers, and traders, who were an influential group and in a good position to arouse popular opposition. The duties imposed by the Sugar Act [and later customs duties] hurt the traders, the small group of rum manufacturers, and consumers of some luxuries; besides they threatened to lower the market prices for exports to the West Indies and check the inflow of specie from that source, thus spreading the losses to other groups. (Wright 1941: 193–94)

The American War of Independence—and perhaps even the very decision to declare independence—was additionally related to the English, French, and Spanish rivalry in the construction of empire and accumulation of capital in the eighteenth century. Already months before the conclusion of the Seven Years War at the Peace of Paris in 1763, the French minister Etienne François de Choiseul had made plans for a future Franco-Spanish alliance, intending to reinitiate hostilities against England within five years (G. Williams 1966: 189). Though de Choiseul was removed from office by his "continentalist" political opponents and the renewal of war did not come to pass in the decade of the 1760s, the underlying conflict and French interest in regaining lost ground remained. It is in this context that the senior American diplomat-statesman, Benjamin Franklin, in a letter dated December 19, 1775, addressed the following inquiry to his contacts in France shortly before the American Declaration of Independence:

> It gives us great pleasure to learn from you that "all Europe wishes us the best success in the maintenance of our liberty." But we wish to

know whether any one of them, from principles of humanity, is disposed magnanimously to step in for the relief of an oppressed people, or whether if, as it seems likely to happen, we should be obliged to break off all connection with Britain, and declare ourselves an independent people, there is any state or power in Europe who would be willing to enter into an alliance with us for the benefit of our commerce, which amounted, before the war, to near seven million sterling per annum, and must continually increase, as our people increase most rapidly, (Franklin, quoted in Callendar 1965: 163)

Another letter, dated March 3, 1776, authorized an American who had been sent to Paris to take the following action:

You will be able to make immediate application to Monsieur de Vergennes, ministre des affaires étrangères . . . that you request an audience . . . and then acquaint him . . . that France had been pitched on for the first application [for arms and munitions], from the opinion that if we should, as there is great appearance we shall, come to a total separation from Great Britain, France would be looked upon as the power whose friendship it would be fittest for us to obtain and cultivate. That the commercial advantages Britain had enjoyed with the Colonies had contributed greatly to her late wealth and importance. That it is likely great part of our commerce will naturally fall to the share of France, especially if she favors us in this application, as that will be a means of gaining and securing the friendship of the Colonies; and that as our trade was rapidly increasing with our increase of people, and, in a greater proportion, her part of it will be extremely valuable. That the supply we at present want is clothing and arms for twenty-five thousand men, with a suitable quantity of ammunition, and one hundred field pieces. That we mean to pay for the same. (Franklin, quoted in Callender 1965: 164–65)

And on January 5, 1777, Franklin wrote further to Vergennes himself:

As other princes of Europe are lending or hiring their troops to Britain against America, it is apprehended that France may, if she thinks fit, afford our independent States the same kind of aid, without giving England any cause of complaint. But if England should on that account declare war, we conceive that by the united force of France, Spain, and America, she will lose all her possessions in the West Indies, much the greatest part of that commerce which has rendered her so opulent, and be reduced to that state of weakness and humiliation which she has, by her perfidy, her insolence, and her cruelty, both in the east and the west, so justly merited. . . . North America now offers to France and Spain her amity and commerce. . . . The interests of three nations are the same. (Franklin, quoted in Callender 1965: 166–67)

France did of course enter the war on the side of America, perhaps less from principles of humanity than from commonality of interest. Although Franklin's promises proved to be exaggerated, British fortunes did indeed fall, obliging that country to cut its losses, acceding to American independence after the battle of Yorktown. When Britain entered the Treaty of Versailles with France and Spain, although tactically strengthened by some last minute victories elsewhere, it was strategically weaker than at any previous peace settlement of the eighteenth century.

Paradoxically, though understandably. it was America's allies who then sought to press their respective claims and to confine the new nation to the Atlantic seaboard; and it was the British secretary of state, the Earl of Shelburne, who, in the anticipation of a larger market for continued Anglo-American trade (an anticipation that was to be confirmed by history) challenged the territorial and strategic pretension of France and Spain, and insisted that American territory should extend to the Mississippi. The Americans, for their part, had to determine what economic and political organization to institute in their new country, or more accurately thirteen countries. Their ill-fated confederation lasted less than a decade and was replaced by the United States of America under the Constitution of 1787. I have no wish to participate in the still-ongoing debate that was launched by Charles Beard with the publication in 1913 of *An Economic Interpretation of the Constitution*, and will here merely register my agreement with Beard's contemporary, Guy Callender, who observed:

There has always been a disposition to hold the old confederation responsible for the economic difficulties of the time, and to give to the new government, which followed it, credit for the prosperity which came with its establishment. There is very good reason, however, for thinking that the causal relation between economic and political conditions is really the reverse of this. Economic conditions, over which government had little or no control, wrecked the old confederation; while a prosperity, slowly prepared by influences that were for the most part independent of politics, smoothed the way for the establishment of the new government and insured it extraordinary success. The reasons for this view may be briefly stated. From an economic point of view, the decade following the Revolution represents one of those cycles of commercial speculation, crisis, hard times and gradual return to conditions of prosperity, which has been repeated so often in our history. . . . It was well recognized that prosperity depended upon foreign trade, and large imports were made in the expectation that even larger markets for exports would be opened than had been enjoyed in colonial times. But these markets were not opened; the expectations of the merchants were not fulfilled; and a crisis followed. . . . It is difficult to see how the old confederation, if it had possessed all the efficiency which had been given to the new government, could have done anything to remedy the situation. The root of the difficulty was the dislocation of our commercial relations with the rest of the world [which was in the throes of recession]. . . . The defects of the old confederation were then in no way responsible for the hard times. It had not produced them, nor could the best government in the world have removed them. It could only have enabled the people to endure them with more equanimity. If it is impossible to connect the hard times of the early part of the period with the old confederation, so it is impossible to attribute the return of prosperity to the influence of the new government. Before it came into existence, the signs of improvement were plainly evident. . . . As has happened so often in our later history, the foundation of returning prosperity was laid before political action was taken. The new government came into existence just in time to receive the credit for improved economic conditions and to be floated into power and popularity by that prestige. (1965: 180–82)

Curtis Nettels seems to agree, and in his recent book, *The Emergence of a National Economy, 1775–1815*, devotes two chapters to "Postwar Trade and Depression" and "Depression Remedies." Nonetheless, he states:

the men who deplored the weaknesses of the postwar economy ascribed them to certain features of the central government under the Articles of Confederation. Congress lacked the power to tax and therefore suffered the inadequacies of poverty. Since the states could levy duties on imports and exports, Congress could not create a national free trade area or put pressure on foreign powers by means of concessions or reprisals. The states possessed the decisive powers over money and credit and did not use them to provide the country with a uniform and stable currency. The Articles did not equip the Union with the money or the authority essential for sustaining a national army. Lack of military force and of diplomatic prowess enfeebled Congress in its efforts to deal with the formidable problems of the West. (Nettels 1962: 90)

These were not abstract weaknesses in general, but institutional, or rather political, limitations that made themselves concretely felt precisely during the depression years, in which internationally the American balance of trade was suffering—exports had declined by half—and the Western frontier required defense, or at least dissuasive power, against the Spaniards and the French. At the same time internal state governments, under the pressure of popular discontent and rebellions such as Shays' in 1786 in Massachusetts, continued to issue paper money, thereby favoring the numerous debtors against the fewer richer lenders and merchants. A brief partial recovery before the middle of the decade, reminiscent of the years just preceding the revolution itself, had reduced political agitation from below and the interest of the propertied groups in more effective—and more repressive—state institutions. But the more acute economic downturn of 1785–1786 and the massive popular political movements, such as Shays' Rebellion in 1786, renewed and increased political support for the federalists (Wright 1941: 230–40).

Writing "beyond Beard" (Staughton Lynd's term), who partially confused agriculturalists, the poor, and southerners in lumping them into the opposition, and beyond Robert Brown, who, in criticizing Beard, went to the extreme of assigning middle-class status to almost everybody in a supposedly classless society, Nettels summarizes:

> The men who wished to strengthen the central government and who took an active part in the movement for the Constitution were designated in 1787–1789 as both "nationalists" and "federalists." . . . The original aim of the nationalists was to provide for the payment in specie of the wartime debts of the Union. The depression of 1785–1787 then emphasized other interests. These included the creation of a single, stable, national currency based on coin—a reform that called for the surrender by the states of their power to issue paper money. The nationalists also wished to deprive state legislatures and state courts of their then uninhibited power of favoring debtors at the expense of creditors. In addition, the nationalists desired to make the central government equal to the task of enlarging foreign markets for the exports and the shipping of the Union. A comparable interest was that of enabling the central authority to foster domestic manufactures. Also, many nationalists regarded a strengthened Union as essential to the defense of the West and to the effective development of its resources. Finally, the social unrest of the 1780's convinced apprehensive men that a potential national government was needed for the suppression of domestic insurrections that might menace the owners of private property. . . . The nationalists anticipated that such powers might be used both to stimulated economic activity and to protect established interests. . . . The program of the nationalists was defensive in several respects. It aimed to protect creditors and investors from hostile acts of state governments. It also promised to safeguard maritime trade, as in the Mediterranean, by means of an adequate navy. To the West, the program offered security from attack by the Indians and from the

encroachments of foreign powers. New bulwarks would guard property owners if imperiled by insurrections such as Shays' Rebellion. The underwriting of property would reinforce slavery and assure federal aid to slaveowners when threatened by revolts too formidable to be put down by local authority. (Nettels 1962: 90–92)

Staughton Lynd adds:

the upper-class leaders of the Revolution were themselves divided into two basic groups, Northern capitalists and Southern plantation owners, and the Constitution represented not a victory of one over the other but a compromise between them. . . . In the 1790's . . . the coalition of sectional leaders which had directed the Revolution and then the movement for the Constitution almost at once broke down. Thus (as in most colonial independence movements) a first revolution for national independence was followed by a second revolution which determined what kind of society the independent nation would become. (Lynd, in Bernstein, ed. 1968: 50–51)

6. *The French Revolution*

Another product of the general 1762–1789 depressive cyclical downswing, it may be said with certainty, was the French Revolution of 1789, despite the fact that after nearly two centuries argument may still continue about the relative economic position and political participation of the various social classes and sectors. During much of the eighteenth century, France had achieved substantial economic and industrial growth, often at a rate exceeding that of Britain (see Chapters 3 and 6). Despite its worldwide defeat at the hands of Britain in the Seven Years War, France and its Caribbean colonies enjoyed golden years of prosperity in the decade following the Peace of Paris in 1763. Yet exports already had begun to stagnate during that decade (Labrousse 1958: 65); and the earlier war (or wars) laid the seeds for the renovation (in connection with the American Revolution) of Franco-Spanish warfare against the British, which together with other factors assumed a critical importance in creating the conditions for the French Revolution, namely, "distinct . . . prolonged stagnation" in trade and industry begun in France by 1772 and "outright recession during the American wars" (Crouzet 1967: 148, 153).

By 1778 France was in full and long general economic depression, and by 1780 agricultural depression as well. A weak recovery in 1786–1787 was followed by a renewed downswing beginning in 1788, lasting until 1791, and marked by the crisis of 1789. Already marked by nearly a decade of depression, France now experienced a sharp decline in profits and wages; in some sectors production and employment fell to 50 percent of 1787 and predepression levels (Labrousse 1958: 68). Moreover, the revolution was born in the midst of a government financial crisis which was itself the result of the debt contracted to carry on the American War of 1777–1783. C. E. Labrousse goes so far as to assert that "without the American War there would have been no financial crisis of the government, no convocation of the Estates General and no Revolution—at least at that time and in the form in which it actually broke out" (Labrousse 1958: 68). Georges Lefebvre makes a similar assessment:

> We now are well aware that the Revolution of 1789 came to pass only as the result of a truly extraordinary and unforeseen coincidence of a whole series of immediate causes: a financial crisis of exceptional gravity stemming from participation in the war of the American colonies; a crisis of unemployment engendered by the treaty of commerce of 1786 with England and war in Eastern Europe; and finally a crisis of rising prices and misery provoked by the bad harvest of 1788 and by the edict of 1787 which, by authorizing the export of grain, had emptied the storehouses. But these are not all the factors. (Lefebvre 1947: 74; see also Lefebvre 1958: ch. 2)

Labrousse summarizes:

> Thus, the revolutionary events themselves, as well as some of the important economic policies and institutions which emerged from the Revolution, had their origin in large part in the decline in profits and wages, in the strained circumstances of the industrialist, the artisan, the tenant farmer, the small owner, and the distress of the wage earner and the day laborer. An unfavourable concatenation of events brought together in a common opposition the bourgeoisie and the proletariat. (Labrousse 1958: 72)

7. *Invention and Enlightenment*

One Sunday afternoon in the spring of 1765 whilst James Watt, mechanical instrument maker, aged twenty-nine, was taking a walk on

Glasgow Green . . . there flashed across his mind the solution of a problem that had long troubled him: how could the cylinder of a steam-engine be both hot and cold at the same time? His solution, known as the device of the separate condenser, made it possible to employ steam as the motive power for industry. Watt's first patent applying his Sunday inspiration was taken out in 1769; his first successful engine was finished in 1776; by 1800, when the patent expired, his engine, improved in several respects, was in use in mines and foundries, in textile and paper mills, and great columns of smoke from innumerable chimneys spoiling the light and colour of the skies declared the triumph of industry and the glory of man. (Hammond and Hammond 1966: 110)

Before Watt's inspiration could become a material reality, Watt himself had to turn to John Roebuck, of the Carron Iron Works, for financial help (in exchange for which Watt sought to pump out by steam power Roebuck's mines which were full of water), until Roebuck went bankrupt in the 1772/1773 depression. Watt then formed a partnership with Matthew Boulton to assure himself of a source of capital. However, this capital (initially £20,000 declined by £11,000 between 1762 and 1780 in Boulton's Soho works (Hammond and Hammond 1966: 116–30).

Watt's case was not an isolated one. The number of patents issued in Britain had doubled from 92 in the years 1750–1759 (and less before that) to 205 between 1760 and 1769, rising to 294 in the decade of the seventies and 477 in that of the 1780s (Musson 1972: 50). Among these were the inventions and innovations that revolutionized the cotton industry and the world: James Hargreaves' spinning jenny in 1764, Richard Arkwright's spinning water frame in 1769, Samuel Crompton's spinning mule in 1779, and Edmund Cartwright's power loom in 1785, which permitted the industrialization of cotton textiles in England. In 1793, Eli Whitney invented the cotton gin, which permitted the efficient separation of the cotton seed from the fibre, and which would make American cotton growing competitive and the continuation of southern slavery profitable. It has often been observed, of course, and was emphasized by Joseph Schumpeter that there is a distinction between invention and its application, or innovation; and that there tends to be a time lag between the two. Trevor Ashton, commenting on the evidence for this alleged time lag, writes:

Kondratieff has argued (though without much supporting evidence) that most major inventions are made during periods of recession and applied during the ensuing periods of recovery. But, at least, the fact that so many patents were taken out in years of prosperity, and so few in years of depression (such as 1775, 1778, 1793, 1797, 1804, 1817, 1820, and 1826) suggests that it was the hope of gain, rather than avoiding loss, that gave the impulse. (Ashton 1972: 118)

Musson (1972: 52–53) casts doubt on "Ashton's theory" by pointing to the lag between the patenting of an invention and its innovation; a position given some support by the fact that so many of the "significant peaks in the [patent] figures for 1766, 1769, 1783, 1792" (Ashton 1972: 117) as well as the nonpeaks and the gestation times of the inventions were in this generally depressive period. The hope of gain does not preclude loss of the attempt to avoid it.

"The [economically depressed] decade of 1760–70 is, on the other hand, a turning point in technical and scientific history" (Bernal 1969, II: 506). The end of the eighteenth century was a time not only for invention, but also for the flowering and fruition of the Enlightenment. By mid-century David Hume had already made his mark in England and Montesquieu and Abbé Reynal had already called for greater libertarianism in France. Voltaire wrote *Candide* in 1759 and the first volume of the *Encyclopedie* had appeared in 1751. But the most earnest work of the middle-class French philosophes and encyclopedistes—Denis Diderot, Paul Holbach, Jean Jacques Rousseau (who wrote *The Social Contract* in 1762)—did not begin until the 1760s and its growing influence did not make itself felt until still later. In Germany, Immanuel Kant reacted with *The Critique of Pure Reason* in 1781. With the pens of Edward Gibbon in England and the Marquis de Condorcet in France, the writing of history became a call to optimistic rationality. Baron Turgot, Jules Quesnay, and the physiocrats called for economic liberalism in France as a crisis remedy. Adam Smith followed up *The Theory of Moral Sentiments* with the publication in 1776 of *The Wealth of Nations*. In Spain, economists like Pedro Rodríguez Campomanos, Bernardo Ward, and Caspar de Jovellanos influenced the liberalization of trade in the empire. Some, like Benjamin Franklin, combined scientific discovery with progressive politics. The Lunar Society of scientists and radicals sought to institutionalize them both in England; and Joseph Priestly practiced near-atheism as a clergyman, advanced the study of chemistry and electricity, and supported the increasing radicalism of the French Revolution (Bernal 1969, I: 531–33).

> The connexion between these different aspects of social change cannot have been a chance one. Indeed, the more closely they are examined the more intricate appear the threads knitting science, technique, economics, and politics together at this time into one pattern of transformation of culture. The period is a crucial one for the development of humanity. (Bernal 1969, I: 518–19)

Chapter 6

The Eighteenth-Century Commercial Revolution in Accumulation

The discovery of America, and that of a passage to the East Indies by the Cape of Good Hope, are the two greatest and most important events recorded in the history of mankind. Their consequences have already been very great. . . . One of the principal effects of those discoveries has been to raise the mercantile system to a degree of splendour and glory which it could never otherwise have attained to. . . . The countries which possess the colonies of America, and which trade directly to the East Indies, enjoy, indeed, the whole shew and splendour of this great commerce. . . . Europe, however, has hitherto derived much less advantage from its commerce with the East Indies, than from that with America. . . . By opening a new and inexhaustible market to all the commodities of Europe, it gave occasion to new division of labour and improvements of art, which, in the narrow circle of ancient commerce, could never have taken place for want of a market to take off the greater part of their produce. The productive powers of labour were improved, and its produce increased in all the different countries of Europe, and together with it the real revenue and wealth of the inhabitants. The commodities of Europe were almost all new to America, and many of those of America were new to Europe. A new set of exchanges, therefore, began to take place which had never been thought of before, and which should naturally have proved as advantageous to the new, as it certainly did to the old continent. The savage injustice of the Europeans rendered an event,

213

which ought to have been beneficial to all, ruinous and destructive to several of those unfortunate countries.
—Adam Smith, *An Inquiry into the Nature and Causes of the Wealth of Nations* (1776)

The colonies secured a market for the budding manufactures, and, through the monopoly of the market, an increasing accumulation. The treasures captured outside Europe by undisguised looting, enslavement, and murder, floated back to the mother-country and were turned into capital. . . . As a matter of fact, the methods of primitive accumulation are anything but idyllic. . . . In actual history it is notorious that conquest, enslavement, robbery, murder, briefly force, play the great part. . . . In fact, the veiled slavery of the wage workers in Europe needed, for its pedestal, slavery pure and simple in the new world. . . . Capital comes [into the world] dripping from head to foot, from every pore, with blood and dirt.
—Karl Marx, *Capital* (1867)

1. Expansion, Direction, and Composition of International Trade in the Eighteenth Century

International trade expanded significantly and rapidly during the eighteenth century. Moreover, it changed in direction, composition, and structure. The slave trade and the triangular trade between Europe, Africa, and the Americas assumed particular importance; and the oriental trade underwent qualitative changes twice during the century. This international trade and the high profits derived from it made an important contribution to the process of capital accumulation in northwestern Europe, particularly England, and northeastern America; and the rapid growth of manufacturing exports significantly facilitated and furthered the development of industry and the Industrial Revolution. Trade and war were intimately—and reciprocally—related to each other and to the process of capital accumulation and economic development as a whole.

These aspects of international trade in the eighteenth century may be examined in turn.

In Britain domestically produced exports increased fivefold during the eighteenth century, compared to a threefold increase of national income. As a percentage of national income, domestic exports rose from 5–6 percent in 1688, to 9–11 percent in 1700–1750; and reached 14 percent by the end of the eighteenth century (Deane and Cole 1967: 28–29). British exports doubled between 1720 and 1760, and again between 1760 and 1795 (Heaton 1967: 36). This expansion of British exports, at first slow and then faster, is further reflected in the three-year moving average of British exports (apparently including re-exports). In 1701, this average was £6 million; it gradually increased to £9 million in 1741. After 1741, this increase accelerated to £13 million in 1751, £16 million in 1771, £21 million in 1791, and £36 million in 1801 (Deane 1967: 86). Over this same period (1701–1801), British imports increased from £5 million to £29 million. Thus throughout the eighteenth century, Britain maintained an almost constant export surplus (Heaton 1967: 86). The exports and trade of France, the other large trading nation, increased even faster than those of Britain, by five times from 1715 to 1789 (the French Antilles' exports increased eight times between 1716 to 1787) so that in 1789 they were even greater than those of Britain absolutely, though they remained smaller relative to France's much larger population (Deane 1967: 36; Vilar 1969: 313).

British foreign trade, and international trade generally, underwent a significant and substantial redirection from Europe to the rest of the world, that is, Asia, Africa, and in particular the Americas, during the first seven decades of the eighteenth century. This redirection was associated with a change in the commodity composition of British foreign trade: the export of woollen manufactures was increasingly matched by that of an ever wider variety of other manufactures; and among British imports, manufactures lost and foodstuffs correspondingly gained in relative importance. These and other changes are summarized in the accompanying Tables 6.1 and 6.2.

The growth of commercial ties between Britain and the colonial world of Asia, Africa, and the Americas—and the further integration of the colonial world into the process of world capital

Table 6.1
British Foreign Trade, 1700–1773
Changes in Direction and Composition
(in percentages)*

	1700[a]		1773[a]	
	Total[b]	To Asia, Africa, & the Americas	Total[b]	To Asia, Africa, & the Americas
Total Exports	100	15	100	38
Domestic exports	69	10	63	31
Woollen manufactures	47	4	27	8
Other manufactures	8	5	27	21
Food & raw materials	13	1	9	1
Re-exports	31	5	37	7
Total Imports	100	32	100	53
Manufactures	32	9	17	6
Raw materials	35	4	32	7
Food	34	18	51	39

SOURCE: R. Davis, in Minchinton 1969: 109.
[a] 1700 means 1699–1701 average; 1773 means 1772–1774 average.
[b] Differences between "Total" and "To Asia, Africa, & the Americas" columns represent trade with Europe, including Ireland and Turkey.
* In interpreting this table, it should be noted that some countries in Europe, notably Spain and Portugal, in turn re-exported to their colonies in Latin America a significant proportion of their imports from Britain. Hence the real share of Asia, Africa, and the Americas in Britain's exports was higher than that indicated. For example, about 10 percent of Britain's exports and 20 percent of manufacturing exports went to Portugal alone, and much of this went from there to Brazil (Fisher 1971: 126; see also Chapter 3, section 2 of this volume).

accumulation—is reflected in Table 6.1 by the increase from 10 percent to 31 percent of domestically produced exports and from 15 percent to 38 percent of total British exports absorbed by these regions of the colonial world. This represents a significant relative re-direction of British foreign trade away from Europe and toward the rest of the world; and, since total exports more than tripled over this period, it reflects a still more substantial increase in the absolute quantity of British exports taken by these colonies.

Furthermore, among domestically produced exports, manufac-

Table 6.2
British Foreign Trade in the Eighteenth Century
by Major World Regions
(in percentages of total in each year)

	1700/1	1750/1	1772/3	1797/8[a]
Domestic Exports to:				
Europe[b]	85	77	49	30
North America	6	11	25	32
West Indies	5	5	12	25
East Indies & Africa	4	7	14	13
Re-exports to:				
Europe[b]	85	79	82	88
North America	5	11	9	3
West Indies	5	4	3	4
East Indies & Africa	4	5	6	4
Imports from:				
Europe[b]	66	55	45	43
North America	6	11	12	7
West Indies	14	19	25	25
East Indies & Africa	14	15	18	25

SOURCE: Deane 1965: 56; for details see Deane and Cole 1967: Table 22.
[a] 1797/8 percentages are for Great Britain; 1700–1773 percentages are for England and Wales.
[b] Europe includes Spain and Portugal, a share of whose imports from Britain went on to their colonies in America and a larger share whose exports to Britain came from those colonies.

tures other than woollens increased their share of total British exports from 8 percent to 27 percent. and from 5 percent to 21 percent of the exports to the colonial world. This change reflected the growing production and export of "nails, axes, firearms, buckets, coaches, clocks, saddles, handkerchiefs, buttons, cordage and a thousand other things; a variety of goods becoming so wide that the compilers of Customs records tired of further extending their long schedules of commodities and lumped an increasing proportion of these exports under the heading 'Goods, several sorts' " (R. Davis 1969: 106).

The bulk of these growing exports went to the West Indies and, after mid century, increasingly to North America. The exports to the

West Indies rose from £205,000 in 1700 to £450,000 in 1750 and to £1,168,000 in 1772; and those to North America from £256,000 in 1700 to £970,000 in 1750 and to £2,460,000 in 1772—out of a total of £4,461,000 in 1700 and £9,739,000 in 1772 (Deane and Cole 1967: 87). Davis summarizes:

> All this time, at England's doorstep there lived a population of 200,000,000 Europeans (as compared with 3,000,000 Americans across the Atlantic). They were England's traditional customers, and until recently their only ones. Yet it was only the old woollen industry that seriously carried on—as it had always done—the "hard sell" on the continent; the newer industries cut their teeth on easier, privileged markets, mostly far away. (R. Davis 1969: 117)

During the final decades of the century, this was even more the case, particularly of the new cotton textiles industry, so that by the end of the eighteenth century, only one-fifth of Britain's exports went to Europe and four-fifths went to the rest of the world (Deane and Cole 1967: 86). In other words, as European (especially French) economic rivalry and political-military opposition increasingly closed the European market to British exports and manufactures, the colonial world and North America were persuaded or obliged to fill—and overfill—the gap.

British imports (i.e., other countries' exports to Britain) also underwent significant modifications during the first seven decades of the eighteenth century, and still more important ones during the last three decades. British imports of manufactures from Europe, except for oriental textiles, experienced a decline from 32 percent to 17 percent of total imports (see Table 6.1). They were increasingly replaced by raw materials, especially iron and timber but also wool, imported from Southern Europe and especially from the Baltic region, which tended to replace northwestern Europe as Britain's European trading partner. This tendency reflected British manufacturing rivalry, especially with France, as well as its manufacturing development, which already in the eighteenth century was partly dependent on the import of raw materials. In trade with the world as a whole, however, the share of raw materials in Britain's import bill remained at roughly one-third until 1773, and did not increase significantly until the advent of the cotton industry, which was entirely dependent on imported raw materials. Up until 1773, the declining relative share of manufacturing imports was replaced by the absolute and relative increase in the import of foodstuffs, largely from the colonial regions, which rose from 34 percent to 51 percent of total imports (see Table 6.1). For agricultural and continental France, the other major European trading country of the eighteenth century, this trend was probably less marked. The major trading nation of the eighteenth century, Holland, maintained the absolute quantity of its exports during the eighteenth century, and hence fell increasingly behind in its relative share.

A further feature of this expansion of international trade and British exports was that at the end of the eighteenth century and again during the third quarter of the eighteenth century British re-exports of goods, previously imported primarily from the colonial regions, increased more than domestically produced exports (and therefore more than total exports). Thus, the share of re-exports in total exports rose from 31 percent in 1700 to 37 percent in 1773 (see Table 6.1). Of these re-exports, only about one-sixth were reshipped to the colonial areas, and the remainder were sold in Europe. The already significant British export surplus to Europe in the eighteenth century was further increased by these re-exports and was used to finance, through multilateral settlements, Britain's deficit with the rest of the world, a deficit that was principally incurred by excessive imports from the Baltic region and India (Saul 1960: 5). Deane (1965: 58) estimates that between one-half and three-quarters of the final value of the re-exports accrued to the original producers in their countries of origin, but that means that one-quarter to one-half of the same accrued to the British, without counting the profits remitted to Britain by those original producers. The original producers in the colonial areas therefore made a not unimportant contribution to British capital accumulation through their supply of re-exported goods, quite apart from their contribution through multilateral settlements to the process of capital accumulation as a whole.

2. Triangular and Slave Trades

The fivefold expansion of trade during the eighteenth century commercial revolution turned on the axis of the so-called triangular trade, and this, in turn, turned on the axis of the slave trade. The pattern of this multilateral trade and settlements system of the eighteenth century is illustrated by the accompanying diagram, but it was in fact very much more complex than this diagram suggests. A classic summary of the triangular trade can be found in Eric Williams' *Capitalism and Slavery:*

> In this triangular trade England—France and Colonial America equally—supplied the exports and the ships; Africa the human merchandize; the plantations the colonial raw materials. The slave ships sailed from the home country with a cargo of manufactured goods. These were exchanged at a profit on the coast of Africa for Negroes, who were traded on the plantations, at another profit, in exchange for a cargo of colonial produce to be taken back to the home country. As the volume of trade increased, the triangular trade was supplemented, but never supplanted, by a direct trade between home country and the West Indies, exchanging home manufactures directly for colonial produce. (E. Williams 1966: 51–52)

The kingpin in the triangle of European manufactures, African labor, and American colonial produce was the supply, transport, sale, exploitation, and replacement of the black slaves, whose work ultimately supported the entire system. The most widely cited estimates of the number of African slaves imported into the Americas are 900,000 in the sixteenth century, 2.75 million in the seventeenth century, 7 million in the eighteenth century, and 4 million in the nineteenth century (Fage 1962: 83; Sheridan 1969: 13). Philip Curtin's estimate for the eighteenth century is 5.5 million (Bohannon and Curtin 1971: 269).* The number of Africans who were forced to leave their homes in the course of this trade was much higher, since it is often estimated that half of them died in the slave wars or during their transport to and confinement at the African coast, and another half of the remaining ones died on the "middle passage" across the Atlantic. The total number of Africans so affected by the slave trade has been estimated, perhaps exaggeratedly, at as high as 100 million. The trade, which was initially in Portuguese and Dutch hands, passed increasingly into the hands of the French and British, especially after the 1713 grant of *asiento* to England. By

---

* The complete recent and lower estimates in Curtin (1969) were not available to the writer at the time of writing.

Multilateral Trade in the Eighteenth Century

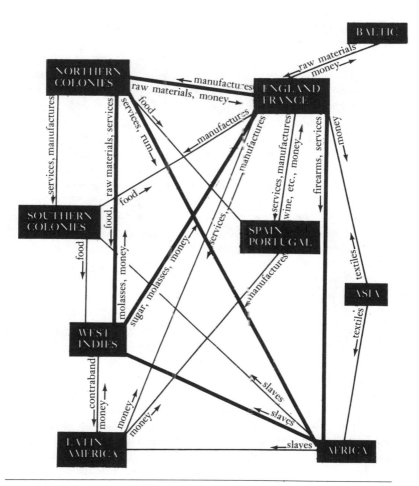

LEGEND:
Manufactures: especially textiles, not necessarily self-produced or consumed
Food: including tobacco and fish
Services: especially shipping
Money: in coin, bullion, and drafts
Raw materials: especially timber and other naval stores, and iron (from Baltic)
SOURCE: adapted from Mauro (1961).

all accounts, the slave trade was the most profitable business of the eighteenth century.

The slaves were purchased on the coast of Africa (see Chapter 3, section 4) by first European and then increasingly also North American traders who paid primarily with firearms and rum, both of which were essential instruments of the intra-African slave business, and secondarily with cotton textiles (provided by Asia) and trinkets. In the Americas, the slaves were sold to planters or miners for their products, sugar and its derivatives especially, but also gold and silver coin and bullion or letters of credit on London, Liverpool, Bordeaux, Nantes, Boston, etc. The American products were sold in Europe, which in turn exported its manufactures (and re-exports derived from Asia) to the colonies throughout the Americas. Only the West Indies, and to some extent the southern plantation colonies of North America, could pay for their manufacturing imports through production of exportable nonmonetary commodities, even though these were produced by alien labor and the import of this labor absorbed the major part of their import capacity. The Latin American mining colonies of Spain and Portugal, of course, paid for most of their imports with the money they mined. Much of this money reached northeastern Europe through Spain and Portugal, who remitted it to settle their own merchandize trade deficits. The Asian and Baltic regions, on the other hand, maintained a merchandize trade surplus with northeastern Europe, much of which was in turn settled by the shipment of money to them.

New England and the Middle Atlantic colonies of North America were in a special intermediary position, which had an important bearing on the course of their future development (see Chapter 5, section 5). They both engaged in and profited from the slave trade as well as their own triangular trade among Africa, the West Indies, and America.

The oriental trade, which in a sense had been the prime cause of all these developments in the fifteenth and sixteenth centuries and which had declined in importance during the seventeenth-century depression, revived during the eighteenth century, but on new bases. The ancient spice trade with the East Indies, particularly the Dutch islands of Indonesia, continued. During the eighteenth century, the spice trade was supplemented by sugar, cotton, and especially coffee, all of which were grown in the islands on Dutch command, often with the specialization of one island–one crop, either by local growers or Dutch plantations. In the last decades of the eighteenth century, the Dutch East India Company ran into increasing economic difficulties at home and in Java; and these difficulties were further aggravated by domestic and international political problems at home and by the British threat in Batavia, which the British ultimately conquered. The Manila Galleon trade from China through the Philippines to Mexico and Spain also revived and attained a scope beyond that of earlier times. But the most important development occurred in the trade in oriental textiles, particularly from India but also from China, for sale in Europe and for re-export to Africa and the Americas (and, in the case of Britain, for re-export to the European continent). The essentials of this trade—with India until about 1760 and with China on into the nineteenth century—may be gleaned from the letter from the emperor of China, Ch'ien Lung, saying that country possessed all things (quoted on p. 160 above) and from the comments of Voltaire, who incidentally was a great admirer of China but also of slave colonies;

> People ask what becomes of all the gold and silver which is continually flowing into Spain from Peru and Mexico It goes into the pockets of Frenchmen and Englishmen and Dutchmen, who carry on trade in Cadiz, and in return send the products of their industries to America. A large part of the money goes to the East Indies and pays for silk, spices, saltpetre, sugar-candy, tea, textiles, diamonds, and curios. (Quoted in Stavrianos 1966a: 169)

Between 1733 and 1766, 65 percent of all English exports to Asia was silver (Vilar 1969: 343), required to pay for Asian exports. This mercantile inconvenience was not remedied until the political power which Clive acquired for the East India Company at the Battle of Plassey in 1757 and in subsequent conquests increasingly permitted the unilateral transfer of Indian production through simple pillage. The British could then also "afford" to accelerate this transfer up to a much higher annual rate. In this way, reminiscent of the Spaniard's plunder of sixteenth-century America, was initiated the "drain" of India and its real incorporation into the process of world capital accumulation, to the acceleration of which India thus contributed significantly (see Chapter 4, especially section 8).

3. *Do Colonies Pay? War and Accumulation*

In connection with several stages of the process of capital accumulation, the question has often been put: "Do colonies pay?" Adam Smith is frequently cited (see, for instance, Thomas 1968: 32) in support of the thesis that they do not. But Smith's argument was principally directed against *monopoly* trade with the colonies, and he insisted that a distinction be drawn between the effects of the colonial trade and the effects of the monopoly of that trade: "The former are always and necessarily beneficial; the latter are always and necessarily hurtful" (Smith 1937: 573). The main thrust of Smith's whole work was, after all, against monopoly. Although he complained about the military expenses of defending the British colonies against France and, to a lesser extent, the administrative expenses of the colonies, for which the colonists themselves were loath to contribute taxes (Smith was writing just as the North American colonies were going to war against "taxation without representation"), nevertheless he devoted long pages to detailing the advantages Europe had derived from the colonial trade (see Smith 1937, chapter "On Colonies"). Yet R. P. Thomas seeks Smith's authority in arguing against R. B. Sheridan and others:

> R. B. Sheridan maintains that the British West Indies made a substantial contribution to the economic development of Great Britain before the end of the eighteenth century. A careful examination of the evidence presented by Sheridan does not support his contention. . . . The possession of the West Indies actually had the effect of retarding the growth of Great Britain. . . . The income of Englishmen would have been at least £500,000 higher in the absence of the West Indies from the Empire. . . . Suppose the West Indies did not belong to the empire and the capital actually invested there had been invested instead in England. What would this amount of capital have earned under this hypothetical alternative?. . . For the year 1773 the income of Englishmen would have been at least £631,750 higher had the West Indies not been part of the empire. It appears from the preceding that Adam Smith was correct. (Thomas 1968: 30, 39)

Sheridan, in his reply to Thomas, disputes his calculations, and points to the fundamental flaw in his argument:

> R. P. Thomas is, in effect, speculating about what would have happened in the event that something else had happened which could not

have happened. . . . Rather than the hypothetical alternative posed by R. P. Thomas, a more fruitful question is whether or not Great Britain would have had sufficient base for her Industrial Revolution in the absence of tropical colonies. . . . Colonial development contributed much to the English "take-off." (Sheridan 1968: 60–61)

In any case, the Industrial Revolution and colonial development were historically quite inseparable.

The exact extent of the contribution that the colonial trade made to the commercial revolution of the eighteenth century will never be known, and it is impossible to calculate the size of the contribution of the colonial trade and the commercial revolution to the process of capital accumulation, industrial revolution, and economic development. But, perhaps more important than how much, is the question of how, directly and indirectly, international and especially colonial trade contributed to this process of accumulation, transformation, and development. Thus, despite his opposition to the mercantilist system, Adam Smith himself was not blind to all the facts. He noted that the "profits of a sugar-plantation in any of our West Indian colonies are generally much greater than those of any other cultivation that is known either in Europe or America" (Smith 1937: 366).

In 1798 the prime minister of England, William Pitt, assessed the annual income from the West Indian plantations alone at £4 million, as compared with £1 million from the rest of the world. E. Williams (1966: 53) writes: "According to Davenant, Britain's total trade at the end of the seventeenth century brought in a profit of £2,000,000. The plantation trade accounted for £600,000; re-export of plantation goods £120,000; European, African and Levant trade £600,000; East India trade £500,00; re-export of East India goods £180,000." Ernest Mandel expands on this account, in an effort "to estimate the most important amounts of this direct robbery slave trade and 'normal' trade between 1500 and 1750":

a) E. J. Hamilton estimates in 500 million gold pesos the value of the gold and silver that the Spaniards took to Europe between 1503 and 1660.
b) Colenbrander calculates 600 million gold florins for the treasure that the Dutch East India Company took out of Indonesia between 1650 and 1780.
c) Father Rinchon estimates as almost 500 million gold florins the profit on only the slave trade of French capital during the eighteenth century,

without counting the profit obtained from the *work* of the slaves in the plantations of the West Indies, which was several times this amount.

d) According to H. Wiseman and the *Cambridge History of the British Empire*, it is considered that the earnings obtained with the work of the slaves in the British West Indies were at least some 200 to 300 million gold pounds.

e) Finally, in the pillage of India in the period of 1750 to 1800 only, the ruling class in Great Britain obtained between 100 and 150 million gold pounds.* If these sums are added up, we get more than 1,000 million gold pounds, that is, more than the value of all of the capital invested in all of the steam-operated industry of Europe around the year 1800. (Mandel 1968: 119–20)

Mandel does not suggest, nor does anyone else, that all of this capital flowed directly into European industry or industrialization. However, Marx, recalling that "Liverpool waxed fat on the slave trade . . . its method of primitive accumulation" and that "the cotton industry introduced child-slavery in England," observed that "in fact, the veiled slavery of the wage workers in Europe needed, for its pedestal, slavery pure and simple in the new world" (Marx 1954, I: 759–60).

The argument has been made, however, that international trade played a minimal role in the process of capital accumulation. R. M. Hartwell, in his introduction to a volume on *The Causes of the Industrial Revolution in England*, states:

On capital accumulation, the crucial fact is that there was at no time in the eighteenth century a marked rise in the rate of investment out of national income. Foreign trade, although expanding, absorbed insufficient a proportion of national output to have been more than a contributing factor to growth. . . . P. Deane and W. A. Cole reckon that net capital formation was about 5 percent of the national income in 1688, no more than 6 percent in 1780, and perhaps 7 percent in 1800. (Hartwell 1967: 17)

Hartwell correctly cites the figures of Deane and Cole, although Deane also comments that nowhere is there "evidence for a disproportionate increase in the rate of national investment in the first three decades of the nineteenth century" (Deane 1965: 154; see also Deane

---

* It must be noted that these sums omit such significant major capital flows as those represented by Spanish American silver and Brazilian gold *after* 1660, the British, Dutch, Portuguese, and North American slave trade, etc.

and Cole 1967: 304–5). Deane and Cole recognize that there was "a slow acceleration of industrial growth beginning in the 1740's and reaching a crescendo in the last two or three decades [of the eighteenth century]" (Deane and Cole 1967: 304), but Hartwell concludes that P. Deane and W. A. Cole, however, reject increasing international trade as the promoter of growth, and find rather that agricultural change and population growth play the vital roles in the "mechanics of eighteenth-century growth" (Hartwell 1967: 63).

Phyllis Deane herself, however, writes elsewhere:

> In sum, and in conclusion, the six main ways in which foreign trade can be said to have helped to precipitate the first industrial revolution are listed below: (1) First of all it created a demand for the products of British industry. . . . Specialization, as Adam Smith recognized in the 1770's, depends on the extent of the market; without specialization it is not possible to obtain the economies of scale and experience which can lower costs and prices sufficiently to bring a product within the reach of the mass of the population. This is the vicious circle of a closed economy. . . . It was access to a world market that broke this vicious circle for Britain. (2) International trade gave access to raw materials which both widened the range and cheapened the products of British industry. Without access to raw cotton Britain could not have shifted from dependence on an industry with a relatively inelastic demand (wool) to a technologically similar industry with a relatively elastic demand (cotton). Unless they had been able to import Swedish bar-iron, Sheffield cutlers could never have built up the trade in quality steel which survived into the period when British bar-iron became good enough to serve their purpose. (3) International trade provided poor, underdeveloped countries with the purchasing power to buy British goods. . . . (4) It provided an economic surplus which helped finance industrial expansion and agricultural improvement. The profits of trade overflowed into agriculture, mining and manufacture. Without them the innovators would have found it difficult to convert the new ideas and rotations and machines into productive enterprise. . . . (5) It also helped to create an institutional structure and a business ethic which was to prove almost as effective in promoting the home-trade as it had been for the foreign trade. The elaborate network of commercial institutions in the city. . . . The systems of orderly marketing, insurance, quality-control and standardization of product which grew up out of the needs of foreign trade were important aids to improving productivity at home. . . . (6) Finally, it is worth noting that the expansion of international trade in the eighteenth century was a prime cause of the growth of large towns and industrial centers. . . . the spectacular expansion of Liverpool and Glasgow was almost entirely a function of foreign trade. (Deane 1965: 66–68)

And in the chapter entitled "In Retrospect: A Summary of Conclusions" of the same book cited by Hartwell, Deane and Cole themselves state:

> Throughout the past two and a half centuries international trade has been a strategic factor in British economic growth. Overseas markets gave an outlet to industries which would have operated far less efficiently within the confines of domestic demand: imported raw materials provided bases for innovation and specialisation: foreign investment offered profitable employment to capital which found home prospects unattractive. . . . It is not too much to say that the foreign-trade sector was setting the pace for British economic growth. . . . Even in the eighteenth century when the absolute weight in the pre-industrial economy of her transactions with the rest of the world was less than half of what it has generally been in the industrialised economy of the past hundred years, it is probable that about a third of British industrial output was exported. The profits earned by the merchants carrying trade between the Americas, the Far East and Europe were a source of finance for investors in British agriculture and industry. The existence of exploitable international markets at the end of the eighteenth and beginning of the nineteenth centuries was probably crucial in initiating the process of industrialisation and the growth in real incomes which was associated with it. (Deane and Cole 1967: 309–12)

Finally, on the very pages that Hartwell cites to advance his conclusion, Deane and Cole write:

> There can, of course, be no doubt of the central importance of overseas trade in the expansion of the economy during this period. . . . it is clear that the major export industries, and those domestic industries which supplied them with some of their raw materials, such as coal-mining and soap-making, enjoyed higher rates of growth than most other branches of economic activity. This does not necessarily mean that the quickening tempo of economic expansion in the second half of the eighteenth century can be directly attributed to the accelerated growth of foreign trade during that period. Indeed, examination of the evidence suggests that, if there was a causal relationship between the growth of foreign trade and the growth of national income, it was of a more complex character and operated in a different direction than has usually been supposed. We shall argue here that the expansion of the British export trade was limited by the purchasing power of Britain's customers, and that this in its turn was limited by what they could earn from exports to Britain. (Deane and Cole 1967: 83)

To this may be added two observations. First, the relationship between Britain's export trade and the purchasing power of Britain's customers was always true. Moreover, the earnings of Britain's customers were augmented by multilaterally settled *world* trade, as Benjamin Franklin, for instance, explained. Second, the relationship between trade and income is not as crucial for the process of capital accumulation and development as that between either trade or income and *investment*. Deane and Cole continue:

> An outstanding feature of British trade during the eighteenth century was its increasing reliance on colonial markets. In 1700, over four-fifths of English exports went to Europe and only a fifth to the rest of the world. By the end of the century, on the other hand, this relationship was almost exactly reversed. Even in absolute terms, British goods made little headway in the protected markets of her European rivals. . . . Hence the increase in British exports in the course of the century was almost entirely due to the expansion of trade with the new, colonial markets in Ireland, America, Africa and the Far East. The most important of these markets from the standpoint of the British manufacturer were North America and the West Indies. (Deane and Cole 1967: 86)

For the process of world capital accumulation, the standpoint of the British manufacturer turned out to be most important. Like the British manufacturer, such analysts of this process as Adam Smith, Friedrich List, and Karl Marx have made the same connection between the expansion of colonial trade and the development of British industry. As already noted, Smith observed that even before 1776, there were "new divisions of labour and improvements of art, which in the narrow circle of ancient commerce, could never have taken place for want of a market to take off the greater part of their produce." He added that Britain had become "the manufacturers for the numerous and thriving cultivators of America and the carriers, and in some respects the manufacturers too, for almost all the different nations of Asia, Africa and America" (Smith 1937: 416, 591).

Friedrich List (1856: 114–20) commented favorably on the success of British commercial policy, as he summarized it, "to buy raw materials and sell manufactured products." Karl Marx noted in *Capital* that "the colonies secured a market for the budding manufactures, and, through the monopoly of the market, an increased accumulation. The treasures captured outside Europe by undisguised looting, enslavement, and murder, floated back to the mother-country and were there turned into capital" (Marx 1954, I: 753–54).

But perhaps the most forceful argument has been made by Eric

Williams, now prime minister of Trinidad and Tobago, in his
Capitalism and Slavery.

The triangular trade thereby gave a triple stimulus to British industry.
The Negroes were purchased with British manufactures; transported to
the plantations, they produced sugar, cotton indigo, molasses and other
tropical products, the processing of which created new industries in
England; while the maintenance of the Negroes and their owners on the
plantations provided another market for British industry, New England agriculture and Newfoundland fisheries. By 1750 there was hardly
a trading or manufacturing town in England which was not in some
way connected with the triangular or direct colonial trade. The profits
obtained provided one of the main streams of that accumulation of
capital in England which financed the Industrial Revolution. . . . This
external trade naturally drew in its wake a tremendous development of
shipping and shipbuilding. Not the least of the advantages of the
triangular trade was its contribution to the wooden walls of England. . . . The development of the triangular trade and shipping and
shipbuilding led to the growth of the great seaport towns. Bristol,
Liverpool and Glasgow occupied, as seaports and trading centers, the
position in the age of trade that Manchester, Birmingham and Sheffield
occupied later in the age of industry. . . . It was the slave and sugar
trades which made Bristol the second city of England for the first
three-quarters of the eighteenth century. . . . When Bristol was out-
stripped in the slave trade by Liverpool, it turned its attention from the
triangular trade to the direct sugar trade. Fewer Bristol ships sailed to
Africa, more went direct to the Caribbean. . . . What the West Indian
trade did for Bristol the slave trade did for Liverpool. . . . The shipping entering Liverpool increased four and a half times between 1709
and 1771; the outward tonnage to six and a half times. The number of
ships owned by the port multiplied four times during the same period,
the tonnage and sailors over six times. . . . It was estimated in 1790
that the 138 ships which sailed from Liverpool for Africa represented a
capital of over a million pounds. . . . Not until the Act of Union of
1707 was Scotland allowed to participate in colonial trade. That permission put Glasgow on the map. Sugar and tobacco underlay the prosperity of the town in the eighteenth century. Colonial commerce stimulated the growth of new industries. . . . It is necessary now to trace
the industrial development in England which was stimulated directly or
indirectly by the goods for the triangular trade and the processing of
colonial produce. . . . wool was the spoiled child of English manufactures. . . . The cargo of a slave ship was incomplete without some
woollen manufactures. . . . But cotton later superseded wool in colonial
markets. . . . What the building of ships for the transport of slaves did
for eighteenth century Liverpool, the manufacture of cotton goods for

the purchase of slaves did for eighteenth century Manchester. The first major stimulus to the growth of Cottonpolis came from the African and West Indian markets. The growth of Manchester was intimately associated with the growth of Liverpool, its outlet to the sea and the world market. The capital accumulated by Liverpool from the slave trade poured into the hinterland to fertilize the energies of Manchester; Manchester goods for Africa were taken to the coast in Liverpool slave vessels. Lancashire's foreign market meant chiefly the West Indian plantations and Africa. The export trade was £14,000 in 1739; in 1759 it had increased nearly eight times; in 1779 t was £303,000. Up to 1770 one-third of this export went to the slave coast, one-half to the American and West Indian colonies. It was this tremendous dependence on the triangular trade that made Manchester. . . . Manchester received a double stimulus from the colonial trade. If it supplied the goods needed on the slave coast and on the plantations, its manufactures depended in turn on the supply of the raw material. Manchester's interest in the islands was twofold. The raw material came to England in the seventeenth and eighteenth centuries chiefly from two sources, the Levant and the West Indies. . . . But in the early eighteenth century England depended on the West Indian islands for between two-thirds and three-quarters of its raw cotton. . . . Sugar refining. . . . Rum distillation. . . . Pacotille. . . . The Metallurgic Industries. . . . Guns formed a regular part of every African cargo. Birmingham became the center of the gun trade as Manchester was of the cotton trade. . . . Along with iron went brass, copper, lead. . . . The needs of shipbuilding gave a further stimulus to heavy industry. (E. Williams 1966: 52, 57, 60–61, 64, 68, 70–73, 78, 81–84)

Another side of the question is posed by David Landes, in his essay devoted to "Technological Change and Industrial Development in Western Europe, 1750–1914," in the *Cambridge Economic History of Europe*, specifically: "How much of the increase in demand and the trend toward mass production of cheaper articles is to be attributed to the expansion of home as against foreign markets is probably impossible to say." His answer is rather equivocal:

One may perhaps attempt this kind of comparison for the wool industry: at the end of the seventeenth century English exports of wool cloth probably accounted for upwards of 30 per cent of the output of the industry; by 1740, the proportion had apparently risen, possibly to over half, and in 1771-2, something under a half. In this important branch, then, the major impetus seems to have come from the export trade, and the most active exporting area in the industry. . . . Yet the answer is not so simple. (Landes 1966: 287–88)

But later Landes continues:

> The commercial frontier of Britain lay overseas—in America, Africa, south and east Asia. The first was by far the most important: the West Indies and mainland colonies together bought 10 per cent of English domestic exports in 1700–1, 37 percent in 1772–3, about 57 percent in 1797–8. Wool had played a big part in these gains: the sale of cloth in the new Atlantic market (America and Africa) grew sixfold from the beginning of the century to the eve of the American Revolution. Now it was cotton's turn. (Landes 1966: 313–14)

Thus, as Deane and Cole also note and even Hartwell recognizes, to understand the contribution or relation of this international and colonial trade to the process of world capital accumulation we must go beyond the statistical correlations between growth of trade and growth of income, beyond even the relationship between the growth of trade and the growth of industry in general, and inquire into the role of particular parts of this trade. This means an examination of particular colonies—their productive forces and their relations of production—and their contribution to the development of particular industries at particular historical junctures and places. The important role of the expansion of world trade during the commercial revolution of the eighteenth century in creating the conditions for the Industrial Revolution at the end of that century has also been observed by, among others, J. L. and Barbara Hammond (*The Rise of Modern Industry*), Paul Mantoux (*The Industrial Revolution in the Eighteenth Century*), and Arnold Toynbee (*The Industrial Revolution*). But perhaps the most important recent research into the issue is Deane and Cole, *British Economic Growth 1688–1959*. Their findings are summarized in Table 6.3.

On the basis of these and other data Christian Palloix concludes:

> One of the fundamental lessons to be drawn from these facts is the marked acceleration of the growth rates from 1780 to 1800—4.6% for exports, 2.1% for national product—at a time when 70% of British exports went to the third world, here defined as the territories that were politically and economically dominated. . . . We may note . . . the particularly high annual rates of growth in the period 1780–1800 for cotton textiles (14.1%), iron and steel (5.1%), and other metal working (5% on the average). Reliance only on the internal market, an agricultural market at the time, would not have allowed such a development of the productive forces. This constraint imposed by the internal market is shown in Table 3 [partially reproduced here in Table 6.3], where the

Table 6.3
Development of Export and Other Production
Compared, 1700–1800

Years	Export industries	Internal market industries	Agricultural production	National income
1700	100	100	100	100
1760	222	114	115	147
1780	246	123	126	167
1800	544	152	143	251

SOURCE: Deane and Cole 1967: 78.

growth rate of agricultural output . . . is effectively imposing strict limits on the growth rate of the industry that is oriented exclusively to this market. (Palloix 1969: 183)

The Industrial Revolution, first in Britain and later in other metropolitan countries, of course involved far-reaching transformations of the metropolitan economy, polity, society, and culture that are beyond the scope of this book. The associated technological revolution and innovation, which has received so much attention, cannot be realistically understood in isolation from this process of capital accumulation and market expansion. For as Eric Hobsbawm (1964a: 47) has pointed out: "Whatever the British advance was due to, it was not scientific and technological superiority." It is at least symbolic that, as Eric Williams recalls, 'it was the capital accumulated in the West Indian trade that financed James Watt and the steam engine. Boulton and Watt received advances from Lowe, Vere, Williams and Jennings." Williams adds that Boulton wrote Watt that "Lowe, Vere and Company may yet be saved, if ye West Indian fleet arrives safe from ye French fleet . . . as many of their securities depend on it" (E. Williams 1956: 102–3).

The authoritative *Cambridge Economic History of Europe* concludes:

The British case is the classic prototype of an industrial revolution based on overseas trade. . . . The growth of English commerce in the eighteenth century provided a large part of the accumulated wealth necessary to finance nascent industry in the last quarter of the century. The opportunity to buy raw materials and sell finished products in foreign markets vastly extended the range of economic opportunity to British industry. (*Cambridge Economic History of Europe* 1965, VI: 51)

The simultaneous importance of trade and war—or of trade war—in the eighteenth century is evident and undeniable. Questions may arise, therefore, about the possible relations, or even causative relations, between them. One may seek, with T. S. Ashton, "the answer to the question whether war increased or decreased economic activity in the nation" (1955: 64) and advanced or retarded the process of capital accumulation and development in the world as a whole. I agree with Ashton that "it admits of no simple answer."

> The gains and losses arising from war were distributed unevenly. Some industries and regions benefited from government orders while others suffered from a decline in civilian demand. Some prospered because of the protection from foreign competition afforded . . . others declined because of curtailment of imports of raw materials or of shrinkage of markets abroad. Enough has been said to indicate that war was an important cause of instability in eighteenth-century commerce. . . . To sum up: the wars of the eighteenth century led to the acquisition of new territories and new markets. They may have created employment for men who would otherwise have been idle or engaged in anti-social activities. They stimulated some branches or production and drew remote communities into the main currents of national life. It is possible to point to a few—very few—technical inventions to which they gave rise. On the other hand, they involved many losses in men and ships, and in intangible human qualities. If there had been no wars the English people would have been better fed, better clad, certainly better housed, than they were. War deflected energies from the course along which—so it seems in retrospect—the permanent interests of England lay. At this stage of development the chief need of the country was an efficient network of main roads and inland waterways; and, as will be seen, war tended to retard the creation of this. If England had enjoyed unbroken peace the Industrial Revolution might have come earlier. These assertions and conjectures will not today find universal acceptance. (Ashton 1955: 68, 83)

They certainly will not, nor should they!

To begin with, Ashton's analysis of the superficial relations between war and trade is equivocal, and the explicit and implicit conclusions that he derives from them are still more so. Although Ashton observes a varied and complex relation between the military and commercial ups and downs and although some periods of war coincided with some phases of general cyclical upswing, the dominant impression is one of coincidence between war and downswing. Ashton, as well as other writers, translates this coincidence into a unidirectional causation to the effect that war interrupts international trade and economic development of progress generally (see also John U. Nef [1963] for a more general argument on the relationship between war and progress). But one could equally well argue that the causation runs the other way: cyclical downswings help to generate or accentuate (the causes of) war, or at least of some kinds of war. This certainly seems to have been the case for the War of Jenkins' Ear/Austrian Succession and for the "Third" English-French war associated with the American Revolution, as well as for the Revolution itself. This cyclical downswing marked the defensive attempts to eliminate the opponent's competitive power, as opposed to the expansive and acquisitive aims of at least Britain in the Seven Years War, the beginning of which coincided with a cyclical upswing.

More important is Ashton's contention that war deflected energies from the course or direction in which England's permanent interests lay and that in their absence the Industrial Revolution would have come earlier. This implies a judgment of what these permanent interests comprised as well as what the necessary and sufficient conditions for the Industrial Revolution comprised. Ashton writes as though these could be summarized (or symbolized) by better domestic transportation facilities and higher domestic consumer incomes. This judgment may be challenged. Certainly it was by the leading statesmen of the time, such as Pitt in England and Choiseul in France. For each, the chief obstacle to national development was the economic and political power of the other; and therefore the chief political objective was the elimination or at least limitation of that power. In retrospect, this objective may be said to be more than just a short-term tactic. Rather it was consistent with the permanent interests of the sector of the ruling class represented by these ministers in their respective countries (against those of the "little Englanders" and the continental French), if Hobsbawm is correct in suggesting that "under pre-industrial conditions there was probably room for only one pioneer national industrialization (as it turned out the British), but not the simultaneous industrialization of several 'advanced economies,' consequently also—at least for some time—for only one 'workshop of the world' "(Hobsbawm 1969: 49n). I believe the evidence on the expansion of foreign trade confirms this argument even more strongly than it confirms the argument about the importance of the export relative to the home market. I thus agree with Hobsbawm when he adds:

> This brings us to the third factor [after domestic and export markets] in the genesis of the Industrial Revolution, *government* [or rather, the state]. Here the advantage of Britain over her potential competitors is quite evident. Unlike some of them (such as France) she was prepared to subordinate *all* foreign policy to economic ends. Her war aims were commercial and (what amounted to much the same thing) naval. (Hobsbawm 1969: 49) (Emphasis in the original)

Even if it is perhaps exaggerated to say *all* foreign policy was subordinated to economic ends, of the occasional replacement of the Pitts by Walpole and Bute, for example, the relative dominance of imperial interests in Britain and the relative advantage of Britain in imperial competition are evident. One might think that the integral role of war in imperial strategy and the process of world capital accumulation should be as evident today as it was then. Adam Smith recalled in 1776 that the last war [of Seven Years] was undertaken altogether on account of the colonies. . . . The Spanish war of 1739 was principally undertaken on their account . . . and in the French war that was a consequence of it . . . a great part of which ought justly be charged to the colonies" (Smith 1937: 899). (It is true that Smith supposed that the wars were also fought for the benefit of the colonists and that they should therefore justly be made to pay for some of the costs of these wars; but this does not diminish his testimony that war was fought on account of colonial trade and for commercial benefit.) And Romesh Dutt writes:

> "I am sure that I can save the country, and that no one else can." So spoke the great William Pitt, afterwards Lord Chatham, not boastfully, but with that consciousness of power, and that clear prevision of great events, which sometimes come to men inspired by a lofty mission. William Pitt more than redeemed his pledge. He directed the administration of his country from 1757 to 1761, and, singularly enough, these five years mark the rise of the modern British Empire. England's ally, Frederick the Great, won the battle of Rossbach in 1757, made Prussia,

and humbled France. Wolfe took Quebec in 1759, and the whole of Canada was conquered from the French in [1760]. Clive won the battle of Plassey in 1757, and Eyre Coote crushed the French power in India in 1761. Within five years England's greatness as a world power was assured; France was humbled in Europe and effaced in Asia and America. (Dutt 1970, I: 1)

Of course, although these years of the Seven Years War may have been decisive, they were not unique. They were, as we have seen, one in a series of such contests, and the French would again try to recoup their losses in the war against England associated with the American War of Independence and in Napoleon's conscious attempts in the wars that carry his name, after which France lacked the strength ever to try again.

The Hammonds write:

> The wars of economic nationalism, which succeeded to the wars of religion of the sixteenth century, have to be considered in two aspects. In the first place they determine which of the states of Europe should be the predominant power in parts of the world which had great economic importance; they decided between England, France and Holland as competitors for ascendancy in India and North America. In the second place the strain of these wars told more severely on industry and commerce in some countries than in others, and thus affected their relative material progress. In both these respects England [an island on whose territory no war was fought and whose navy and commerce were ultimately strengthened by this fact] gained at the expense of her neighbors. (Hammond and Hammond 1966: 38–39)

Hobsbawm agrees:

> British policy in the eighteenth century was one of systematic aggressiveness—most obviously against the chief rival, France. Of the five great wars of the period, Britain was clearly on the defensive in only one. The result of this century of intermittent warfare was the greatest triumph ever achieved by any state: the virtual monopoly among European powers of overseas colonies, and the virtual monopoly of world-wide naval power. (Hobsbawm 1969: 59-60)

The Hammonds conclude that "if the wars of the seventeenth and eighteenth centuries helped to determine the time, place, and course of Industrial Revolution, they were themselves effects, rather than the cause, of the changes that came over Western Europe between the discovery of the new world and the establishment of a series of independent American states (Hammond and Hammond 1966: 50).

Chapter 7

Conclusions: On So-Called Primitive Accumulation

I have not answered all the questions that my readers will pose themselves at the end of this excessively long trip that I have imposed on them. But in history the perfect book, the book that never again shall be written, does not exist. On the contrary, history is an ever changing interrogation of the past, inasmuch as it must adapt itself to the necessities and sometimes the anxieties of the present. History offers itself as a means for the knowledge of man and not as an end in itself. I do not know what, in this context, the reader will be able to get out of a book like this one; everyone has his own way of dialoging with a book. As for me, this Mediterranean, magnificent and charged with the ages of the sixteenth century, today buried in the world of shadows, has made me pass over many paths, pursuing many problems that are problems of today, and not of yesterday or the day before. . . .
—Fernand Braudel, *La Méditerranée et le Monde méditerranéen à l'Epoque de Philippe II*

The process of capital accumulation is a, if not the, principal motor of modern history and constitutes the central problem examined in this book. Yet capital accumulation, and its treatment here, poses a number of fundamental theoretical and therefore also empirical questions that remain largely unresolved. These questions fall into four related categories: (1) primitive, primary, and capitalist capital accumulation; (2) the unequal structure and relations of production, circulation, and realization in capital accumulation; (3) uneven transformation of capital accumulation through stages, cycles, and crises; and (4) unending class struggle in capital accumulation, through the state, war, and revolution. Insofar as one single and continuous process of capital accumulation has existed in this world for several centuries, this heuristic division of the problem into unequal structure, uneven process, and so on is necessarily arbitrary. The structural inequality and temporal unevenness of capital accumulation, on the other hand, are inherent to capitalism.

1. On Primitive, Primary, and Capitalist Accumulation

A major open question concerns the basis and modalities of capitalist accumulation of capital itself, and particularly the transition to this process through "so-called primitive accumulation"—as well as the transition again from capitalist to "socialist accumulation." Insofar as I argue that during the past few centuries the world has experienced a single, all-embracing, albeit unequal and uneven, process of capital accumulation that has been capitalist for at least two centuries, it is necessary to inquire how this process began, on what bases it developed, and to what extent it has undergone important changes.

Marx wrote, "employing surplus-value as capital, reconverting it into capital, is called accumulation of capital" (Marx 1954, I: 579). Marx broke down surplus value as follows: "The surplus-value reproduced by prolongation of the working-day, I call *absolute surplus-value*. On the other hand, the surplus-value arising from the curtailment of the necessary labour-time, and from the corresponding alteration in the respective lengths of the two components (necessary and unnecessary for reproduction) of the working-day, I call *relative surplus-value*" (1954, I: 315). Although absolute surplus value has certainly been important for accumulation, the most important recent capitalist accumulation, and Marx's analysis of it, has been based on the increasing production of relative surplus value. However, although Marx mentions it "only empirically"—in five lines as "one of the most important factors checking the tendency of the rate of profit to fall" (1962, III: 230) and in four pages as among the "circumstances that . . . determine the amount of accumulation" (1954, I: 599–602), he also wrote: "in the chapters on the production of surplus-value it was constantly pre-supposed that wages are at least equal to the value of labour-power. Forcible reduction of wages below this value plays, however, in practice too important a part, for us not to pause upon it for a moment. It, in fact, transforms, within certain limits, the labourer's necessary consumption-fund into a fund for the accumulation of capital" (1954, I: 599); and: "The part played in our days by the direct robbery from the labourer's necessary consumption-fund in the formation of surplus-value, and, therefore, of the accumulation of the accumulation-fund of capital, the so-called domestic [or putting-out] industry has served to show" (1954, I: 602). That is, capitalist accumulation of capital is also based on a superexploitation of labor power through excess-surplus value, which often—and not only in British domestic industry—denies the laborer even the minimum necessary for subsistence by any definition and which, at some times and places, prohibits even the reproduction of labor power. Moreover, this less-than-subsistence superexploitation occurs both through wage labor and through other relations of production, as well as through the connection between the two.

A related question refers to the kind or modality of capital accumulation. In one sense, capital accumulation is by definition "capitalist" and has been defined and analyzed by Marx and Marxists in terms of the creation of a free labor force through the separation of previous owners from their means of production, the production of absolute surplus value and (through technological innovation and increasing organic composition of capital) of relative surplus value, the reproduction of this cycle through the realization of surplus value and its application in new production and innovation, the concentration and centralization of capital, etc.—that is, in terms which define industrial capitalism and imperialism. But before this industrial capitalist process of capital accumulation became, and could become, self-sustaining, apparently around 1800, there was a long period of so-called primitive accumulation, *prior to* "capitalist" accumulation and importantly based on precapitalist relations of production and/or their transformation into capitalist ones. The meaning of this "so-called primitive accumulation" that occurred in the several centuries prior to 1800 bears further consideration. During this period of *previous*, prior (in German, *ursprüngliche*), original, precapitalist accumulation, in precapitalist times and based on precapitalist relations of production, these relations and the mode of production they formed were, in that sense, also noncapitalist. Accumulation, then, could not be said to have been directly based on surplus value, insofar as it was not produced by free wage laborers. Nonetheless, the value that the producers received was, in some sense, less than that which they produced, or no accumulation would have been possible. The consumption that producers were allowed may or may not have been equal to, greater than, or lesser than their needs for subsistence and the requirements for the reproduction of the productive force.

If precapitalist means previous to capitalist, then, by definition, it is also noncapitalist. If precapitalist means the beginning of capitalist, then it is part capitalist, part noncapitalist. But in either event, noncapitalist need not be precapitalist, since it can also be simultaneous with capitalist accumulation or even postcapitalist. Thus, insofar as primitive accumulation refers to accumulation on the basis of production with noncapitalist relations of production, it need not be prior to, but can also be contemporary with capitalist production and accumulation. Such noncapitalist production, and the accumulation based on it, may be called *primary* accumulation, to distinguish it from precapitalist primitive accumulation and production (Roger Bartra calls it permanent primitive accumulation). Such primary accumulation, based in part on production through noncapitalist relations of production, has been a frequent, if not constant, companion of the capitalist process of capital accumulation even in its developed stages of the dominance of wage labor and later of relative surplus value. Indeed, such primary accumulation has made a substantial, if not essential, contribution to capitalist accumulation of capital. Such primary accumulation of capital may or may not also imply superexploitation of the non-wage labor producer beyond his or her needs for minimum subsistence and reproduction. It implies superexploitation of wage labor insofar as its consumption fund and the reproduction of its labor power draws directly on this noncapitalist production.

Drawing on these conceptual distinctions, we may pose a series of further questions that arise out of our examination of the genesis, bases, and modalities of capital accumulation and especially of the "so-called primitive accumulation" that Marx discusses in Volume 1 of *Capital*. If this process of "so-called primitive accumulation" occurred in the three or more centuries prior to the capitalist process of capital accumulation that began with the Industrial Revolution, in what sense did it involve any accumulation of capital? In what sense was it "so-called primitive?" In what sense did it lead and/or contribute to the later capitalist process of accumulation? And in what way is the earlier process (or processes) similar to or different from the later process of capital accumulation?

Marx made the following argument about "the secret of primitive accumulation":

> But the accumulation of capital pre-supposes surplus-value; surplus value pre-supposes capitalistic production; capitalistic production pre-supposes the pre-existence of considerable masses of capital and of labour-power in the hands of producers of commodities. The whole movement, therefore, seems to turn in a vicious circle, out of which we can only get by supposing a primitive accumulation (previous accumulation of Adam Smith) preceding capitalist accumulation; an accumulation not the result of the capitalist mode of production, but its starting point. . . . The so-called primitive accumulation, therefore, is nothing else than the historical process of divorcing the producer from the means of production. It appears as primitive, because it forms the pre-historic stage of capital and of the mode of production corresponding with it. (Marx, 1954, I: 713–14)

But this formulation raises more questions than it answers. Two of these questions, to begin with, are: How does the *amassing* of considerable masses of capital take place, and what bearing on this has the process of divorcing the producers from their means of production? Marx himself argues that a considerable mass of the capital amassed in the prehistoric stage of capital before the Industrial Revolution was produced with relations of production that did not imply, require, or even permit the wage labor divorce of producers from their means of production. A variety of noncapitalist and precapitalist relations of production—colonial, slave, second serf, but also first serf and feudal—both inside and outside Europe and Western Europe, contributed to this amassing of capital before the Industrial Revolution.

Marx's rhetorical observation that "the veiled slavery of the wage-workers in Europe needed, for its pedestal, slavery pure and simple in the new world" and that "capital comes [into the world] dripping from head to foot from every pore, with blood and dirt" (1954, I: 759–60) suggests not only that these "noncapitalist" sources and relations of production were essential to capitalist accumulation of capital, but that they implied the forcible robbery of parts of these producers' consumption fund for the accumulation of capital. The seven "useful" years of a slave's life in many parts of the New World, the decline in Indian population in Mexico from 25 million to 1.5 million (and the rise in labor costs for mining) in little more than a century after the Conquest, not to mention the total decimation of the indigenous population of the Caribbean in half a century, the increased incidence and depth of famine in Bengal after its rape by the British, and many less massive failures of the population to reproduce itself after being incorporated into the process of capital accumulation, all testify to the superexploitative character of these relations of production, social formations, and the process of accumulation in its preindustrial stage.

Many of these same relations of production, and the production derived from them, continued to be and are still important for the capitalist process of capital accumulation An important question, for then and now, is exactly how production under noncapitalist relations of production contributed to or was transformed into capitalist accumulation, both previous to its beginning per se and simultaneously with it since. The insistence on the importance of these relations and the surplus value ultimately produced by them both previous to the Industrial Revolution and since (during the period of classical imperialism studied by Rosa Luxemburg and Lenin, for instance), does not, of course, deny the importance of the historical process of divorcing producers from their means of production and their transformation into wage earners. Indeed, this process underlay the development not only of capitalist relations of production, but part of the process of accumulation also, in that the producers' divorce from their instruments of production also contributed to the concentration of capital. Moreover, it may be argued that the divorce of many producers from their means of production in the Third World during the imperialist period and the denial of the minimum means of subsistence to either the resulting wage laborers or the remaining non-wage producers (obliging one to subsist with the support or at the expense of the other) or both, made a material contribution not only to the accumulation of capital but also to the elevation of the wage rate in metropolitan countries.*

Thus, the process of divorcing owners from their means of production and converting them into wage laborers was not only primitive, original, or previous to the capitalist stage, but also continued during the capitalist stage, as it still does. And so primary noncapitalist accumulation also continues, feeding into the capitalist process of capital accumulation. But the latter continues not simply because capitalist development of wage labor divorces producers from their means, but also *despite* this divorce through the maintenance and even re-creation of not strictly wage labor relations. The question of how and why this so-called primitive, nondivorcing, primary, noncapitalist accumulation has taken place and continues long after the Industrial Revolution is still the subject of considerable debate. But the problem of the relation and contribution of primary accumulation to capitalist accumulation of capital is similar to and brings us back to the question of the relation and contribution of primitive, precapitalist accumulation to capitalist accumulation itself: How do we escape from the vicious circle around the starting point of capitalist capital accumulation by supposing a primitive accumulation (previous accumulation) preceding capitalist accumulation? When, then, *was* the starting point of the capitalist mode of production? How did the precapitalist (and therefore noncapitalist) primitive original accumulation take place and amass capital, if there was no capitalist-expanded reproduction? And how did this previous accumulation fulfill a necessary, if not sufficient, condition for the starting point of capitalist accumulation of capital? Indeed, when was the starting point, not of capitalist accumulation, but of precapitalist accumulation that materially and economically contributed to real capitalist accumulation?

Marx seems to exclude the fourteenth- and fifteenth-century "beginnings of capitalist production" from the beginning of the "modern history of capital" which dates from "the creation in the sixteenth

---

* For estimates of unequal exchange, see Amin (1974) and for estimates of the underdeveloped countries' excess of merchandise exports over imports between 1880 and 1930, see Frank (1978, ch. 7, and in press).

century of a world-embracing commerce and a world-embracing market. . . . The colonies secured a market for the budding manufactures, and, through the monopoly of the market, an increasing accumulation. The treasures captured outside Europe by undisguised looting, enslavement and murder, floated back to the mother-country and were turned into capital" (1954, I: 146, 753–54). But the production and the concentration of productively based merchant capital in the Italian cities was essential to the voyages of discovery and the early creation of a world-embracing commerce. Then, *how* were the treasures turned into capital? And how important in this process was the unrequited loot and how important the market sale of manufactures? How, specifically, did the digging-out of silver in the Americas and its transport to Europe contribute to amassing capital in Europe? One answer, examined in this book, is that this silver and gold financed the purchase of use value and exchange value from the Orient and Eastern Europe. (But what did the countries of the latter, in turn, do with the precious metals, apart from partially sterilizing them, in other words, using some measure to keep the increase in the supply of money from circulating and raising prices?) Another answer is that the resulting inflation, insofar as the precious metals were not sterilized, led directly and indirectly to the concentration of capital, the divorce from means of production, and the increase in exploitation of more, and less well-paid, labor. How did the looted and slave-produced, as well as European wage labor- and non-wage-labor-produced, use values and their conversion into exchange values contribute to amassing and concentrating capital? How was the capital that was amassed in the sixteenth, seventeenth, and eighteenth centuries then reproduced—in the absence of developed capitalist relations of production—and then finally converted into capital that was able to reproduce itself at least partly through wage labor industrial production and reproduction? The question of when and how original precapitalist, primitive accumulation of capital became (the starting point of) the capitalist process of capital accumulation remains substantially open.

A further question of immediate political and economic relevance concerns the possible persistence and importance of so-called primitive, or rather primary, accumulation today. Certainly the production of use values through noncapitalist and precapitalist relations of production continues today and is still directly converted into exchange value for the process of capitalist accumulation, though perhaps their importance is no longer so great. But we may inquire how important noncapitalist relations of production are for the capitalist process of capital accumulation today in terms of three functions: (1) the sustenance and, in time of need, provision of a potential reserve army of labor and pool of labor power; (2) the contribution to the sustenance and the reproduction of wage labor power for which capital pays a less-than-subsistence wage that is too low for the wage laborer's sustenance and reproduction; and (3) the use of noncapitalist "socialist" relations of production to produce value that enters into the world capitalist process of capital accumulation.

The sustenance of a potential reserve army of labor through partially noncapitalist relations of production, which offers capital new labor power and, at the same time, helps to depress the wages of existing labor, can be observed today in the massive flow of "guest workers" from rural Southern to industrial Northern Europe, albeit by way of the southern regional centers, and in the increasing transfer from industrial to some underdeveloped countries of industrial production, or assembly, for export. The quantitative importance of this set of relations for the accumulation of capital is difficult to define and estimate, but these relations are certainly significant.

Noncapitalist village production contributes substantially to the sustenenace of labor power and the retirement of wage laborers, who receive literally less than a living wage, in African and Asian mines, plantations, and urban employments, as Meillassoux, Rey, and others have pointed out. Although the extended family members of these migrant and other wage laborers in Southern and Western Africa may produce substantial use value that does not directly enter the process of circulation, part of this use value is consumed by those wage laboring family members who do directly produce exchange and surplus value (often excess surplus value and frequently for export), so that the nonexchanged, noncapitalist production indirectly contributes to the capitalist process of capital accumulation. Indeed, if these workers were dependent only on the share of their value production that capital returns to them in the form of wages, some of them would be unable to produce any surplus value for capital at all, so that for the surplus value that they do produce, capital has their "noncapitalist" family members to thank. (Of course, far from doing so, it maligns them as a further "welfare" charge on capital.) The same principle of "noncapitalist" primary accumulation of capital is also partly at work in the situation of the European "guest workers," insofar as they are reared and again received by communities in Southern Europe, Asia, or the Caribbean, where part of the production is through "noncapitalist" productive relations. Extending this argument to its logical conclusion, the most widespread and important incidence of this phenomenon (i.e., the capitalist accumulation of capital partly on the basis of primary accumulation through "noncapitalist" relations of production) is the unrequited production and reproduction performed by the wife and mother within the bourgeois and working-class families! For, if capital had to pay the housewife for the total contribution she, like the family of the African migrant worker, makes to the ability of the worker to produce surplus value, and if capital did not have her as a further underpaid labor force and reserve army of labor to boot, capitalist accumulation of capital would be difficult, if not impossible.

Finally, if precapitalist-noncapitalist relations of production produce value that directly or indirectly enters the process of circulation in such a way as to permit or contribute to capitalist realization and accumulation, then does not production through postcapitalist-noncapitalist relations of production do the same? What else is the significance for the process of capital accumulation of imperialist capital's current interest in cheap, well-trained, and disciplined labor in the socialist economies of the Soviet Union and Eastern Europe? Imperialist capital may have to directly or indirectly pay more than a subsistence income to the socialist countries' producers, or the socialist state may subsidize their social consumption. But whether imperialist firms proceed through "contract processing" of industrial production for re-export from the socialist countries or simply buy their manufactures and raw materials, part of the value produced by work in these economies is transferred to the capitalists whose profit realization and accumulation is enhanced either by the goods they receive from the socialist countries or by the capitalist-produced goods they exchange for them, or both. At a time when this East-

West economic integration proceeds apace under the political um-
brella of détente, the question arises to what extent the social formations with socialist, "noncapitalist" relations of production are or are
not isolated from the single, capitalist process of capital accumulation. And, after the debates—between followers and opponents of
Althusser in France, between communists and the "new" left in
Europe, Asia, Africa, and Latin America—about the ways and
means of the transition from feudalism to capitalism and from
capitalism to socialism, the question arises (or remains): What do we
mean by *transition*? A transition between two transitions? And are
transitions necessarily cumulative and unidirectional?*

2. On Unequal Relations of Production, Circulation, and Resolution in Accumulation

The *extent* of the single, worldwide process of capital accumulation and of the capitalist *system* it has formed over several centuries
remains an important open question. Clarity in the debate is rendered difficult by what may be called the inherent structural inequality in the pattern of capitalist development itself, which admits
of varying interpretation. The question has had important theoretical and political relevance for over a century. Marx distilled his
theory of capital primarily from its most developed manifestation in
England and left unelaborated how far the latter included the less
developed and undeveloped sectors of Europe and the world, which
he examined more through historical description than through
theoretical categories (such as primitive accumulation, Asiatic mode
of production, etc.). Moreover, in his newspaper accounts, of Brit-

---

* Addressing the Congress of the Hungarian Communist Party in Budapest on
March 19, 1975, the head of the Soviet party, Leonid Brezhnev, said that because of
"broad economic links between capitalist and socialist countries, the ill effects of the
current crisis in the West also had an impact on the socialist world." This impact,
moreover, was neither casual or unintentional: in its 1966 resolution the Central
Committee of the Hungarian party said "the new economic mechanism should
establish a close relationship between internal and external markets. It should increase
the impact of influences originating in foreign markets on domestic."

ain's role in India, the Mexican-American War, and the American Civil War, among others, Marx thought that the extension of *the* process of capital accumulation and of its most developed social formations to these sectors was progressive and held out the hope that Britain presented them with the mirror of the their own future. Rosa Luxemburg regarded the incorporation of seemingly external noncapitalist and precapitalist economies into *the* process of capital accumulation as necessary for the resolution of its internal problems of realization. For Lenin, Trotsky, and Stalin, Asia, Africa, and Latin America, not to mention non-European Russia, were objects of imperialist expansion which generated immediate nationalities questions for the continuing and uninterrupted revolution. The Third International subordinated both the theoretical elaboration and the political solution of these questions to the construction of socialism in one country, and some of its heirs still seek to do so today. In recent years, after the replacement of colonialism by neocolonialism, struggles for national liberation, and, in some countries, the construction of socialism, questions relating to the extent of capital accumulation and the structure of the capitalist system are increasingly expressed in the following terms: (a) the "primacy" of "internal" "productive" relations rather than "external" "circulation," or commercial, relations, and (b) supposing the former, the nature, extent, and combination of capitalist and noncapitalist relations of production, modes of production, and social formations, and their ripeness for socialist revolution.

If capitalist production is the production of exchange value, then it also involves the circulation or exchange of use value. Capitalist accumulation involves the expanded re-production of exchange value through the cycle of realization of exchange value through the exchange of use value. "Circulation is itself a moment of production, since capital becomes capital only through circulation" (Marx 1973: 520), and circulation can continue to produce exchange value only through continued production of use value. Thus, however central the production of exchange value (not simply of use value, which is equally essential to any productive system) may be to capitalist accumulation of capital, the realization of capital through the exchange of use and exchange values in the process of circulation is also an essential part of the process of capitalist production and accumulation—and should be an essential part of its definition. Therefore, neither the relations of the production of use value nor the production of exchange value through wage labor can be in and of itself a sufficient criterion for the existence or nonexistence of capitalist production and accumulation, since each leaves out of account other relations that are essential to the realization and reproduction of capital, and therefore to the accumulation of capital.

The reaches of the capitalist system or the extent to which particular economic activities or social formations are incorporated in the capitalist process of capital accumulation may and must then be examined in terms of the relations of production, exchange, and realization of capital that contribute to this process of accumulation. To identify the reaches of capitalist accumulation and the capitalist system, the relevant question is not simply the existing relations of production per se, and still less the existence of wage labor (since the latter can exist in isolation without contributing to the reproduction and accumulation of capital, while production with relations of production other than wage labor can be and is exchanged and realized as capital, and therefore can and does contribute importantly to the accumulation of capital throughout its history). Insofar as relations of production—in relation to exchange and realization—are the significant criterion, it is the *transformation* of the relations of production, circulation, and realization through their incorporation into the process of capital accumulation that is, in principle, the relevant criterion of the existence of capitalism. (This is so, even though the far-reaching transformation of preexisting relations of production was not necessary in parts of India and China to permit some of their production to contribute to capital accumulation elsewhere for a time—until these areas too had to undergo transformation in order to continue their contribution.) In historical practice, however, participation in the world process of capital accumulation and the transformation of the relations of production have gone together, each being necessary for the other, although the transformation of preexisting relations of production does not necessarily entail the establishment of wage labor everywhere. Instead, incorporation into the worldwide process of capital accumulation may entail trans-*formation* of relations of production from one "non-capitalist" form to another or the utilization of preexisting forms of production to contribute to capital accumulation in combination with different circuits of circulation.

The formulation of this theoretical approach to the diversity of forms in the process of capital accumulation and the inequality in the structure of the capitalist system, as well as the considerations below about the uneven process of accumulation (and the use of this approach in the examination of the worldwide process of capital accumulation until 1790 undertaken in the text) may help to resolve some controversies about the extent of capitalism.

Most easy to resolve, in principle, is the question of the extent of the global system as an alternative to the ideal and often idealized units of analysis that are so widely used in social and historical studies, such as the village, tribe, nation (state), or (European) continent and their supposed past or present defining characteristics. It may easily be argued that most of these do not exist in the past or the present, and cannot be understood in isolation from each other and from the process of world history as a whole.*

However difficult it may be in practice to demonstrate exactly the mutual and determinant relation of any or each of these to the process of world history, it may be argued that the existence, the essential characteristics, and much of the recent development of most of these social "units" has been substantially shaped by their participation in the worldwide process of capital accumulation and in the world capitalist system. The early history of such participation is painted with broad brush strokes in the text of the book. From this account it would appear that capital has not so much transgressed state boundaries to become international in recent times, as that the nation-state itself was formed long ago as a byproduct and servant of capital, whose existence and accumulation had already been "international" from its inception, before the nation-state was born. Turning to the present, it is clear that there still exists no independent international socialist economy, market, or accumula-

---

* I have previously argued as much under the titles "Sociology of Development and Underdevelopment of Sociology" and "Functionalism and Dialectics" (Frank 1969) and "On Dalton's 'Theoretical Issues in Economic Anthropology' " (Frank 1970a).

tion, as Stalin, for one, had anticipated. What remains open to question is to what extent the socialist countries are in or out of capitalist accumulation and world capitalism.

More difficult is the question posed by those who argue that relations of production are "internal" and therefore determinant, while exchange relations or circulation are "external" and superficial, or virtually irrelevant to capitalist accumulation and its definition. Is capitalism, and still more the transition to capitalism and the determinants of its development, confined to certain centers of economic activity, leaving most of the world for a long time and still much of the world today outside the capitalist system (with, at most, some exchange relations with the centers of capitalist production that are external to both the capitalist and the noncapitalist relations of production)? Not in my opinion. Without necessarily implying such a formulation, the question of production vs. circulation emerges from Marx's priority in the analysis of the determination of and determinant role of the relations of production (but of exchange value) that underlie capitalist accumulation, as against the more superficially visible relations of exchange. The issue of the determinant priority of the relations of production over the relations of exchange also arose in Lenin's critique of the populist Narodniks in tsarist Russia. In the debate about the transition from feudalism to capitalism, Maurice Dobb subscribed to the determinant role of production relations that were supposedly "internal" to the declining feudalism and the emerging capitalism and "internal" to some parts of Western Europe. Paul Sweezy was ascribed a "circulationist" position that supposedly interpreted the transition as arising from exchange relations that were "external" to both feudal and capitalist productive relations and supposedly "external" to Europe in that they stressed the importance of the commercial expansion of Europe and the *productive* incorporation, particularly of the mining economies of the New World, into the process of accumulation. The debate has often been regarded as a chicken-and-egg one, in which Dobb was said to argue that the transformation of European "internal" productive relations (in the "center") caused its commercial expansion, while Sweezy was supposed to have argued that Europe's "external" commercial expansion (in the periphery) determined the transformation of the relations of production from feudalism to capitalism in Europe. Toshio Takahashi is regarded to have attempted a resolution which leaned toward Dobb's analysis, if only because, in Marxism and in fact, internal contradictions determine external ones. (Thus, in his essay *On Contradiction*, Mao Tsetung illustrated this principle by recalling that with equal external heat applied to an egg and a stone, a chicken emerges from the former and nothing from the latter— because of their different ' internal" compositions.)*

The analysis of a single process of accumulation and the development of a single world capitalist system renders the question of the internality or externality of the determination, at least of this process itself, irrelevant and unanswerable. The determination is, of course, geographically and sectorally internal to where this process takes place, and it must scientifically be sought internally to the human activities—including population changes—and their relations which give rise to and participate in this process, although climatic or other physical circumstances may be contributory factors.** The predominance of "internal" relations of production over "external" relations of exchange is rendered more questionable, in turn, if we consider the necessary connection of both of these relations for the realization of, and therefore for the expanded reproduction and accumulation of, capital, with successive relations and modes of production.

The debate about the capitalist and other modes of production and their relations has recently assumed new vigor in many parts of the

---

* The present author has frequently been criticized as a "Narodnik" circulationist, who, in the tradition of such less guilty parties as Baran and Sweezy, has supposedly confused capitalism with exchange to the total or virtual exclusion of production and for mistakenly arguing that external relations in or with the periphery are determinant instead of internal ones in the center. A citation, classification of, and partial answer to some one hundred critiques was attempted in an answer to critics (Frank 1977). Though I admit having examined relations of exchange, perhaps overly so, I have rejected the contention that I entirely neglected relations of production, in the prefaces to the revised edition of *Capitalism and Underdevelopment* (1969) and to *Lumpenbourgeoisie* (1972).

**This book is intended as a step toward the internal explanation of this worldwide process. Another major step is Immanuel Wallerstein's *The Modern World-System*. Vol. I (of four planned volumes): *Capitalist Agriculture and the Origins of the European World-Economy in the Sixteenth Century* (1974a).

world.* The result is the agreement that Stalin's formulation of universally progressive transition from communalism to slavery, to feudalism, to capitalism, must be abandoned as schematically un-Marxist and altogether out of keeping with historical reality. There is increasing, but not entire, agreement that the precapitalist modes and relations of production that remain, and many that existed until not long ago, are neither "feudal" nor "Asiatic," and certainly need not be so. There is a variety of modes or, at least, of relations of production and of combinations among them and between them and the capitalist mode of production. Many of them are preserved or even created by the incorporation into the capitalist process of capital accumulation of the production that is organized through this variety of "noncapitalist" relations or modes of production. Though there is substantial agreement that only one mode of production can be dominant at one time and place, there is some disagreement as to whether here or there the dominant mode of production is indeed the capitalist one. Perhaps because the question is related to political

---

* In India, the *Economic and Political Weekly* has carried an ongoing debate on modes of production in Indian agriculture and colonial modes of production since 1971 (summarized in Alavi 1975; Cleaver 1976) and the *Journal for Contemporary Asia* has done so for other areas. In France, Recherches Internationales à la Lumière du Marxisme and the Centre d'Etudes et de Recherches Marxistes have published collective volumes on the second serfdom in Eastern Europe and on feudalism, respectively, while *La Pensée* carries occasional individual articles, and Amin, Meillassoux, Rey and others have published major books advancing my analysis, especially for Africa, of the problem of modes of production. Ahlers et al. in West Germany and Kossok in East Germany have prepared new analyses of modes of production in Latin America. In Latin America itself, *Cuadernos del Pasado y Presente* in Buenos Aires, *Cuadernos de la Realidad Nacional* in Chile before the coup, *Estudios Centroamericanos* in San José, Costa Rica, *Historia y Sociedad* in its new series in Mexico, and *Ciencias Economicas y Sociales* in Caracas have, over the past four or five years, devoted well over a thousand pages of analysis by Laclau, Sempat, Cardoso, Cordova, Semo, Cuevas, Bartra and others to colonial and other modes of production and social formations in Latin America and the Caribbean. The more or less common denominator of terminological use in this discussion, which I shall adopt here, is that "relations of production" concretely refer to these in the narrower sense; "mode of production" is a more abstract concept referring to ideal type combinations of one or more relations of production with forces of production, and therefore sometimes also of extraction of surplus and the related superstructure; and "social (and economic) formation" refers to a particular concrete combination of relations of modes of production and superstructure in a particular time and place. Though of these, "mode of production" has the most currency in the discussion, I prefer whenever possible to refer to the more concretely identifiable "relations of production."

strategy for national liberation and democratic or socialist revolution, there is more disagreement about which regions, productive and exchange activities, and relations of production or social formations do and do not form part of the capitalist system and its process of capital accumulation, or, to put it the other way around, how far capitalism extends today or extended at particular times and places in the past. Arguing that capitalism can only be said to exist where production is entirely or predominantly undertaken by wage labor, and denying that category to hundreds of millions of people employed in agriculture in India and Latin America, despite the existence of nearly half of these without land ownership and often even without tenancy, some conclude that Indian agriculture or entire countries in Latin America are feudal. Patnaik (1971, 1972), for example, takes this position regarding India, while Raúl Fernández and José Ocampo (1974) claim the same for Latin America, though, at the same time, they ascribe this circumstance to the existence and predominance of imperialism. In terms of the criteria proposed above, this conclusion is, of course, entirely unacceptable. The argument is an extreme version of a tendency to regard the past and present relations of production of particular parts of the world in isolation from the worldwide capitalist process of capital accumulation and to take account of only part of the capitalist process of re-production of capital.

In other words, without denying or neglecting the importance of the detailed analysis that others make of the transformation of productive relations in Europe in the past, or in other parts of the world more recently, I argue that their analysis as part of a single worldwide process of capital accumulation also requires more attention. Most economic histories of the "world" not only omit most extra-European production and exchange (even most of that outside West Europe or even northwest Europe); they neglect the participation of the productive and exchange activities of extra-European countries in the European, not to say world, process of accumulation and development. Moreover, they disregard the part that these productive and exchange relations played in the developing world system. The argument here is that, whatever the answer to these questions, it must be sought where the world process of accumulation took place, in the colonial periphery of the world system as well as in the metropolitan center. Indeed, as this review of the early part of this process indicates, particular peripheries and particular parts of the metropolis have participated differently in this process. Moreover, I agree with Wallerstein that the role and changing participation of various "intermediate" mediating "semiperipheries"— once the Iberian peninsula and Eastern Europe, later the United States and perhaps Russia, now possibly the emerging "subimperialist" centers and/or the Soviet Union and the socialist economies of Eastern Europe—has received particularly little attention and remains very inadequately understood.

The attempt to examine the process of reproduction and accumulation of capital "on a world scale," to use the terminology of Amin's title, and to inquire into "the origins of the European world-economy," to cite Wallerstein's subtitle, is the purpose of this book. It leads to the following further questions and possible answers about the extent and structure of capitalist production, exchange, and realization.

Where and when is capitalism to be found? More precisely, what parts of the earth (or which productive activities and social formations) participated in the single worldwide capitalist process of capital accumulation? Marx can be considered to have identified the existence of capital (if not capitalism) in "the creation of a world-embracing commerce and world-embracing market" dating from the sixteenth century, "although we come across the first beginnings of capitalist production as early as the fourteenth and fifteenth century, sporadically, in certain towns of the Mediterranean" (1954, I: 715, 146); in "the transition from feudal to capitalist mode of production" in the sixteenth and seventeenth centuries (1962, III: 327–30); or in the development of industrial capital in England and parts of Europe in the first half of the eighteenth century. Some would interpret him as claiming that large parts of Asia, Africa, and Latin America are still untouched by capitalism today. Slavery, for instance, is not wage labor. Does this justify interpreting Marx as saying that the slave plantations in the U.S. South and the Caribbean were not capitalist? What use is such an interpretation? We must reject as misleading at best, if not altogether useless, a criterion that does not lead us to recognize that the sugar slave plantations of Brazil in the sixteenth century, those of more and more Caribbean islands in the seventeenth and eighteenth centuries, and the cotton slave plantations of the U.S. South in the nineteenth century were essential parts of a single system and historic process in which they contributed materially to the primitive and then industrial accumulation of capital concentrated in particular parts of the system and times of the process. Does this mean that the escaped black slaves and small yeoman farmers practicing subsistence agriculture at the margin of plantations were "outside" of the capitalist system? If the slave-using economies of the Americas were integral parts of the system and essential contributors to its development, then were the "single export" slave-producing societies of Africa not equally essential parts of and participants in a process of accumulation? Of course they were. But exactly how far into the interior of Africa did the slave trade and slave wars extend to incorporate precapitalist societies into the world process of accumulation? Irrespective of which "colonial" mode of production was generated in or imposed on the mining activities of Mexico, Peru, and Minas Gerais, and through them on the surrounding areas, peoples, and their social formations, the latter also participated materially in the same system and process. Does this mean that all of Mexico, Peru, and other surrounding areas and peoples were integral parts of the worldwide, if not all-embracing, system by colonial times? Were the mining and even backward-linked argicultural and other supply-producing activities metropolitan overseas enclaves? If so, when, if ever, did these enclaves and activities impose the process of their development on the others and/or begin to generate a process of accumulation that came to be partially autonomous, if not independent of accumulation elsewhere in the world?

The Ottoman Empire was instrumental in the long-distance oriental and African trade, and this trade encouraged the expansion of the Ottoman Empire, which, in the fifteenth century, led to the discovery of America; both were intimately related to the transition from feudalism to capitalism in Western Europe. In the fifteenth and particularly sixteenth centuries, the regions bordering the Mediterranean on the north also became prominent in this trade and associated activities. In the seventeenth century, the entire Mediterranean area and its peoples bordering it in Southern Europe, North Africa, and the Middle East or Western Asia again lost this prominent place and participation. If Southern Europe's participation in capitalist development was then slowed down, was the Ottoman and

Arab people's place in the system eliminated entirely? More likely, one might argue that they experienced an involution, differing according to differences in their internal structure (as suggested by Amin), not unlike that of other areas in recent history. The same increase of production and expansion of trade thus visited upon the productive activities and social formations in the aforementioned regions nonetheless did not require, induce, or impose a far-reaching transformation of the mode of production in South and Southeast Asia until the second half of the eighteenth century and later, despite the active participation in this same process of substantial productive activities of large regions in these subcontinents, or in China and Japan, which remained wholly or substantially isolated from this process until the mid-nineteenth century. These major regions of the world long remained unincorporated, or only marginally incorporated, in the process of capital accumulation, even though some, particularly parts of India, contributed to the process before their incorporation. We may ask to what extent and how the sacrifice of Indian labor in the silver mines of Mexico and Peru or of African labor in the slave plantations of the Caribbean (and the transformation and formation of productive relations there) for a time postponed—but ultimately made all the more necessary—the transformation of "Asiatic" modes of production and the sacrifice of Indian labor in India.

Beginning in the sixteenth century, Eastern Europe experienced a "second serfdom" at the same time that Western Europe increasingly freed itself from its first. Through the production and export of cereals and raw materials (for which Western Europe paid the Eastern European landlords partially with silver and sugar imported from the Americas and spices from the Orient) the "second serfs" of Eastern Europe helped Western Europe overcome its shortage of grain. This shortage had in turn been caused by the enclosure of agricultural land to graze sheep (who therefore were said to "eat men") to produce wool for textiles (which were also in part exported to Eastern Europe), thus promoting the migration of former peasants and serfs to the towns (whose "air makes free") in the transition from feudalism to capitalism in Western Europe. Russia did not seem to be part or participant yet at all, until Peter the Great opened a window in Petrograd. Can we account for all of this content and extent of capitalist, albeit protocapitalist, development?

Then there is the ethnocentric question: "Why didn't 'they' col-onize 'us'?" Why did the Chinese, who sent merchant fleets of 200 ships, each one larger than any the Europeans would have until years to come, to the coast of East Africa in the fifteenth century, not develop and dominate a long-distance trade? Instead, they hemmed the trade and bridled their merchants—for "internal" reasons. Why did the Indians, whose cotton textile technology was the world's most advanced and whose export of textile production was by far the greatest until 1800, not carry through the Industrial Revolution? Ernest Mandel (personal communication, February 19, 1975) writes: "You know my answer: because the more advanced agriculture in the East led to a bigger increase in population, which made irrigation works imperative; therefore, centralization of the agrarian surplus; therefore, political weakness of the bourgeoisie; therefore, discon-tinuous process of primitive accumulation. In the West, the lower labor productivity in agriculture, with more limited population, made possible fragmentation of political power, thereby enabling the rise of a politically more powerful bourgeoisie, and a big reverse from discontinuous to continuous accumulation of capital in the fifteenth century." However that may be (and the question remains open despite the answers of Mandel, Barrington Moore, Amin, and others), even Max Weber recognized, through his comparative study of oriental and Western society and religion, that the answer lies not in the realm of "ethics" or "spirit," but in the forces and relations of production and exchange, as well as in the associated political or-ganization of society. These same circumstances, which impeded prior capitalist development and expansion in the East, also offered it the strength for a long time to resist substantial incursion from the West and/or to render Western and capitalist geographic, economic, and politico-military incursion beyond isolated spots on the coast and, of course, structurally different parts of Southeast Asia too costly and unattractive before the late eighteenth and the nineteenth centuries.

3. On Uneven Stages, Cycles, and Crises in Accumulation

Another set of questions concerns the temporal unevenness of the process of capital accumulation and capitalist development. We face again the question of distinguishing phases, stages, or epochs in this process and the problem of the transition from one to another. Related to these difficulties is the problem of observing and analyzing the fluctuations or cycles, short, medium, and long, in the process of accumulation. If in the centuries prior to the Industrial Revolution there was a previous so-called primitive accumulation during the prehistory of capital, how were the starting point of this precapitalist history, its own phases of transition, and its transition to capitalist accumulation and development related to observed fluctuations or perhaps even cycles in this so-called process of primitive accumulation?

Along with some students of history, I suggested in Chapter 1 that there may have existed a long "up-and-down-swing," not to call it a wave, fluctuation, or cycle, which manifested itself in the expansion associated with the crusades of the twelfth and part of the thirteenth centuries, followed by a long downswing in the fourteenth and part of the fifteenth centuries, which brought in its train the Black Death, among other socioeconomic and demographic convulsions. Apparently, there was an economic recuperation in parts of Europe, beginning at the end of the fifteenth and running through much of the sixteenth century, of which the discovery, conquest, and exploitation of America was but a part. Can these hypotheses be sustained, and if so, do they imply that so-called primitive accumulation began, in some sense, as early as this time?

If there were such precapitalist and even pre-precapitalist economic fluctuations, in what sense were they related to the process—not to say cycles—of accumulation, at a time when there was no industrial capitalist cycle of capital accumulation? Were these ups and downs totally random fluctuations or reflections of climatically generated and/or demographic fluctuations that should not be called "cycles" in that the germ of the downswing was not already contained in the upswing, and still less vice versa? Insofar as these long swings were reflected in prices, were they, as Braudel and Spooner (1967) seem to argue, *only* variations in price (and below them of agricultural and money supply) or were they more than that, as is suggested here? And *what* more? Can we distinguish long swings in production or in rates of growth of production? Can we go further and find fluctuations in investment and even in profitability, which could be termed cycles, in that the downswing is *caused* by the upswing itself? In that case, is it valid to suggest that these were up-and-down cycles in the process of accumulation or so-called primitive accumulation of merchant capital? Did the downswings, and especially the crises, bring with them disadjustments that permitted and/or obliged readjustments in economic (including productive) relations so that even during the prehistory of industrial capital the economic crises played an essential cathartic role in the development of the process of accumulation through transformations in productive and exchange relations? In sum, even though the reproduction cycle of industrial capital was not yet developed, is it legitimate to argue that the process of accumulation had begun already prior to the Industrial Revolution? In that case, how did that process of accumulation compare with or differ from the cycle of industrial capital?

The historical process of capital accumulation and capitalist development has occured in phases or stages. Of course, these phases do not have an existence independent from the process itself, nor does the process exist without its phases. Similarly, the process of accumulation and its phases of development have been temporally uneven, in that they have had expansive upswings and contractive downswings, which are also integral parts of the process. It is apparently possible to distinguish so-called long economic up-and-down-swings; but the process of accumulation is also marked by "medium" and short fluctuations and cycles. Of course, these latter are also integral parts of the longer swings, as daily and momentary events are also integral aspects of these and of the whole historical process. That is, history and its cycles do not have a reified existence apart from the multiple events that compose them, and the events and their uneven occurrence do not take place outside of history.*

---

* Thus, Pierre and Huguette Chaunu (1974) observe in their classic study of the Atlantic economy:

The economy of the Spanish-American Atlantic . . . is thus an economy of long phases, those long phases so dear to the hearts of French historians. It is, however, possible to discern within these great movements—first the rise, then the leveling-off or decline—a series . . . of short-term cyclical fluctuations in sixteenth—and seventeenth—century economies: fluctuations which in the absence of statistics can be guessed at rather than perceived. Cyclical fluctuations ripple through . . . from 1504 to 1650. From 1590 to 1650, a cycle of about 10 to

This obliges us to ask which events, which regularities and which patterns of unevenness, and which economic cycles to select for observation and study. The choice depends, of course, on the purpose. A short-term speculator may be most interested in the minute-to-minute fluctuations of the stockmarket. During the so-called inventory cycles, inventories are built up and run down. In the classical Juglar eight-to-ten-year business cycles, investment is accelerated and decelerated, but using essentially the same technology and productive relations. Construction varies in the eighteen-to twenty-year Kuznets cycles. The major changes and transformations in the process of capital accumulation include all of these, of course, but seem to be particularly related to the innovations in technology or productive forces and the transformations in productive relations associated with the so-called fifty-year-long waves sometimes associated with the name of Kondratieff (without implying acceptance of his theory of cycles, however) or with sets of them and with the transformation of the mode of production from one stage of development to another. It is these latter, and within them the periods of economic and political crisis, which receive preferential attention in this book. But this raises the threefold question of whether these long waves exist at all, inasmuch as their very existence has been challenged even for our times; whether they existed (and how they could exist) before the advent of industrial capitalism; and how they can supposedly be identified to be a century or more long during the prehistory of capital.

More concretely, we should ask: In what sense was there a seventeenth-century depression? Chapter 2 documents that beginning late in the century, the expansion of the sixteenth-century let-off. Compared to the previous uneven expansion, much of the seventeenth century witnessed, most visibly, a decline in the production of silver and in the growth of the money supply, long periods of deflation,

11 years may be clearly distinguished, lagging slightly behind the decade—the declining phase corresponding roughly to the first half of the decade, the rising phase to the second half. It remains to be seen what these short fluctuations imply. . . . Nor is it impossible that between the 10-11 year fluctuations and the centennial ones (rising phase 1508-1620, declining phase 1620-1680) we may be able to discover intermediate fluctuations known to historians of the French school as "interdecennial fluctuation." . . . To sum up, there is no golden rule for determining short- and medium-term fluctuations in the Spanish-Atlantic economy from 1504 to 1650. (1974: 122–23)

very much reduced transatlantic trade, less or slower expansion of oriental trade, and perhaps lower production or a slower rate of growth. Certainly, there were more, longer, and more severe economic and political crises. The Mediterranean area, Portugal, Spain, Italy, and the Ottoman Empire, which had been in economic ascendency in the sixteenth century, suffered a decline which was in many respects absolute (and until today permanent) and also relative to the Northwest of Europe.*

Why then did the Mediterranean decline? Some suggestions are offered in Chapter 2, but they do not go very far. Did the Mediterranean regions become less competitive? Were they, in response to a general decline in demand at least in internationally traded goods, less able to reduce costs of production and to undertake the social changes in productive relations and/or technological changes in pro-

---

* On the other hand, the Chaunus also write: "Nor is there a *single* economic cycle for the Spanish Atlantic. . . . There are *several* economic cycles, of which that of the Spanish Atlantic is at most a resultant. The economic space of the sixteenth century, and even more that of the seventeenth, was certainly much more partitioned than that of the twentieth, and *a forteriori* the nineteenth" (1974: 123). And the student of the French Languedoc region, Le Roy Ladurie objects:

Is it correct, in connection with such a period, to employ catch-all phrases like 'the crisis of the seventeenth century' or to speak of the 'reversal of the conjuncture' beginning in the early decades of the century? Such expressions are perfectly valid in regard to the Spanish-colonial conjuncture, to Ibero America. . . . They are equally valid in regard to Castile and Italy; and a few decades later could be applied to Germany and neighboring Burgundy devastated by the Thirty Years War. But outside these geographical limits, vast as they are, simple extrapolation is impossible. One cannot even assert that the 'Mediterranean conjuncture,' as a whole, supports the thesis of a change of direction around 1620: some violent short-lived crises, yes; a demographic slowdown (beginning in the last third of the sixteenth century), without a doubt; a universal secular depression, no—at least not yet because Provence, Languedoc, and Catalonia—all of the considerable Mediterranean Littoral of the Gulf of Lion, from Tarragona to Toulon—escaped the radical reversal of the economic conjuncture which assumed henceforth a southern, peninsular, and from a European point of view, almost marginal character. On the northernmost shores of the Mediterranean, the conjuncture subsided; it changed pace; it grew *sluggish;* it did not yet *reverse itself.* (Le Roy Ladurie 1974: 146)

I would, on the contrary, argue that Le Roy Ladurie's own account suggests that the conjuncture was not so "marginal" after all, and still less so if we observe that it also appeared in England, Portugal, and the Eastern Mediterranean, as well as parts of Eastern Europe. It is inherent in this process that crises affect different sectors and regions unequally and even unevenly, permitting some of them relative—and eventually some of them also absolute—advantages over others.

ductive forces necessary to remain competitive? In the Italian cities, it has been suggested, the effective opposition of the guilds prevented such changes. What prevented them in Spain and Portugal, where the state was relatively strong? In Portugal this relative strength perhaps was canceled out by the economic concessions made to Britain in return for political protection against Spain. And in the latter? Some of Spain's economic weakness and "antinational" economic policies, dating from the sixteenth century may be traced to the Habsburg emperors, who were in permanent debt to foreign bankers to finance their European wars.

Returning to the question of international competitiveness, were costs of production, in textiles for instance, higher in the South than in the North of Europe? The sixteenth-century inflation had been more severe in the South (which was closer to the source of money) than in the North, raising prices more in the former than in the latter, and encouraging exports from the North to the South. But insofar as the inflation was an important instrument in the decline of real wages, had they not declined more and perhaps farther in the South of Europe than in the North? What accounts for the increasing differentiation of Northern Europe during the seventeenth century as well? Germany was effectively taken out of the running by the Thirty Years War.* But was this war a cause or, as we may suspect, a result of this German decline? Holland enjoyed its "golden seventeenth century," but it was based on commerce: Dutch expansion in the Orient was more at the expense of Portugal than representative of a net growth of European trade, partially also at the expense of Britain and northern Germany, and did not last beyond the century. Why was this commerce, as well as Dutch finishing of raw British cloth, not translated into productive development, taking advantage also of the textile productive capacity and experience in the Flemish regions (of present-day Belgium)? Why, finally, was Britain, which at the beginning of the century was uncompetitive even with Holland, by the end of the century able to challenge the much larger France, and go on in the eighteenth century effectively to win out over its French rival?

---

* Yet it has been claimed that the "Thirty Years War . . . did not entail long-lasting economic decline in the countries in which it was waged. . . . . In Germany, too, industry recovered quite rapidly . . . but rather industry modified its organization by returning to more primitive forms" (Topolski 1974).

The development in Britain of the "new draperies" through the putting-out system was a factor, as were the associated "bourgeois" revolutions of 1640 and 1688, and the intervening anti-Dutch Navigation Acts. That is, British manufacturing and overseas commerce could count increasingly on the effective support of a growing state. But did not Louis XIV's "l'état-c'est-mo" France also have a strong state? Was not Colbert the archetype of overseas state-supported mercantilism? One answer is that Colbert nevertheless represented only the relatively weak merchant and manufacturing interests against the stronger, landed, continent-oriented interests defended by Louis XIV's minister of war. And if in England the merchant and manufacturing interests (and we must ask what were the conflicts of interest between these) so effectively gained the upper hand under Cromwell after 1640, then why was the bourgeois Glorious Revolution of 1688 necessary?

Returning to the question of long cyclical swings in silver and gold production, prices, and production or even investment in general, was the decline in silver production and in the growth of the money supply the "cause" of the depression, or were they rather the consequences of an already existing cycle of over-and-under accumulation that was determined otherwise, but still within the process of accumulation itself? And why was recovery uneven in the eighteenth century? If there was an "investment cycle," how so? And in that case, how did the process of so-called primitive accumulation differ from that of capitalist accumulation?

Skipping over the first half of the eighteenth century (dealt with in Chapter 3 and elsewhere), we may turn to some major questions raised by the treatment in Chapter 5 of the period 1762 to 1789 as a long crisis-ridden downswing, which brought with it not only the American and French, but also the Industrial revolutions. A first question, of course, is whether it can be satisfactorily established that there was an economic downturn (from what?) during these three decades. Was there a slowdown in production as well as in productive or at least commercial investment? There is evidence that there was a decline, at least, in profitability in the British-related world economy, and that an attempt was made to counteract this decline through measures such as paper increases in the supply of money by the Bank of England and the establishment of country banks. The production of gold fell off, and toward the end of the century the production and supply of silver began to rise sharply again.

One of the hypotheses of this book is that in each major economic crisis the process of accumulation turns to depend significantly and critically on a sharp increase of superexploitation and so-called primitive accumulation. This apparent tendency seems to have been reflected after 1760 in the sharp acceleration of the enclosure movement in Britain, which inspired Oliver Goldsmith's "Deserted Village," and by the plunder of Bengal after the Battle of Plassey of 1757 in India. Both represent sharp increases of primitive accumulation, but the former also generated wage labor and the latter did not. Can we say that these and other changes in the relations of production and in the amount of capital that was amassed represent the crisis-generated adjustment in the process of capital accumulation that followed upon a previous overaccumulation through other means? If the previous (mid-century and earlier) accumulation had "run out of steam" and led to declining rates of profitability, had this been in the realm of merchant capital only? Or is it more likely that European productive capital (invested, for instance, in overseas sugar plantations, domestic agriculture, and certain lines of manufacturing) was also affected by a crisis of profitability? (There is no doubt that the British-owned sugar plantations in the Caribbean began their decline after 1763, but the French plantations at the same time began their "golden age," only to sink into oblivion by the revolution in Haiti in 1794. This was perhaps the consequence of overexploitation by the French, after they had lost all further opportunities in India, North America, and Africa with the Peace of Paris in 1763). Again, if these events already represent cyclical fluctuations in productive investment, how did this prehistory of capital differ from its history, which began with the Industrial Revolution? And what were "the causes of the Industrial Revolution"? Chapter 5 explores the possiblity that part of the causes lie in this post-1762 economic crisis. But it may be, and has been, objected that even if all the other questions about this post-1762 period could be satisfactorily answered, so momentous a transformation in world history as the Industrial Revolution cannot be ascribed solely to a supposed thirty-year economic crisis. Perhaps; but I am suggesting only that the crisis accelerated and made definitive a transformation that was already underway earlier in the eighteenth century, and before, as Chapter 6 makes clear. Moreover, neither I nor anyone else, as that chapter also suggests, has yet been able to offer a complete or wholly satisfactory explanation of the causes of the Industrial Revolution.

4. *On Unending Class Struggle in Accumulation*

"The history of all hitherto existing society is the history of class struggle," Marx and Engels wrote in *The Communist Manifesto*. Nonetheless, notwithstanding numerous studies of various of its aspects and despite the prevalence of schoolbook "political" history, a real history of the class struggle remains one of the least developed of Marxist, let alone other, social and economic historiography. Particularly weak is the analysis of class formation and struggle in relation to the process of capital accumulation as a whole, a weakness reflected in this book. Here I shall confine myself to a few isolated and superficial observations and questions about capital accumulation, class formation and composition, and class conflict and struggle as manifested through the state, warfare, and religious or ideological and political conflict, or revolution.

The unequal and uneven process of accumulation was both cause and consequence of increasing differentation of productive forces and relations, and these of differences in class composition and interests. For instance, as Chapter 1 tries to demonstrate, relatively minor variations in productive and social circumstances between Eastern and Western Europe in the late Middle Ages nonetheless permitted, through the sixteenth-century economic expansion, the decline of serfdom and the development of manufactures in some parts of the West, while generating or reinforcing a class of landowners in the East whose interests were opposed to a similar development and were tied instead to the production of staples for export. For the production of these, in the absence of sufficient urban opposition, they successfully forced the peasantry into a second serfdom. In the New World also, and through the slave trade in Africa, the place of the local organization of production in the international division of labor generated the development of power-

ful classes of productive, commercial, political, and military entrepreneurs and officials (the distinction was often hard to make) whose
immediate economic interests were tied to production for and trade
with Europe at the expense of the masses of the local population and
consequently these regions did not experience any autonomous development and suffered the development of undevelopment in much
the same way as did Asia and other parts of Africa later. Less clear is
how and why these metropolitan and local interests were so successfully able to impose themselves and their economic, social, and
political order, despite the frequent, if not constant, opposition of
the oppressed and exploited sectors of the population. (Their passive, active, and violent opposition has, with some exceptions, gone
largely unrecorded by the ruling groups who have written history.)
In Europe itself, the process of differentation and generation of
conflicting interests was, of course, also far from uniform and contributed to an agitated history of domestic and foreign conflict.

As Marx observed, force and violence were the midwives of this
process throughout. Much of this force and violence was organized
and institutionalized by the state, whose principal *raison d'être* it and
the associated subsidy of one social class and sector at the expense of
another has been and remains. Though perhaps still insufficiently
studied, the importance of the state in the colonial system, both in
the motherland and the colony, and in the associated mercantile
system and the commercial wars is intuitively evident. But, as Adam
Smith, if not all those who recognize him as the father of their
discipline, emphasized and Marx again reiterated, the emergence
and action of the state played an equally essential role in the development of "domestic" or "national" capitalism: by enforcing the
separation of producers from their means of production and the
provision of a labor force capable of producing surplus, not to say
extra, surplus value, or through the provision of laws and measures
that facilitate the realization of surplus value by capital. The development of the state, and particularly of the absolute state in the
seventeenth century, did not take place until the attempts at empire
building, especially of the Habsburgs had failed (Wallerstein 1974a:
132 ff.). But insofar as this is the case, it may also be suggested
(although Wallerstein says it was inherently impossible) that the
failure of empire itself was in part immediately occasioned by the

end of economic expansion. Similarly, it may be suggested that the rise of the strong state with more limited national sovereignty was the result of economic depression in the seventeenth, and in France already in part of the sixteenth, century. This imposed economic retrenchment and exacerbated economic, social, and political conflict within neighboring regions and socioeconomic groups at the same time that it made them rivals for more limited opportunities of those in other nations in formation. Louis XIV and Colbert on the one hand and Cromwell and the Long Parliament on the other represented results of the seventeenth-century depression, even if they did not represent the only possible solutions. The "nationalist" policies of their states were the response, in times of economic difficulties, of compromise and arbitration between contending economic interest groups and the conversion of the winner's interests into state and national policy. This was most clearly visible in the increasingly commercially motivated international alliances and Anglo-Dutch, Anglo-French, and Hispanic wars of the seventeenth and eighteenth centuries. Chapters 2 and 3 distinguish among these between "offensive" wars, or military campaigns and international diplomacy during or immediately following periods of economic upswing, and "defensive" wars, during times of economic downswing and depression. The place of "religious" wars and those of dynastic succession, as well as of all war, in the worldwide process of capital accumulation is, of course, in need of much more study.

The relation of ideological and religious conflict to the process of capital accumulation, and to its unequal incidence and uneven tempo, also requires more systematic study. In the context of historical materialism, R. H. Tawney's argument in *Religion and the Rise of Capitalism* (1947) that the conditions of the latter provide the context of the former, are more persuasive than Weber's in *The Protestant Ethic and the Spirit of Capitalism* (1958) that the former generates the latter. I have argued (1974, 1978) how unsatisfactory this Weber thesis is in contrast to the analysis of relations of production and exchange in the process of capital accumulation. Thus, if Jews and Protestants were in Europe associated with economic expansion (albeit not for reasons of their "ethic"), their expulsion here and there, and the Counter-Reformation in one principality or another, would seem to have been immediately related to economic contraction and/or renewed dominance of landed interests and/or economic contraction. (For a related argument see Wallerstein 1974a.) That rebellion and revolution are related to alterations in class composition arising out of changes in forces and relations of production, and particularly that they are often sparked by economic crises, is amply documented but not systematically analyzed in the context of the process of accumulation as a whole. The English, French, and American revolutions of the seventeenth and eighteenth centuries, analyzed in Chapters 2 and 5, not to mention later and contemporary revolutions and counter-revolutions, are related to such economic and political crises.

To observe and to argue that these political and ideological ("superstructural") events are not arbitrarily or simply self-determined but have for centuries been determined parts of the unequal incidence and uneven tempo of the process of capital accumulation, and this, moreover, not only on a local or national but on a world scale, is not to deny that they in turn exercise qualitatively crucial and far-reaching influences on this process of accumulation and its "infrastructure." On the contrary, although my analysis is particularly inadequate in this regard, the argument is that political and ideological, as well as cultural and scientific, movements are decisive for the "economic" process.

One of my hypotheses in this regard (presented in Chapters 2 and 5) is that the incidence of major scientific and technical invention, as well as of philosophical and artistic "revolution," is coincident with and generated or accelerated by economic—and therewith political—crisis. Perhaps cumulative step-wise scientific and cultural advance is fed by and achieved during periods of economic expansion, to the continuance of which they may also help to contribute.

But my hypothesis is that "Kuhnian revolutions" in scientific, philosphical, or cultural paradigms arise directly or indirectly out of economic crisis in which "necessity is the mother of invention." In Chapters 2 and 5 I suggest that the seventeenth-century scientific revolution associated with Galileo, Leibniz, Descartes, and others and the late eighteenth-century technological revolution associated with Watt, Arkwright, Ely, and others were in part economic crises generated by attempts at reducing costs of production and expanding economic frontiers under economic limitations. Although there is some evidence of state and other institutionally sponsored and financed technological research (and the establishment of scientific societies and institutes) associated with the crisis of the seventeenth century, the fact that many major scientific and technological advances then and since came from extra-institutional outsiders or loners (*Einzelgänger*, autodidacta) would seem to lend still more plausibility to my hypothesis since it is they who are particularly convulsed by the agitation of the times, and that is why they are outsiders.

My hypothesis is that the economic crisis also becomes indirectly effective through the political crisis that it engenders and this effect is particularly strong on those individuals (also loners or rebels) who suggest the revolutionary advances in philosophy and the arts, as well as in the sciences. Most of the Renaissance was coincident with the fourteenth- and fifteenth-century crisis or crises, and many of its most important figures were politically moved thereby (although the "High Renaissance" in Italy coincided with what was apparently already a period of economic upswing). But many of the leading figures of seventeenth-century philosophical and artistic renovation and of the late eighteenth-century Enlightment worked and gained acceptance in times of economic and political crisis. Similarly, scientific, philosophical, and cultural "revolutions" in the nineteenth and twentieth centuries may be said to have occurred during, or to have been generated by, periods of particular economic and political crises and through the mediation of minds that were particularly agitated by these crises. The work of such minds in turn has had far-reaching influence on the course of human history and on the process of capital accumulation thereafter. To some extent even the "revolutionary" interpretation and writing of history thus has had and can have some influence on the course of history itself!

Bibliography

Adams, Robert McC. *The Evolution of Urban Society: Early Mesopotamia and Prehistoric Mexico*. Chicago: Aldine, 1966.

——————. "Early Civilizations, Subsistence and Environment." In Carl H. Kraeling and Robert McC. Adams, eds., *City Invincible: An Oriental Institute Symposium*. Chicago: University of Chicago Press, 1960.

Akerman, Johan. *Estructures y ciclos económicos*. Madrid: Aguilar, 1962.

Alavi, Hamza. "India and the Colonial Mode of Production," *Economic and Political Weekly* (Bombay), Special Number (August 1975): 1235–62.

Amin, Samir. *Unequal Development*. New York: Monthly Review Press, 1976, pp. 317–33.

——————. *Accumulation on a World Scale*. New York: Monthly Review Press, 1974.

Anderson, Perry. *Lineages of the Absolutist State*. London: New Left Books, 1974; New York: Humanities, 1975.

Aptheker, Herbert. *The American Revolution 1763–1783*. New York: International Publishers, 1960.

——————. *The Colonial Era*. New York: International Publishers, 1959.

Arcila Farías, Eduardo. *Comercio entre Venezuela y México en los siglos XVII y XVIII*. Mexico: Fondo de Cultura Económica, 1950; also available from El Colegio de México.

Arrighi, Giovanni. "The Relations Between the Colonial and Class Structures: A Critique of A. G. Frank's Theory of the Development of Underdevelopment." Dakar: IDEP, mimeo., 1972.

——————. "Struttura di classe e struttura coloniale nell' analisi del sottosviluppo," *Giovane Critica* 22–23 (1970).

Ashton, Thomas S. "Some Statistics of the Industrial Revolution in Britain." In A. E. Moussan, ed., *Science, Technology, and Economic Growth in the Eighteenth Century*. London: Methuen, 1972.

————. *An Economic History of England: The Eighteenth Century*. London: Methuen, 1955; New York: Barnes and Noble, 1969.

————. *Economic Fluctuations in England, 1700–1800*. Oxford: Clarendon Press, 1959; New York: Oxford University Press, 1959.

Ashworth, William. *A Short History of the International Economy since 1870*. 2nd ed. London: Longmans, 1962; New York: Humanities, 1970.

Aston, Trevor, ed. *Crisis in Europe, 1560–1660: Essays from Past and Present*. London: Routledge & Kegan Paul, 1965.

Bagú, Sergío. *Economía de la sociedad colonial: Ensayo de la historia comparada de América Latina*. Buenos Aires: El Ateneo, 1949.

Bairoch, Paul. *Revolución industrial y subdesarrollo*. Havana: Instituto de Libro, 1969; (orig. French ed. 1965).

Baran, Paul. *The Political Economy of Growth*. New York: Monthly Review Press, 1957.

Barbour, Violet. *Capitalism in Amsterdam in the Seventeenth Century*. Ann Arbor: University of Michigan Press, 1963.

Bartra, Roger. "Modos de producción y estructura agraria en México," *Historia y Sociedad* (Mexico) 2, no. 1 (1974).

————. *El modo de producción asiático: Problemas de la historia de los paises coloniales*. Mexico: Era, 1969.

Bastin, John, and Benda, Harry J. *A History of Modern Southeast Asia*. Englewood Cliffs, N.J.: Prentice Hall, 1968.

Baudin, Louis. *Der sozialistische Staat der Inka*. Hamburg: Rohwolt Verlag, 1956.

Beard, Charles A. *An Economic Interpretation of the Constitution of the United States*. 1913; New York: Macmillan, 1941.

Bernal, J. D. *Science in History*. 4 vols. Harmondsworth: Penguin Books, 1969; Cambridge: MIT Press, 1969.

Bernstein, Barton J., ed. *Towards a New Past: Dissenting Essays in American History*. New York: Pantheon, 1968.

Bertram, G. W. "Economic Growth in Canadian Industry, 1870–1915." In W. T. Easterbrook and M. H. Watkins, eds., *Approaches to Canadian Economic History*. Toronto: McClelland and Stewart, 1967.

Birnbaum, Norman. "The Rise of Capitalism: Marx and Weber." In Neil J. Smelser, ed., *Readings on Economic Sociology*. Englewood Cliffs, N.J.: Prentice-Hall, 1965.

Bloch, Marc. *Feudal Society*. Chicago: University of Chicago Press, 1961.

Blum, Jerome. "Rise of Serfdom in Eastern Europe," *American Historical Review* 42, no. 2 (July 1957).

Boeke, J. H. *Economics and Economic Policy of Dual Societies*. New York: Institute of Pacific Relations, 1953.

————. *The Structure of the Netherlands Indian Economy.* New York: Institute of Pacific Relations, 1942.

Bogart, Ernest Ludlow. *Economic History of the American People.* New York: Longmans, 1938.

Bohannon, Paul, and Curtin, Philip. *Africa and Africans.* Rev. ed. Garden City, N.Y.: Natural History Press, 1971.

Borah, Woodrow. "America as Model: The Demographic Impact of European Expansion upon the Non-European World." Paper presented at the Thirty-fifth International Congress of Americanists, Mexico, 1962; reprinted by Center for Latin American Studies, University of California, reprint no. 292.

————. "New Spain's Century of Depression," *Ibero-American* 35. Berkeley: University of California Press, 1951.

————, and Cook, Sherburne F. "New Demographic Research on the Sixteenth Century in Mexico." In Howard F. Cline, ed., *Latin American History: Essays on Its Study and Teaching, 1898–1965.* Vol. 2. Austin: University of Texas Press, 1967; reprinted by the Center for Latin American Studies, University of California, reprint no. 288.

Boxer, C. R. *The Golden Age of Brazil 1695–1750: Growing Pains of a Colonial Society.* Berkeley: University of California Press, 1962.

Brading, D. A. *Miners and Merchants in Bourbon Mexico, 1763–1810.* Cambridge: Cambridge University Press, 1971.

Braudel, Fernand. *El Mediterráneo y el mundo mediterráneo en la época de Felipe II.* 2 vols. Mexico: Fondo de Cultura Económica, 1953; originally published in French (Paris: Armand Colin, 1951; later revised and published in English (New York: Harper and Row, 1972).

————, and Spooner, Frank "Prices in Europe from 1450 to 1750." In *Cambridge Economic History of Europe.* Vol. 5. E. E. Rich and C. H. Wilson, eds., *The Economy of Expanding Europe in the Sixteenth and Seventeenth Centuries.* Cambridge and New York: Cambridge University Press, 1967 and 1977.

Bruchey, Stuart. *The Colonial Merchant: Sources and Readings.* New York: Harcourt, Brace & World, 1966.

Buchanan, Keith. *The Southeast Asian World.* New York: Doubleday-Anchor, 1968.

Callender, Guy Stevens. *Selections from the Economic History of the United States, 1765–1860.* New York: Augustus M. Kelley, 1965.

Cambridge Economic History of Europe. 6 vols. Cambridge and New York: Cambridge University Press. 1965—.

Carande, Ramón. *Carlos V y sus banqueros: la vida económica de Castilla 1516–1556.* 2 vols., 2nd ed. Madrid: Sociedad de Estudios y Publicaciones, 1965.

Carssten, F. L. "The Origin of the Junkers," *English Historical Review* 243 (1947).

Centre d'Etudes et de Recherches Marxistes (CERM). *Sur le féodalism.* Paris: Editions Sociales, 1971.

——————. *Sur le "mode de production asiatique."* Paris: Editions Sociales, 1969.

Céspedes del Castillo, Guillermo. "La sociedad colonial americana en los siglos XVI y XVII." In J. Vicens Vives, ed., *Historia económica y social de España y America.* Vol. 3. Barcelona: Editorial Teide, 1957.

——————. *Lima y Buenos Aires: Repercusiones económicas y políticas de la creación del Virreinato de La Plata.* Seville, 1947.

Chandra, Bipan. *The Rise and Growth of Economic Nationalism in India.* New Delhi: Peoples Publishing House, 1966.

Chaudhuri, K. H. "The East India Company and the Export of Treasury in the Early 17th Century," *The Economic History Review* 16, no. 1 (August 1963).

Chaunu, Pierre and Huguette. "The Atlantic Economy." In Peter Earle, ed., *Essays in European Economic History, 1500–1800.* Oxford: Clarendon Press, 1974; New York: Oxford University Press, 1974.

——————. *Seville et l'Atlantique.* 7 vols. Paris, 1959.

Chesneaux, Jean. "Le mode de production asiatique: Quelques perspectives de recherche." In CERM, *Sur le "mode de production asiatique."* Paris: Editions Sociales, 1969; also in Roger Bartra, *El modo de producción asiático.* Mexico: Era, 1969.

Chevalier, François. *Land and Society in Colonial Mexico.* Berkeley: University of California Press, 1963.

Chicherov, A. I. *India: Economic Development in the Sixteenth to Eighteenth Centuries.* Moscow: Vauka Publishing House, 1971.

Cipolla, Carlo M. "The Economic Decline of Italy." In Carlo M. Cipolla, ed., *The Decline of Empires.* London: Metheun, 1970.

——————. *Cañones y velas en la primera fase de la expansión europea, 1400–1700.* Barcelona: Ariel, 1965; published in English as *Guns, Sails, and Empires: Technological Innovation and the Early Phases of European Expansion, 1400–1700.* New York: Funk and Wagnalls, 1965.

——————; López, Robert S.; and Miskimin, Harry A. "Economic Depression of the Renaissance?" *The Economic History Review* 16, no. 3 (April 1964).

Cleaver, Harry. "Internationalisation of Capital and Mode of Production in Agriculture," *Economic and Political Weekly* (Bombay), "Review of Agriculture" (March 1976): A2–A15.

Clough, Shepard B. *European Economic History: The Economic Development of Western Civilization.* 2nd ed. New York: McGraw-Hill, 1968.

Cook, Sherburne F., and Borah, Woodrow. "The Indian Population of Central Mexico, 1531–1610." *Ibero-Americana* 44. Berkeley: University of California Press, 1960.

————, and Simpson, Lesley Byrd. *The Population of Central Mexico in the Sixteenth Century.* 1948; New York: AMS Press, 1977.

Cox, Oliver. *Capitalism as a System.* New York: Monthly Review Press, 1964.

————. *The Foundations of Capitalism.* New York: Philosophical Library, 1959.

Crombie, A. C. *Medieval and Early Modern Science.* Vol. 2. New York: Doubleday-Anchor, 1959.

Crouzet, F. "England and France in the Eighteenth Century: A Comparative Analysis of the Two Economic Growths." In R. M. Hartwell, ed., *The Causes of the Industrial Revolution.* London: Methuen, 1967; New York: Barnes and Noble, 1967.

Curtin, Philip D. *The Atlantic Slave Trade.* Madison: University of Wisconsin Press, 1969.

Davidson, Basil. *The African Slave Trade: Precolonial History, 1450–1850.* Boston: Atlantic-Little Brown, 1961.

————. *Lost Cities of Africa.* Boston: Atlantic-Little Brown, 1959.

Davis, David Brion. "The Comparative Approach to American History: Slavery." In Laura Foner and Eugene Genovese, eds., *Slavery in the New World.* Englewood Cliffs, N.J.: Prentice-Hall, 1969.

————. *The Problem of Slavery in Western Culture.* Ithaca, N.Y.: Cornell University Press, 1966.

Davis, Ralph. "English Foreign Trade, 1660–1700," and "English Foreign Trade, 1700–1774." In W. E. Minchinton, ed., *The Growth of English Foreign Trade in the Seventeenth and Eighteenth Centuries.* London: Methuen, 1969.

Deane, Phyllis. "Industrial Revolution and Economic Growth: The Evidence of Early British National Income Estimates." In R. M. Hartwell, ed., *The Causes of the Industrial Revolution.* London: Methuen, 1967; New York: Barnes and Noble, 1967.

————. *The First Industrial Revolution.* Cambridge: Cambridge University Press, 1965.

————, and Cole, W. A. *British Economic Growth, 1688–1959.* 2nd ed. *Trends and Structure.* New York and Cambridge: Cambridge University Press, 1967.

Desai, A. R., ed. *Rural Sociology in India.* 4th ed. Bombay: Popular Prakashan, 1969.

De Tocqueville, Alexis. *Democracy in America.* 2 vols. New York: Vintage Books, 1954 (orig. French ed. 1835).

Devèze, Michel. *L'Europe et le monde à la fin du XVIIIe siècle*. Paris: Editions Albin Michel, 1970.

Digby, William. *"Prosperous" British India: A Revelation from Official Records*. 1901; New Delhi: Sagar Publications, 1969.

Dobb, Maurice. *Studies in the Development of Capitalism*. Rev. ed. London: Routledge & Kegan Paul, 1963; New York: International Publishers, 1969.

————; Sweezy, Paul; Takahashi, Kohachiro, et al. *The Transition from Feudalism to Capitalism*. London: New Left Books, 1976.

Dopsch, Alfons. *Fundamentos económicos y socialies de la cultura europea*. Mexico: Fondo de Cultura Económica, 1951 (orig. German ed. 1918).

Dorn, Walter D. *Competition for Empire, 1740–1763*. New York: Harper & Row, 1963.

Dutt, Romesh (Chunder). *The Economic History of India*. 2 vols. 1901; New Delhi: Publications Division, Ministry of Information and Broadcasting, Government of India, 1970.

Easterbrook, W. T., and Aitken, Hugh G. J. *Canadian Economic History*. Toronto: Macmillan, 1967.

Elkins, Stanley M. *Slavery: A Problem in American Institutional and Intellectual Life*. Chicago: University of Chicago Press, 1969.

Elliot, J. H. "The Decline of Spain." In Carlo M. Cipolla, ed., *The Decline of Empires*. London: Methuen, 1970.

————. *Imperial Spain, 1469–1716*. Harmondsworth: Penguin, 1970.

Emmanuel, A. *Unequal Exchange*. New York: Monthly Review Press, 1972; first published in French (Paris: Maspero, 1969).

Engels, Friedrich. *The Peasant War in Germany*. Moscow: Foreign Languages Publishing House, 1956.

Fage, J. D. *An Introduction to the History of West Africa*. 3rd ed. New York and Cambridge: Cambridge University Press, 1962, 1964.

Fairbank, John King. *Trade and Diplomacy on the China Coast*. Stanford: Stanford University Press, 1969.

Farnell, J. E. "The Navigation Act of 1651, The First Dutch War, and the London Merchant Community," *The Economic History Review* 16, no. 3 (April 1964).

Faulkner, Harold Underwood. *American Economic History*. 8th ed. New York: Harper & Brothers, 1960.

Fernández, Raúl A., and Ocampo, José F. "The Latin American Revolution: A Theory of Imperialism, Not a Theory of Dependence," *Latin American Perspectives* 1, no. 1 (Spring 1974): 30–61.

Fisher, H. E. S. *The Portugal Trade: A Study of Anglo-Portuguese Commerce, 1700–1770*. London: Methuen, 1971.

————. "Anglo-Portuguese Trade: 1700–1770." In W. E. Minchinton, ed., *The Growth of English Overseas Trade in the Seventeenth and Eighteenth Centuries*. London: Methuen, 1969.

Florescano, Enrique. *Precios del maíz y crisis agrícolas en México, 1708–1810*. Mexico: El Colegio de México, 1969.

Foner, Laura, and Genovese, Eugene, eds. *Slavery in the New World: A Reader in Comparative History*. Englewood Cliffs, N.J.: Prentice Hall, 1969.

Frank, Andre Gunder. *Dependent Accumulation and Underdevelopment*. New York: Monthly Review Press, 1978; London: Macmillan, 1978.

————. *Mexican Agriculture 1521–1630: Transformation of the Mode of Production*. Cambridge: Cambridge University Press, in press; also published in Mexico (Escuela Nacional de Antropología e Historia, 1976).

————. *On Capitalist Underdevelopment*. Bombay: Oxford University Press, 1975.

————. "Multilateral Merchandise Trade Imbalances and Uneven Economic Development," *The Journal of European Economic History* (Rome) 5, no. 5 (Fall 1976); also published in A. G. Frank, *Dependent Accumulation and Underdevelopment*. New York: Monthly Review Press, 1978; London: Macmillan, 1978, ch. 7.

————. "On the Roots of Development and Underdevelopment in the New World: Smith and Marx vs. The Weberians," *Theory and Society* (Amsterdam) 2 (1975); also in *Revue Internationale de Sociologie* 10, nos. 2–3 (August-December 1974); also published in A. G. Frank, *Dependent Accumulation and Undevelopment*. New York: Monthly Review Press, 1978; London: Macmillan, 1978, ch. 3.

————. "Dependence Is Dead, Long Live Dependence and the Class Struggle: A Reply to Critics,' *Latin American Perspectives* 1, no. 1 (Spring 1974): 87–106; revised version in *World Development* (Oxford) 5, no. 4 (1977).

————. *Lumpenbourgeoisie: Lumpendevelopment*. New York: Monthly Review Press, 1972.

————. "On Dalton's 'Theoretical Issues in Economic Anthropology,' " *Current Anthropology* 11, no. 1 (February 1970a): 67–71.

————. "Toward a Theory of Capitalist Development." Paper presented to the Thirty-ninth International Congress of Americanists, Lima, Peru, August 1970b.

————. *Latin America: Underdevelopment or Revolution*. New York: Monthly Review Press, 1969

————. *Capitalism and Underdevelopment in Latin America*. 1967; rev. ed. New York: Monthly Review Press, 1969; London: Penguin Books, 1971.

————, and Shah, Said A. *Underdevelopment: Theory Is History*. Bombay: Oxford University Press, in press.

Fromm, Erich, and Maccoby, Michael. *Social Character in a Mexican Village: A Sociopsychoanalytic Study*. Englewood Cliffs, N.J.: Prentice-Hall, 1970.

Furnivall, J. S. *Colonial Policy and Practice*. Cambridge: Cambridge University Press, 1948; New York: New York University Press, 1956.

————. *Netherlands India*. Cambridge: Cambridge University Press, 1944.

Furtado, Celso. *The Economic Growth of Brazil*. Berkeley: University of California Press, 1965.

Fynn, J. K. *Asante and Its Neighbours, 1700–1807*. London: Longmans, 1971; Evanston, Ill.: Northwestern University Press, 1972.

Ganguli, B. N., ed. *Readings in Indian Economic History*. Bombay: Asia Publishing House, 1964.

Galeano, Eduardo. *Open Veins of Latin America*. New York: Monthly Review Press, 1973; first published in Spanish (Mexico and Buenos Aires: Siglo XXI Editores, 1972).

Geertz, Clifford. *Agricultural Involution: The Processes of Ecological Change in Indonesia*. Berkeley: University of California Press, 1963.

Genovese, Eugene. *The World the Slave-Owners Made*. New York: Pantheon, 1969.

————. "Rebelliousness and Docility in the Negro Slave. Critique of the Elkins Thesis," *Civil War History* 13, no. 4 (December 1967).

Gibb, H. A. R. *Mohammedanism. A Historical Study*. New York: Mentor, 1955.

Gibson, Charles. *The Aztecs Under Spanish Rule*. Stanford: Stanford University Press, 1964.

Glamann, Kristof. *European Trade, 1500–1750*. Vol. 2. London: Fontana, 1971.

Godelier, Maurice. "Le notion de 'mode de production asiatique' et les schémas marxistes d'évolution des sociétés." In CERM, *Sur le "mode de production asiatique."* Paris: Editions Sociales, 1969a; in part also in Roger Bartra, *El modo de producción asiático* (Mexico: Era, 1969).

————. *Las sociedades primitivas y el nacimiento de las sociedades de clases según Marx y Engels*. Medellín, Colombia: LaOveja Negra, 1969b.

Góngora, Mario. *Origen de los "inquilinos" de Chile Central*. Santiago: Editorial Universitaria, 1960.

Goveia, Elsa V. "Comment on 'Anglicanism, Catholicism, and the Negro Slave.' " In Laura Foner and Eugene Genovese, eds., *Slavery in the New World*. Englewood Cliffs, N.J.: Prentice-Hall, 1969.

Gray, Lewis C. *History of Agriculture in the Southern United States to 1860*. 2 vols. Gloucester, Mass.: Peter Smith, 1958.

Habib, Irfan. "Potentialities of Capitalistic Development in the Economy of Mughal India," *The Journal of Economic History* 29, no. 1 (March 1969a).

————. "Problems of Marxist Historical Analysis," *Enquiry* (New Delhi) (1969b): 52–68.

Hamilton, Earl J. "American Treasure and the Rise of Capitalism, 1500–1700," *Economica* (November 1929).

Hammond, J. L. and Barbara. *The Village Labourer, 1760–1832*. London: Longmans, Green, 1927; New York: Harper & Row, 1970.

————. *The Rise of Modern Industry*. 1925; London: Methuen, 1966.

Hargreaves, J. D. *West Africa: The Former French States*. Englewood Cliffs, N.J.: Prentice-Hall, 1967.

Harlow, Vincent. *A History of Barbados: 1625–1685*. London: Clarendon Press, 1926; reprint ed., Westport, Conn.: Greenwood Press.

Harper, Lawrence A. "The Effect of the Navigation Acts on the Thirteen Colonies." In Harry N. Scheiber, ed., *United States Economic History: Selected Readings*. New York: Alfred A. Knopf, 1964.

Hartwell, R. M. "The Causes of the Industrial Revolution: An Essay in Methodology." In R. M. Hartwell, ed., *The Causes of the Industrial Revolution*. London: Methuen, 1967; New York: Barnes & Noble, 1967.

Heaton, H. "Industrial Revolution." In R. M. Hartwell, ed., *The Causes of the Industrial Revolution*. London: Methuen, 1967; New York: Barnes and Noble, 1967.

Hill, Christopher. *Reformation to Industrial Revolution, 1530–1780*. Gloucester, Mass: Peter Smith, 1967; Harmondsworth: Penguin Books, 1969.

————. *The Century of Revolution, 1663–1714*. London: Sphere Books, 1969; New York: Norton, 1966.

Hinton, R. W. K. *The Eastland Trade and the Common Weal in the Seventeenth Century*. Cambridge: Cambridge University Press, 1959.

Hobsbawm, E. I. *Industry and Empire*. Harmondsworth: Penguin Books, 1969; New York: Pantheon, 1968.

————. *The Age of Revolution, 1789–1848*. New York: Mentor, 1964a.

————. "Introduction." In Karl Marx, *Pre-Cepitalist Economic Formations*. New York: International Publishers, 1964b.

————. "The Seventeenth Century in the Development of Capitalism," *Science and Society* 24, no. 2 (1960).

————. "The Crisis of the Seventeenth Century," *Past and Present* 5 & 6 (1954); also published in Spanish, together with the above article, in Eric Hobsbawm, *En torno a los origenes de la revolución industrial*. Buenos Aires: Siglo XXI Editores, 1971.

Hoetink, Harry. "Race Relations in Curacao and Surinam." In Laura Foner and Eugene Genovese, eds., *Slavery in the New World*. Englewood Cliffs, N.J.: Prentice-Hall, 1969.

Hoffmann, Walter G. *The Growth of Industrial Economies*. Manchester: Manchester University Press, 1958; Dobbs Ferry, N.Y.: Oceana, 1958.

Humboldt, Alexander von. *Political Essay on the Kingdom of New Spain*. 4 vols. London, 1811.

Hymer, Stephen. "Robinson Crusoe and the Secret of Primitive Accumulation," *Monthly Review* 4 (September 1971).

James, C. L. R. *The Black Jacobins*. 2nd rev. ed. New York: Vintage, 1963.

Jara, Alvaro. *Problemas y métodos de la historia económica hispanoamericana*. Caracas: Universidad Central de Venezuela, n.d.

——. *Tres ensayos sobre economía minera hispanoamericana*. Santiago: Universidad de Chile, Centro de Investigaciónes de Historia Americana, 1966.

Jones, J. R. *Britain and Europe in the Seventeenth Century*. New York: Norton, 1966.

Katz, Friedrich. *Situación social y económica de los Aztecas durante los siglos XV y XVI*. Mexico: UNAM, 1966.

Kay, Cristóbal. *Comparative Development of the European Manorial System and the Latin American Hacienda System: An Approach to a Theory of Agrarian Change for Chile*, Ph.d. diss., School of Arts and Social Studies of the University of Sussex, England, 1971; also published in Spanish (Santiago: CESO-Prensa Latinoamericana, 1973).

Keynes, John Maynard. *A Treatise on Money*. 2 vols. London: Macmillan, 1930; New York: St. Martin's, 1972.

Kosambi, D. D. "Indian Feudalism." In A. R. Desai, ed., *Rural Sociology in India*. 4th ed. Bombay: Popular Prakashan, 1969.

——. *An Introduction to the Study of Indian History*. Bombay, 1956.

Kosminsky, E. A. *Studies in the Agrarian History of England in the Thirteenth Century*. Oxford: Basil Blackwell, 1956.

Kossok, Manfred. *El Virreynato de La Plata. Su estructura económica social*. Buenos Aires: Editorial Futuro, 1959.

Kula, Witold. *Teoria econòmica del sistèma feudale*. Turin: Einaudi, 1970a; also published in English as *An Economic Theory of the World System*. New York: Humanities, 1976.

——. "Una economía agraria sin acumulación: La Polonia de los siglos XVI-XVIII," *Desarrollo Económico* (Buenos Aires) 9, no. 36 (January-March 1970b).

——. "Il sottosviluppo econòmico in una prospectiva storica," *Annali della Fondazione Luigi Einaudi* (Turin) 3 (1969).

Labrousse, C. E. "The Crisis in the French Economy at the End of the Old Regime." In Ralph W. Greenlaw, ed., *The Economic Origins of the French Revolution: Poverty or Prosperity?* Boston: D.C. Heath, 1958.

Laclau, Ernesto. "Feudalism and Capitalism in Latin America," *New Left Review* 67 (May-June 1971).

Landes, David. "Technological Change and Industrial Development in Western Europe, 1750–1914." In *Cambridge Economic History of Europe*. Vol. 6, part 1. Cambridge: Cambridge University Press, 1966.

Larraz, José. *La época del mercantilismo en Castilla, 1500–1700*. Madrid: Atlas, 1943.

League of Nations (Folke Hilgerdt). *Industrielization and Foreign Trade*. Geneva, 1945.

————. *Network of World Trade*. Geneva, 1942.

Lefebvre, Georges. "French Revolution and the Peasants." In Ralph W. Greenlaw, ed., *The Economic Origins of the French Revolution: Poverty or Prosperity?* Boston: D.C. Heath, 1958.

————. *The Coming of the French Revolution*. New York: Random House, 1947 (orig. French ed. 1939).

Legge, J. D. *Indonesia*. Englewood Cliffs, N.J. Prentice-Hall, 1964.

Le Roy Ladurie, Emmanuel. "A Long Agrarian Cycle." In Peter Earle, ed., *Essays in European Economic History, 1500–1800*. Oxford: Clarendon Press, 1974; New York: Oxford University Press, 1974.

Levkovsky, A. I. *Capitalism in India: Basic Trends in Its Development*. New Delhi: Peoples Publishing House, 1966.

Lewis, Bernard. "The Arabs in Eclipse," and "Some Reflections on the Decline of the Ottoman Empire." In Carlo M. Cipolla, ed., *The Decline of Empires*. London: Methuen, 1970.

List, Friedrich. *National System of Political Economy*. Philadelphia: J. B. Lippincott, 1856.

López, Robert S., and Miskimin, Harry A. "The Economic Depression of the Renaissance," *The Economic History Review* 14, no. 3 (1962).

Lynd, Staughton. "Beyond Beard." In Barton J. Bernstein, ed., *Towards a New Past: Dissenting Essays in American History*. New York: Pantheon, 1968.

Maddison, Angus. *Class Structure and Economic Growth: India and Pakistan Since the Moghuls*. London: George Allen & Unwin, 1971; New York: Norton, 1972.

Mandel, Ernest. *Marxist Economic Theory*. 2 vols. New York: Monthly Review Press, 1970.

————. "L'accumulation primitive et l'industrialisation du Tiers-Monde." In Victor Fay, ed., *En Partant du capital*. Paris: Editions Anthropos, 1968; corrected version in *Pensamiento Crítico* (Havana) 36 (January 1970).

Mannix, Daniel P., and Cowley, Malcolm. *Black Cargoes: A History of the Atlantic Slave Trade, 1518–1865*. New York: Viking Press, 1962.

Mantoux, Paul. *The Industrial Revolution in the Eighteenth Century.* London: Methuen, 1964 (orig. French ed. 1907).

Marx, Karl. *Grundrisse.* London: Penguin Books, 1973; New York: Vintage, 1973.

————. *Pre-Capitalist Economic Formations.* With an Introduction by Eric J. Hobsbawm. New York: International Publishers, 1964.

————. *Capital.* 3 vols. Moscow: Foreign Languages Publishing House, Vol. I, 1954; Vol. II, 1961; Vol. III, 1962.

Marini, Ruy Mauro. *La dialéctica de la dependencia.* Mexico: Era, 1973.

Mauro, Frederic. *L'expansion européenne, 1600–1870.* Paris: Presses Universitaires de France, 1964.

————. "Towards an Intercontinental Model. European Overseas Expansion Between 1500 and 1800," *The Economic History Review* 14, no. 1 (August 1961).

Minchinton, W. E., ed. *The Growth of English Overseas Trade in the Seventeenth and Eighteenth Centuries.* London: Methuen, 1969.

Mintz, Sidney. "The Caribbean as a Socio-Cultural Area," *Journal of World History* 9, no. 4 (1966).

————. "Review of Stanley M. Elkins' *Slavery,*" *American Anthropologist* 63 (June 1961): 579–87.

Miskimin, Harry A. "Monetary Movements and Market Structure: Forces for Contradiction in Fourteenth- and Fifteenth-Century England," *Journal of Economic History* 24, no. 4 (December 1964).

Mukherjee, Ramkrishna. *The Rise and Fall of the East India Company.* New York: Monthly Review Press, 1974; first published in Germany (Berlin: Deutscher Verlag der Wissenschaften, 1955).

Musson, A. E., ed. *Science, Technology and Economic Growth in the Eighteenth Century.* London: Methuen, 1972.

Nef, John U. *War and Human Progress.* New York: Norton, 1963.

Nehru, Jawaharlal. *The Discovery of India.* New York: Doubleday-Anchor, 1960.

Nettels, Curtis P. *The Emergence of a National Economy, 1775–1815.* New York: Harper, 1962.

————. "British Mercantilism and the Economic Development of the Thirteen Colonies," *The Journal of Economic History* 12, no. 2 (Spring 1952); reprinted in William Appleman Williams, ed., *The Shaping of American Diplomacy: 1900.* Chicago: Rand McNally, 1956.

Nichtweiss, Johannes. "Zur Frage der Zweiten Leibeigenschaft und des Sogennanten Preussischen Weges der Entwicklung des Kapitalismus in der Lanwirtschaft Ostdeutschlands." *Zeitschrift Fuer Geschichtswissenshaft* (East Berlin) 5 (1953); also in RILM, *Le deuxième servage en Europe Centrale et Orientale.* Paris: Editions de la Nouvelle Critique, 1970.

North, Douglass C., and Thomas, Robert Paul. "An Economic Theory of the Growth of the Western World," *The Economic History Review* 23, no. 1 (April 1970).

———. *The Economic Growth of the United States, 1790–1860.* New York: Norton, 1966.

Nutting, Anthony. *The Arabs.* New York: Mentor, 1964.

Oliver, Roland, and Fage, J. D. *A Short History of Africa.* Harmondsworth and Baltimore, Md.: Penguin Books, 1962.

Palerm, Angel. "The Agricultural Bases of Urban Civilization in Mesoamerica." In Julian H Steward, ed , *Irrigation Civilizations: A Comparative Study.* Washington, D.C.: Pan American Union Social Science Monographs #1, 1955.

Palloix, Christian. "Impérialisme et mode de production capitaliste," *L'homme et la Société* (Paris) no. 12 (1969).

Parain, Charles. "Caracteres généraux du féodalisme," and "Evolution du système féodale européen." In CERM, *Sur le féodalisme.* Paris: Editions Sociales, 1971.

Parry, J. H. *The Age of Reconaissance.* New York: Mentor, 1964.

———. *The Establishment of the European Hegemony, 1415–1715. Trade and Exploration in the Age of the Renaissance.* New York: Harper & Row, 1961.

———. *Europe and a Wider World, 1415–1715.* London: Hutchison, 1949.

———, and Sherlock, Philip. *A Short History of the West Indies.* 3rd ed. London: Macmillan and St. Martin's Press, 1971.

Patnaik, Utsa. "Development of Capitalism in Agriculture," *Economic and Political Weekly* (Bombay), September 30, 1972.

———. "Capitalist Development in Agriculture," *Economic and Political Weekly* (Bombay), September 25, 1971, pp. A123–30.

Pavlov, V. I. *The Indian Capitalist Class.* New Delhi: Peoples Publishing House, 1964.

Pearn, B. R. *An Introduction to the History of South-East Asia.* Kuala Lumpur: Longmans of Malaysia, 1963; New York: Humanities, 1965.

Phipps, Helen. "Some Aspects of the Agrarian Question in Mexico. A Historical Study." *University of Texas Bulletin* 2512 (April 1925).

Pirenne, Henri. *Economic and Social History of Medieval Europe.* London: Routledge & Kegan Paul, 1936; New York: Harcourt Brace Jovanovitch, 1956.

Postan, M. M. "The Chronology of Labour Services," *Transactions of the Royal Historical Society,* 4th ser , 20 (1937): 169–93.

———; Rich, E. E.; and Miller, Edward, eds. "Economic Organisation and Policies in the Middle Ages." In *Cambridge Economic History of Europe.* Vol. 3. Cambridge: Cambridge University Press, 1965.

Pressnell, L. S. "The Rate of Interest in the Eighteenth Century." In L. S. Pressnell, ed., *Studies in the Industrial Revolution.* London: Athlone Press, 1960.

Price, Jacob M. "Multilaterialism and/or Bilaterialism: The Settlement of British Trade Balances with 'The North,' c. 1700," *The Economic History Review* 14, no. 2 (1962).

Ramírez Nicochea, Hernán. *Antecedentes económicos de la independencia de Chile.* 2nd ed. Santiago: Facultad de Filosofía y Educacion, Universidad de Chile, 1967.

Recherches Internationales à la Lumière du Marxisme (RILM). *Le deuxième servage en Europe Centrale et Orientale.* Paris: Editions de la Nouvelle Critique, 1970.

Reglá, Juan. "La época de los tres primeros Austrias." In J. Vicens Vives, ed., *Historia de España y América.* Vol. 3. Barcelona: Editorial Vicens Vives, 1961.

Revillagigedo, Conde de. *Informe sobre las Misiones 1793 e Instrucción Reservada al Marqués de Branciforte, 1794.* 2 vols. Mexico: Editorial Jus, Colección México Heroico, 1966.

Ribeiro, Darcy. "The Culture-Historical Configurations of the American Peoples," *Current Anthropology* 11, no. 3 (September 1970).

————. *Las Américas y la Civilisación.* 3 vols. Buenos Aires: Centro Editora de América Latina, 1969. In English as *The Americas and Civilization.* New York: Dutton, 1971.

Rodney, Walter. "The Impact of the African Slave Trade on West Africa." In Roland Oliver, ed., *The Middle Age of African History.* London and New York: Oxford University Press, 1967.

————. "African Slavery and Other Forms of Social Oppression on the Upper Guinea Coast in the Context of the Atlantic Slave Trade," *Journal of African History* 2, no. 3 (1966): 431–43.

Rosenberg, H. "The Rise of the Junkers in Brandenburg-Prussia, 1410–1653," *American Historical Review* 49, nos. 1 & 2 (1943–1944).

Sauer, Carl O. *The Early Spanish Main.* Berkeley: University of California Press, 1966.

Saul, S. B. *Studies in British Overseas Trade, 1870–1914.* Liverpool: Liverpool University Press, 1960.

Scheiber, Harry N., ed. *United States Economic History: Selected Readings.* New York: Knopf, 1964.

Schlesinger, A. H. *The Colonial Merchants and the American Revolution, 1763–1776.* New York: 1918.

Schlote, W. *British Overseas Trade from 1700 to the 1930s.* Oxford: Oxford University Press, 1952.

Schumpeter, Joseph A. *Business Cycles: A Theoretical, Historical, and Statistical Analysis of the Capitalist Process.* 2 vols. New York: McGraw-Hill, 1939.

Schurmann, Franz, and Schell, Orville. *The China Reader. I: Imperial China.* New York: Vintage, 1967.

Sen, Bhowani. *Evolution of Agrarian Relations in India*. New Delhi: Peoples Publishing House, 1962.

Sepúlveda, Sergio. *El trigo chileno en el mercado mundial*. Santiago: Editorial Universitaria, 1959.

Shelvankar, K. S. "Indian Feudalism, Its Characteristics." In A. R. Desai, ed., *Rural Sociology in India*. 4th ed. Bombay: Popular Prakashan, 1969.

Shepherd, James F., and Walton, Gary M. "Estimates of 'Invisible' Earnings in the Balance of Payments of the British North American Colonies, 1768–1772," *The Journal of Economic History* 29, no. 2 (June 1969).

Sheridan, Richard. *The Development of the Plantations to 1750: An Era of West Indian Prosperity, 1750–1775*. Barbados: Caribbean University Press, 1970; London: Ginn & Co., 1970.

————. "The Plantation Revolution and the Industrial Revolution, 1625–1775," *Caribbean Studies* 9, no. 3 (October 1969).

————. "The Wealth of Jamaica in the Eighteenth Century: A Rejoinder," *The Economic History Review* 21, no. 1 (April 1968).

Sideri, Sandro. *Trade and Power: Informal Colonialism in Anglo-Portuguese Relations*. Rotterdam: Rotterdam University Press, 1970.

Simonsen, Roberto C. *Historia econômica do Brasil, 1500–1820*. São Paulo: Companhia Editora Nacional, 1962.

Singh, V. B. *Indian Economy Yesterday and Today*. 2nd ed. New Delhi: Peoples Publishing House, 1970.

Sinha, Narendra Krishna. *The Economic History of Bengal from Plassey to the Permanent Settlement*. 3 vols. Calcutta: Firma K. L. Mukhopadhyay, 1961–1970.

Smith, Adam. *An Inquiry into the Nature and Causes of the Wealth of Nations*. 1776; New York: Random House, 1937.

Sombart, Werner. *Der Moderne Kapitalismus*. 5th ed. Munich: Duncker & Humboldt, 1922.

Soustelle, Jacques. *The Daily Life of the Aztecs on the Eve of the Spanish Conquest*. New York: Macmillan, 1962.

Sperling, J. "The International Payments Mechanism in the Seventeenth and Eighteenth Centuries," *The Economic History Review* 14, no. 3 (1969).

Stahl, H. H. "Les anciennes communautés villageoises roumaines (extraits)." In RILM, *Le deuxième servage en Europe Central et Orientale*. Paris: Editions de la Nouvelle Critique, 1970.

Stavrianos, L. S. *The World Since 1500: A Global History*. Englewood Cliffs, N.J.: Prentice-Hall, 1966a.

————. *The Epic of Modern Man. A Collection of Readings*. 2nd ed. Englewood Cliffs, N.J.: Prentice-Hall, 1966b.

Stein, Stanley J., and Barbara H. *The Colonial Heritage of Latin America*. New York: Oxford University Press, 1970.

Steward, Julian H., ed. *Handbook of South American Indians.* Washington D.C.: Bureau of American Ethnology Bulletin 143, Smithsonian Institute, 1946–1950.

Supple, Barry. *Commercial Crisis and Change in England, 1600–1642.* New York and Cambridge: Cambridge University Press, 1969.

Suret-Canale, Jean. "Les sociétés traditionelles en Afrique tropicale et le concept de mode de production asiatique." In CERM, *Sur le "mode de production asiatique."* Paris: Editions Sociales, 1969; also in Roger Bartra, *El modo de producción asiático.* Mexico: Era, 1969.

Tawney, R. H. *Religion and the Rise of Capitalism.* 1926; New York: Mentor, 1947.

Taylor, Philip A. M. *The Origins of the English Civil War: Conspiracy, Crusade, or Class Conflict?* Boston: D.C. Heath, 1960.

Thomas, Robert Paul. "The Sugar Colonies of the Old Empire: Profit or Loss for Great Britain?" *The Economic History Review* 21, no. 1 (April 1968).

Topolski, Jerzy. "Polish Economic Decline." In Peter Earle, ed., *Essays in European Economic History, 1500–1800.* Oxford: Clarendon Press, 1974; New York: Oxford University Press, 1974.

Toynbee, Arnold. *The Industrial Revolution.* 1884; Boston: Beacon Press, 1956.

U.S. Bureau of the Census. *Historical Statistics of the United States: Colonial Times to 1957.* Washington, D.C.: U.S. Government Printing Office, 1960.

Van Alstyne, Richard W. *Empire and Independence. The International History of the American Revolution.* New York: Wiley, 1967.

Van Leur, J. C. *Indonesian Trade and Society: Essays in Asian Social and Economic History.* The Hague: W. Van Hoeve, 1955; Elmsford, N.Y.: Mouton, 1969.

Verlinden, Charles. "Italian Influence in Iberian Colonization," *Hispanic American Historical Review* 33, no. 2 (May 1953).

Vicens Vives, J. *Coyuntura económica y reformismo burgués.* Barcelona: Ariel, 1969.

————. *Aproximación a la historia de España.* 4 vols. Barcelona: Editorial Vicens Vives, 1962.

Vilar, Pierre. "Quelques thèmes de recherche." In CERM, *Sur le féodolisme.* Paris: Editions Sociales, 1971.

————. *Oro y moneda en la historia (1450–1920).* Barcelona: Ariel, 1969; also published in English as *A History of Gold and Money, 1450–1920.* New York: Humanities, 1976.

————. *Crecimiento y Desarrollo.* Barcelona: Ariel, 1964.

Villalobos, Sergio. *El comercio y le crisis colonial. Un mito de la Independencia.* Santiago: Universidad de Chile, 1968.

──────. *Comercio y contrabando en el Rio de la Plata y Chile 1700–1811.* Buenos Aires: Eudeba, 1965.

Wallerstein, Immanuel. *The Modern World-System.* Vol. I. *Capitalist Agriculture and the Origins of the European World-Economy in the Sixteenth Century.* New York: Academic Press, 1974a.

──────. "The Rise and Future Demise of the World Capitalist System: Concepts for a Comparative Analysis," *Comparative Studies in Society and History* 16, no. 4 (September 1974b).

Walton, Gary M. "New Evidence on Colonial Commerce," *The Journal of Economic History* 28, no. 3 (September 1968).

Weber, Max. *The Protestant Ethic and the Spirit of Capitalism.* New York: Scribners, 1958.

Wertheim, W. F. *East-West Parallels: Sociological Approaches to Modern Asia.* The Hague: W. van Hoeve, 1964; Elmsford, N.Y.: Mouton, 1964.

Williams, Eric. *Capitalism and Slavery.* 1944: New York: Capricorn Books, 1966.

──────. *History of the People of Trinidad and Tobago.* London: Andre Deutsch, 1964: New York: Transatlantic Arts, 1962.

Williams, Glyndwr. *The Expansion of Europe in the Eighteenth Century.* London: Blanford Press, 1966

Wilson, Charles. *England's Apprenticeship, 1603–1763.* New York: St. Martin's, 1965; London: Longmans, 1971.

──────. *Profit and Power. A Study of England and the Dutch Wars.* London: Longmans, 1957.

Wittfogel, Karl. *Oriental Despotism: A Comparative Study of Total Power.* New Haven: Yale University Press, 1957.

Wolf, Eric. *Sons of the Shaking Earth.* Chicago: University of Chicago Press, 1959.

──────. *The Mexican Bajío in the Eighteenth Century.* New Orleans: Middle American Research Institute of Tulane University Publications no. 17, 1955.

Wolpert, Stanley. *India.* Englewood Cliffs, N.J.: Prentice-Hall, 1965.

Wright, Chester W. *Economic History of the United States.* New York: McGraw-Hill, 1941.

Zurita, Alonso de. *Breve y sumaria relación de los señores y maneras y diferencias que había de ellos en Nueva-España.* 1550; Mexico: Salvador Chávez Hayhoe, 1941; also published in English (New Brunswick, N.J.: Rutgers University Press).

Index